The NARRATIVE IMPULSE

Short Stories for Analysis

The NARRATIVE IMPULSE

Short Stories for Analysis

MARY PURCELL &
ROBERT C. WYLDER

Bobbs-Merrill Educational Publishing
Indianapolis

The Bobbs-Merrill Company, Inc.
4300 West 62nd Street
Indianapolis, Indiana 46268

First Edition
Tenth Printing—1979

Library of Congress Catalog Card Number 63–14021
ISBN 0–672–63067–2

ACKNOWLEDGMENTS

Butch Minds the Baby: From *Guys and Dolls*, by Damon Runyon. Copyright 1930, 1957 by Damon Runyon, Jr. and Mary Runyon McCann. Published by J. B. Lippincott Company.

By the Waters of Babylon: From *Selected Works of Stephen Vincent Benét*, Holt, Rinehart and Winston, Inc. Copyright, 1937, by Stephen Vincent Benét. Reprinted by permission of Brandt & Brandt.

The Circus: From *My Name Is Aram*, copyright, 1937, 1938, 1939, 1940, by William Saroyan. Reprinted by permission of Harcourt, Brace & World, Inc.

The Facts of Life: From *The Mixture as Before* by W. Somerset Maugham. Copyright 1939 by W. Somerset Maugham. Reprinted by permission of Doubleday & Co., Inc.

Flight: From *The Long Valley* by John Steinbeck. Copyright 1938 by John Steinbeck. Reprinted by permission of The Viking Press, Inc. All rights reserved.

How Beautiful with Shoes: Copyright 1932 by Wilbur Daniel Steele. Reprinted by permission of the Harold Matson Co.

The Lottery: Reprinted from *The Lottery* by Shirley Jackson, by permission of Farrar, Straus and Cudahy, Inc. Copyright 1948 by the New Yorker Magazine. Copyright 1949 by Shirley Jackson.

Love Is a Fallacy: From *The Many Lives of Dobie Gillis* by Max Shulman. Copyright 1951 by Max Shulman. Reprinted by permission of Doubleday & Co., Inc.

The Man Who Could Work Miracles: Reprinted from *The Short Stories of H. G. Wells* by permission of the executors of Mr. Wells.

The Monkey's Paw: Reprinted by permission of Dodd, Mead & Company, Inc. from *The Lady of the Barge* by W. W. Jacobs.

The Most Dangerous Game: Copyright, 1924, by Richard Connell. Copyright renewed, 1952, by Louise Fox Connell. Reprinted by permission of Brandt & Brandt.

Mr. Kaplan and Shakespeare: From *The Education of Hyman Kaplan* by Leonard Q. Ross. Copyright, 1937, by Harcourt, Brace & World, Inc. and reprinted with their permission.

The Open Window: From *The Short Stories of Saki* by H. H. Munro. Reprinted by permission of The Viking Press, Inc. All rights reserved.

A Rose for Emily: Copyright 1930 and renewed 1957 by William Faulkner. Reprinted from *Collected Stories of William Faulkner*, by permission of Random House, Inc.

To Build a Fire: Reprinted by permission of Irving Shepard, copyright owner.

You Could Look It Up: Reprinted by permission; copyright 1941, The Curtis Publishing Co.

PREFACE

Although some of the stories in this volume have been anthologized many times before, and some have appeared only rarely, neither familiarity nor novelty was the criterion for our choice. Because the purpose of this book is to provide students with good stories that they will enjoy reading, and further, to provide them with methods and terminology for reading stories and talking about them, three other criteria guided our selection: strong story line, proven interest to students, excellence of writing.

The first two of these criteria are closely related, and may be examined together. Stories with a strong story line concentrate on the narrative sequence and hold the readers' interest because they are interrupted relatively little by the author's suggestions and commentary. Experience in the classroom has shown us that long blocks of description and numerous paragraphs of background commentary, introspection, or interpretation will appeal to a seasoned reader but not to a novice. On the other hand, a story which moves along quickly, with little interruption, is appealing to both types of readers. This is not to say that the stories in this volume are without meaning and depth, but that the emphasis is on the narrative and that the meaning comes out of the action of the story. They are good stories of a particular kind.

This brings us to the third criterion—excellence of writing. It is obvious that short stories with strong story lines are not necessarily well written. For instance, many westerns have plenty of action but are badly written. However, stories with a good deal of action may be competently or even superbly written, and these are. The authors know how to handle narrative so that it is exciting and meaningful at the same time. They observe consistency of style and clarity of characterization. It is difficult to write as a small boy speaks, but Saroyan does so in "The Circus." Benét creates a

relatively primitive but wise speaker in "By the Waters of Babylon" and never loses sight of his creation. When Thurber casts
his erstwhile trainer of a baseball club into the role of narrator
in "You Could Look it Up," the reader never forgets who is telling the story. In other words, the authors of these works are
careful craftsmen.

In order to aid the teacher, the stories are presented in a
sequence of complexity and of difficulty of understanding (although, of course, difficulty will vary with the student as well as
with the story). While the stories may be assigned in any order,
the sequence suggested is probably best because the questions
and suggestions for reading have been carefully arranged in an
order of progression and point up the outstanding or representa-
tive feature in each case. The first story provides questions and
comments on action and conflict; the second story on foreshadowing, suspense, and setting; the third on dialogue and
point of view; and so on. Followed by a rather full discussion,
the fourteenth story utilizes almost all of the terms considered
previously, while the last two stories are without any apparatus.
These last three selections should show the student how one can
apply all the terms learned to a single selection and also allow
him to do so without help. The section entitled "Terms to Know"
will be useful to him for reference and review.

At the end of each story there is also a short vocabulary exercise, keyed to the "Questions and Suggestions for Reading"
which follow, which brings up questions of the meaning of words
in the context of the story. Naturally, not all of the words which
may cause students difficulty are included in this exercise, and
each teacher may add more as the occasion demands.

This volume is designed for a student who has had little experience in reading or analyzing fiction. By learning everything
the volume teaches, he should become a more perceptive reader
—and a more enthusiastic one.

TO THE STUDENT: HOW TO READ A SHORT STORY

        In running and in walking we use the same muscles
but in different ways. Similarly, when we read fiction or non-
fiction we use the same basic facilities but not to the same end.

The words in both cases may be identical, or nearly so, but the purposes and effects are quite different. Knowing something about these differences will make the reading of both kinds of prose easier and more meaningful.

The most important distinction between the kind of prose we call non-fiction and that we call fiction is that non-fiction deals in some way with the world as it is and fiction with a world that exists only in the imagination of the writer and, if he is successful, of his readers. Non-fiction reports upon events and people, conveys judgments on various matters, describes or explains things and processes, tries to convince us to adopt a point of view or undertake an action, and performs other similar tasks which have a direct relationship with the actual world about us.

Fiction, on the other hand, does not reflect a world, but creates it. This does not mean that the created world has no relationship to the actual world, but only that its relationship is indirect. The hero of a novel may have many of the human characteristics we observe in actual men, but he is not a portrait of a particular actual man. Instead, he is made up by the author to be the kind of person he is. If he is well drawn, he will strike us as "real," even though we know he has no existence outside the work of fiction where we find him.

The secret of reading fiction, then, is not to expect from it the kinds of information, directly conveyed, that non-fiction deals with, but to enter fully into its created world and to become, for the time of the reading, a part of it. Only by experiencing it, by participating in it, can the reader expect to get the most out of a short story or novel.

Entering into the created world of fiction is in itself a kind of creative performance, and demands that the reader make an active attempt to understand what the author is saying. If he does not try, he will not be participating in a story but merely observing it. He must try to understand the characters and their actions, but more than that he must try to feel with the characters to whatever extent he can. He is not trying to *find out about* the characters from outside as much as he is trying to *become* the characters so that he can know them from the inside.

His way of getting himself into the story is, of course, the printed word, and careful attention to language is the technical means of achieving the end of full participation in a fictional creation. In reading the short story, the kind of fiction contained in this collection, the student needs to be particularly alert because of the shortness of the form. If he does not enter into the created world quickly, he may not get into it at all. This means that he must pay especial attention to each word, each action, each bit of information. He must find out what kind of world he is inhabiting, what kind of people are inhabiting it with him, what the nature of their activity is, and, most of all, what the significance of the activity is. He must at the same time resist the temptation to create his own world, to "read into" the story his own ideas and biases. In addition, he should be willing to suspend judgment on the story until he has read it carefully all the way through. Once he has read it and perhaps re-read it, he has the right to decide whether the author has created a convincing world and whether the reader's own entry into it has been either enjoyable or useful or both.

The practical implications in the previous paragraph are fairly clear: 1) the reader must pay attention to details, looking up words he doesn't know and making sure that the meanings of individual sentences are clear, and 2) he must at the same time be sure that he relates the parts of the story to one another and to the story as a whole, so that he can see the total action as a coherent unity. Unless he is skilled and experienced enough to do both of these things simultaneously, he should probably read the story at least twice, once rapidly for its overall effect, once more slowly for the details. Most good stories will, of course, reward repeated further readings as well.

Once the student has had a little practice in reading short stories, he should have no trouble entering into the worlds they offer. When he has finished a number of them, he will find that his own world is a richer and fuller one for his having done so. In viewing new horizons he will have widened his own.

CONTENTS

The NARRATIVE IMPULSE

Short Stories for Analysis

Jack London

TO BUILD A FIRE

Day had broken cold and gray, exceedingly cold
and gray, when the man turned aside from the main Yukon
trail and climbed the high earth-bank, where a dim and little-
traveled trail led eastward through the fat spruce timberland.
It was a steep bank, and he paused for breath at the top, ex- 5
cusing the act to himself by looking at his watch. It was nine
o'clock. There was no sun nor hint of sun, though there was
not a cloud in the sky. It was a clear day, and yet there seemed
an intangible pall over the face of things, a subtle gloom that
made the day dark, and that was due to the absence of sun. 10
This fact did not worry the man. He was used to the lack of
sun. It had been days since he had seen the sun, and he knew
that a few more days must pass before that cheerful orb, due
south, would just peep above the sky-line and dip immediately from view. 15
The man flung a look back along the way he had come. The
Yukon lay a mile wide and hidden under three feet of ice. On
top of this ice were as many feet of snow. It was all pure white,
rolling in gentle undulations where the ice-jams of the freeze-
up had formed. North and south, as far as his eye could see, it 20
was unbroken white, save for a dark hairline that curved and
twisted from around the spruce-covered island to the south,
and that curved and twisted away into the north, where it disappeared behind another spruce-covered island. This dark hair-
line was the trail—the main trail—that led south five hundred 25
miles to the Chilcoot Pass, Dyea, and salt water; and that led
north seventy miles to Dawson, and still on to the north a thou-

1

sand miles to Nulato, and finally to St. Michael on Bering Sea, a thousand miles and half a thousand more.

But all this—the mysterious, far-reaching hair-line trail, the absence of sun from the sky, the tremendous cold, and the strangeness and weirdness of it all—made no impression on the man. It was not because he was long used to it. He was a newcomer in the land, a *chechaquo*, and this was his first winter. The trouble with him was that he was without imagination. He was quick and alert in the things of life, but only in the things, and not in the significances. Fifty degrees below zero meant eighty-odd degrees of frost. Such fact impressed him as being cold and uncomfortable, and that was all. It did not lead him to meditate upon his frailty as a creature of temperature, and upon man's frailty in general, able only to live within certain narrow limits of heat and cold; and from there on it did not lead him to the conjectural field of immortality and man's place in the universe. Fifty degrees below zero stood for a bite of frost that hurt and that must be guarded against by the use of mittens, ear-flaps, warm moccasins, and thick socks. Fifty degrees below zero was to him just precisely fifty degrees below zero. That there should be anything more to it than that was a thought that never entered his head.

As he turned to go on, he spat speculatively. There was a sharp, explosive crackle that startled him. He spat again. And again, in the air, before it could fall to the snow, the spittle crackled. He knew that at fifty below spittle crackled on the snow, but this spittle had crackled in the air. Undoubtedly it was colder than fifty below—how much colder he did not know. But the temperature did not matter. He was bound for the old claim on the left fork of Henderson Creek, where the boys were already. They had come over across the divide from the Indian Creek country, while he had come the roundabout way to take a look at the possibilities of getting out logs in the spring from the islands in the Yukon. He would be in to camp by six o'clock; a bit after dark, it was true, but the boys would be there, a fire would be going, and a hot supper would be ready. As for lunch, he pressed his hand against the protruding bundle under his jacket. It was also under his shirt, wrapped up in a handkerchief and lying against the naked skin. It was the only way to keep the biscuits from freezing. He smiled agreeably to himself as he thought of those biscuits, each cut open and sopped in bacon grease, and each enclos- 5 ing a generous slice of fried bacon.

He plunged in among the big spruce trees. The trail was faint. A foot of snow had fallen since the last sled had passed over, and he was glad he was without a sled, traveling light. In fact, he carried nothing but the lunch wrapped in the hand- 10 kerchief. He was surprised, however, at the cold. It certainly was cold, he concluded, as he rubbed his numb nose and cheek-bones with his mittened hand. He was a warm-whiskered man, but the hair on his face did not protect the high cheek-bones and the eager nose that thrust itself aggressively into the frosty 15 air.

At the man's heels trotted a dog, a big native husky, the proper wolf-dog, gray-coated and without any visible or tem-peramental difference from its brother, the wild wolf. The ani-mal was depressed by the tremendous cold. It knew that it 20 was no time for traveling. Its instinct told it a truer tale than was told to the man by the man's judgment. In reality, it was not merely colder than fifty below zero; it was colder than sixty below, than seventy below. It was seventy-five below zero. Since the freezing point is thirty-two above zero, it meant that 25 one hundred and seven degrees of frost obtained. The dog did not know anything about thermometers. Possibly in its brain there was no sharp consciousness of a condition of very cold such as was in the man's brain. But the brute had its in-stinct. It experienced a vague but menacing apprehension that 30 subdued it and made it slink along at the man's heels, and that made it question eagerly every unwonted movement of the man as if expecting him to go into camp or to seek shelter somewhere and build a fire. The dog had learned fire, and it wanted fire, or else to burrow under the snow and cuddle its 35 warmth away from the air.

The frozen moisture of its breathing had settled on its fur

in a fine powder of frost, and especially were its jowls, muzzle, and eyelashes whitened by its crystalled breath. The man's red beard and mustache were likewise frosted, but more solidly, the deposit taking the form of ice and increasing with every warm, moist breath he exhaled. Also, the man was chewing tobacco, and the muzzle of ice held his lips so rigidly that he was unable to clear his chin when he expelled the juice. The result was that a crystal beard of the color and solidity of amber was increasing its length on his chin. If he fell down it would shatter itself, like glass, into brittle fragments. But he did not mind the appendage. It was the penalty all tobacco-chewers paid in that country, and he had been out before in two cold snaps. They had not been so cold as this, he knew, but by the spirit thermometer at Sixty Mile he knew they had been registered at fifty below and at fifty-five.

He held on through the level stretch of woods for several miles, crossed a wide flat of nigger-heads, and dropped down a bank to the frozen bed of a small stream. This was Henderson Creek, and he knew he was ten miles from the forks. He looked at his watch. It was ten o'clock. He was making four miles an hour, and he calculated that he would arrive at the forks at half-past twelve. He decided to celebrate that event by eating his lunch there.

The dog dropped in again at his heels, with a tail drooping discouragement, as the man swung along the creek-bed. The furrow of the old sled-trail was plainly visible, but a dozen inches of snow covered the marks of the last runners. In a month no man had come up or down that silent creek. The man held steadily on. He was not much given to thinking, and just then particularly he had nothing to think about save that he would eat lunch at the forks and that at six o'clock he would be in camp with the boys. There was nobody to talk to; and, had there been, speech would have been impossible because of the ice-muzzle on his mouth. So he continued monotonously to chew tobacco and to increase the length of his amber beard. Once in a while the thought reiterated itself that it was very cold and that he had never experienced such cold. As he

walked along he rubbed his cheek-bones and nose with the
back of his mittened hand. He did this automatically, now and
again changing hands. But rub as he would, the instant he
stopped his cheek-bones went numb, and the following instant
the end of his nose went numb. He was sure to frost his cheeks;   5
he knew that, and experienced a pang of regret that he had
not devised a nose-strap of the sort Bud wore in cold snaps.
Such a strap passed across the cheeks, as well, and saved them.
But it didn't matter much, after all. What were frosted cheeks?
A bit painful, that was all; they were never serious.   10

Empty as the man's mind was of thoughts, he was keenly
observant, and he noticed the changes in the creek, the curves
and bends and timber-jams, and always he sharply noted
where he placed his feet. Once, coming around a bend, he
shied abruptly, like a startled horse, curved away from the   15
place where he had been walking, and retreated several paces
back along the trail. The creek he knew was frozen clear to
the bottom,—no creek could contain water in that arctic winter,—but he knew also that there were springs that bubbled out
from the hillsides and ran along under the snow and on top   20
the ice of the creek. He knew that the coldest snaps never
froze these springs, and he knew likewise their danger. They
were traps. They hid pools of water under the snow that
might be three inches deep, or three feet. Sometimes a skin
of ice half an inch thick covered them, and in turn was cov-   25
ered by the snow. Sometimes there were alternate layers of
water and ice-skin, so that when one broke through he kept
on breaking through for a while, sometimes wetting himself
to the waist.

That was why he had shied in such panic. He had felt the   30
give under his feet and heard the crackle of a snow-hidden
ice-skin. And to get his feet wet in such a temperature meant
trouble and danger. At the very least it meant delay, for he
would be forced to stop and build a fire, and under its protection to bare his feet while he dried his socks and moccasins. He 35
stood and studied the creek-bed and its banks, and decided
that the flow of water came from the right. He reflected a

while, rubbing his nose and cheeks, then skirted to the left, stepping gingerly and testing the footing for each step. Once clear of the danger, he took a fresh chew of tobacco and swung along at his four-mile gait.

In the course of the next two hours he came upon several similar traps. Usually the snow above the hidden pools had a sunken, candid appearance that advertised the danger. Once again, however, he had a close call; and once, suspecting danger, he compelled the dog to go on in front. The dog did not want to go. It hung back until the man shoved it forward, and then it went quickly across the white, unbroken surface. Suddenly it broke through, floundered to one side, and got away to firmer footing. It had wet its forefeet and legs, and almost immediately the water that clung to it turned to ice. It made quick efforts to lick the ice off its legs, then dropped down in the snow and began to bite out the ice that had formed between the toes. This was a matter of instinct. To permit the ice to remain would mean sore feet. It did not know this. It merely obeyed the mysterious prompting that arose from the deep crypts of its being. But the man knew, having achieved a judgment on the subject, and he removed the mitten from his right hand and helped tear out the ice-particles. He did not expose his fingers more than a minute, and was astonished at the swift numbness that smote them. It certainly was cold. He pulled on the mitten hastily, and beat the hand savagely across his chest.

At twelve o'clock the day was at its brightest. Yet the sun was too far south on its winter journey to clear the horizon. The bulge of the earth intervened between it and Henderson Creek, where the man walked under a clear sky at noon and cast no shadow. At half-past twelve, to the minute, he arrived at the forks of the creek. He was pleased at the speed he had made. If he kept it up, he would certainly be with the boys by six. He unbuttoned his jacket and shirt and drew forth his lunch. The action consumed no more than a quarter of a minute, yet in that brief moment the numbness laid hold of the exposed fingers. He did not put the mitten on, but, instead, struck the fingers a dozen sharp smashes against his leg. Then he sat down on a snow-covered log to eat. The sting that followed upon the striking of his fingers against his leg ceased so quickly that he was startled. He had had no chance to take a bite of biscuit. He struck the fingers repeatedly and returned them to the mitten, baring the other hand for the purpose of 5 eating. He tried to take a mouthful, but the ice-muzzle prevented. He had forgotten to build a fire and thaw out. He chuckled at his foolishness, and as he chuckled he noted the numbness creeping into the exposed fingers. Also, he noted that the stinging which had first come to his toes when he sat 10 down was already passing away. He wondered whether the toes were warm or numb. He moved them inside the moccasins and decided that they were numb.

He pulled the mitten on hurriedly and stood up. He was a bit frightened. He stamped up and down until the stinging re- 15 turned into the feet. It certainly was cold, was his thought. That man from Sulphur Creek had spoken the truth when telling how cold it sometimes got in the country. And he had laughed at him at the time! That showed one must not be too sure of things. There was no mistake about it, it *was* cold. He 20 strode up and down, stamping his feet and threshing his arms, until reassured by the returning warmth. Then he got out matches and proceeded to make a fire. From the undergrowth, where high water of the previous spring had lodged a supply of seasoned twigs, he got his firewood. Working carefully from 25 a small beginning, he soon had a roaring fire, over which he thawed the ice from his face and in the protection of which he ate his biscuits. For the moment the cold of space was outwitted. The dog took satisfaction in the fire, stretching out close enough for warmth and far enough away to escape being 30 singed.

When the man had finished, he filled his pipe and took his comfortable time over a smoke. Then he pulled on his mittens, settled the ear-flaps of his cap firmly about his ears, and took the creek trail up the left fork. The dog was disappointed and 35 yearned back toward the fire. This man did not know cold. Possibly all the generations of his ancestry had been ignorant

of cold, of real cold, of cold one hundred and seven degrees
below freezing point. But the dog knew; all its ancestry knew,
and it had inherited the knowledge. And it knew that it was
not good to walk abroad in such fearful cold. It was the time
to lie snug in a hole in the snow and wait for a curtain of cloud   5
to be drawn across the face of outer space whence this cold
came. On the other hand, there was no keen intimacy between
the dog and the man. The one was the toil-slave of the other,
and the only caresses it had ever received were the caresses
of the whiplash and of harsh and menacing throat-sounds that   10
threatened the whiplash. So the dog made no effort to com-
municate its apprehension to the man. It was not concerned in
the welfare of the man; it was for its own sake that it yearned
back toward the fire. But the man whistled, and spoke to it
with the sound of whiplashes, and the dog swung in at the   15
man's heel and followed after.

The man took a chew of tobacco and proceeded to start a
new amber beard. Also, his moist breath quickly powdered
with white his mustache, eyebrows, and lashes. There did not
seem to be so many springs on the left fork of the Henderson,   20
and for half an hour the man saw no signs of any. And then it
happened. At a place where there were no signs, where the
soft, unbroken snow seemed to advertise solidity beneath, the
man broke through. It was not deep. He wet himself halfway
to the knees before he floundered out to the firm crust.   25

He was angry, and cursed his luck aloud. He had hoped
to get into camp with the boys at six o'clock, and this would
delay him an hour, for he would have to build a fire and dry
out his foot-gear. This was imperative at that low temperature—
he knew that much; and he turned aside to the bank, which   30
he climbed. On top, tangled in the underbrush about the
trunks of several small spruce trees, was a high-water deposit
of dry firewood—sticks and twigs, principally, but also larger
portions of seasoned branches and fine, dry, last-year's grasses.
He threw down several large pieces on top of the snow. This   35
served for a foundation and prevented the young flame from
drowning itself in the snow it otherwise would melt. The flame

he got by touching a match to a small shred of birch bark that he took from his pocket. This burned even more readily than paper. Placing it on the foundation, he fed the young flame with wisps of dry grass and with the tiniest dry twigs. He worked slowly and carefully, keenly aware of his dan- 5 ger. Gradually, as the flame grew stronger, he increased the size of the twigs with which he fed it. He squatted in the snow, pulling the twigs out from their entanglement in the brush and feeding directly to the flame. He knew there must be no fail- ure. When it is seventy-five below zero, a man must not fail in 10 his first attempt to build a fire—that is, if his feet are wet. If his feet are dry, and he fails, he can run along the trail for half a mile and restore his circulation. But the circulation of wet and freezing feet cannot be restored by running when it is seventy-five below. No matter how fast he runs, the wet feet 15 will freeze the harder.

All this the man knew. The old-timer on Sulphur Creek had told him about it the previous fall, and now he was appreciat- ing the advice. Already all sensation had gone out of his feet. To build the fire he had been forced to remove his mittens, 20 and the fingers had quickly gone numb. His pace of four miles an hour had kept his heart pumping blood to the surface of his body and to all the extremities. But the instant he stopped, the action of the pump eased down. The cold of space smote the unprotected tip of the planet, and he, being on that unpro- 25 tected tip, received the full force of the blow. The blood of his body recoiled before it. The blood was alive, like the dog, and like the dog it wanted to hide away and cover itself up from the fearful cold. So long as he walked four miles an hour, he pumped that blood, willy-nilly, to the surface; but now it 30 ebbed away and sank down into the recesses of his body. The extremities were the first to feel its absence. His wet feet froze the faster, and his exposed fingers numbed the faster, though they had not yet begun to freeze. Nose and cheeks were al- ready freezing, while the skin of all his body chilled as it lost 35 its blood.

But he was safe. Toes and nose and cheeks would be only

touched by the frost, for the fire was beginning to burn with strength. He was feeding it with twigs the size of his finger. In another minute he would be able to feed it with branches the size of his wrist, and then he could remove his wet foot-gear, and, while it dried, he could keep his naked feet warm 5 by the fire, rubbing them at first, of course, with snow. The fire was a success. He was safe. He remembered the advice of the old-timer on Sulphur Creek, and smiled. The old-timer had been very serious in laying down the law that no man must travel alone in the Klondike after fifty below. Well, here he 10 was; he had had the accident; he was alone; and he had saved himself. Those old-timers were rather womanish, some of them, he thought. All a man had to do was to keep his head, and he was all right. Any man who was a man could travel alone. But it was surprising, the rapidity with which his cheeks and nose 15 were freezing. And he had not thought his fingers could go life-less in so short a time. Lifeless they were, for he could scarcely make them move together to grip a twig, and they seemed re-mote from his body and from him. When he touched a twig, he had to look and see whether or not he had hold of it. The 20 wires were pretty well down between him and his finger-ends.

 All of which counted for little. There was the fire, snapping and crackling and promising life with every dancing flame. He started to untie his moccasins. They were coated with ice; the thick German socks were like sheaths of iron halfway to the 25 knees; and the moccasin strings were like rods of steel all twisted and knotted as by some conflagration. For a moment he tugged with his numb fingers, then, realizing the folly of it, he drew his sheath-knife.

 But before he could cut the strings, it happened. It was his 30 own fault or, rather, his mistake. He should not have built the fire under the spruce tree. He should have built it in the open. But it had been easier to pull the twigs from the brush and drop them directly on the fire. Now the tree under which he had done this carried a weight of snow on its boughs. No wind 35 had blown for weeks, and each bough was fully freighted. Each time he had pulled a twig he had communicated a slight agitation to the tree—an imperceptible agitation, so far as he was concerned, but an agitation sufficient to bring about the disaster. High up in the tree one bough capsized its load of snow. This fell on the boughs beneath, capsizing them. This process continued, spreading out and involving the whole tree.   5 It grew like an avalanche, and it descended without warning upon the man and the fire, and the fire was blotted out! Where it had burned was a mantle of fresh and disordered snow.

The man was shocked. It was as though he had just heard his own sentence of death. For a moment he sat and stared at   10 the spot where the fire had been. Then he grew very calm. Perhaps the old-timer on Sulphur Creek was right. If he had only had a trail-mate he would have been in no danger now. The trail-mate could have built the fire. Well, it was up to him to build the fire over again, and this second time there must be   15 no failure. Even if he succeeded, he would most likely lose some toes. His feet must be badly frozen by now, and there would be some time before the second fire was ready.

Such were his thoughts, but he did not sit and think them. He was busy all the time they were passing through his mind.   20 He made a new foundation for a fire, this time in the open, where no treacherous tree could blot it out. Next, he gathered dry grasses and tiny twigs from the high-water flotsam. He could not bring his fingers together to pull them out, but he was able to gather by the handful. In this way he got   25 many rotten twigs and bits of green moss that were undesirable, but it was the best he could do. He worked methodically, even collecting an armful of the larger branches to be used later when the fire gathered strength. And all the while the dog sat and watched him, a certain yearning wistfulness in its   30 eyes, for it looked upon him as the fire-provider, and the fire was slow in coming.

When all was ready, the man reached in his pocket for a second piece of birch bark. He knew the bark was there, and, though he could not feel it with his fingers, he could hear its   35 crisp rustling as he fumbled for it. Try as he would, he could not clutch hold of it. And all the time, in his consciousness,

was the knowledge that each instant his feet were freezing.
This thought tended to put him in a panic, but he fought
against it and kept calm. He pulled on his mittens with his
teeth, and threshed his arms back and forth, beating his hands
with all his might against his sides. He did this sitting down,   5
and he stood up to do it; and all the while the dog sat in the
snow, its wolf-brush of a tail curled around warmly over its
forefeet, its sharp wolf-ears pricked forward intently as it
watched the man. And the man, as he beat and threshed with
his arms and hands, felt a great surge of envy as he regarded   10
the creature that was warm and secure in its natural covering.

After a time he was aware of the first far-away signals of
sensation in his beaten fingers. The faint tingling grew stronger
till it evolved into a stinging ache that was excruciating, but
which the man hailed with satisfaction. He stripped the mit-   15
ten from his right hand and fetched forth the birch bark. The
exposed fingers were quickly going numb again. Next he
brought out his bunch of sulphur matches. But the tremendous cold had already driven the life out of his fingers. In his
effort to separate one match from the others, the whole bunch   20
fell in the snow. He tried to pick it out of the snow, but failed.
The dead fingers could neither touch nor clutch. He was very
careful. He drove the thought of his freezing feet, and nose,
and cheeks, out of his mind, devoting his whole soul to the
matches. He watched, using the sense of vision in place of that 25
of touch, and when he saw his fingers on each side the bunch,
he closed them—that is, he willed to close them, for the wires
were down, and the fingers did not obey. He pulled the mitten on the right hand, and beat it fiercely against his knee.
Then, with both mittened hands, he scooped the bunch of   30
matches, along with much snow, into his lap. Yet he was no
better off.

After some manipulation he managed to get the bunch between the heels of his mittened hands. In this fashion he carried it to his mouth. The ice crackled and snapped when by a   35
violent effort he opened his mouth. He drew the lower jaw in,
curled the upper lip out of the way, and scraped the bunch

with his upper teeth in order to separate a match. He succeeded in getting one, which he dropped on his lap. He was no better off. He could not pick it up. Then he devised a way. He picked it up in his teeth and scratched it on his leg. Twenty times he scratched before he succeeded in lighting it. As it flamed he held it with his teeth to the birch bark. But the burning brimstone went up his nostrils and into his lungs, causing him to cough spasmodically. The match fell into the snow and went out.

The old-timer on Sulphur Creek was right, he thought in the moment of controlled despair that ensued: after fifty below, a man should travel with a partner. He beat his hands, but failed in exciting any sensation. Suddenly he bared both hands, removing the mittens with his teeth. He caught the whole bunch between the heels of his hands. His arm-muscles not being frozen enabled him to press the hand-heels tightly against the matches. Then he scratched the bunch along his leg. It flared into flame, seventy sulphur matches at once! There was no wind to blow them out. He kept his head to one side to escape the strangling fumes, and held the blazing bunch to the birch bark. As he so held it, he became aware of sensation in his hand. His flesh was burning. He could smell it. Deep down below the surface he could feel it. The sensation developed into pain that grew acute. And still he endured it, holding the flame of the matches clumsily to the bark that would not light readily because his own burning hands were in the way, absorbing most of the flame.

At last, when he could endure no more, he jerked his hands apart. The blazing matches fell sizzling into the snow, but the birch bark was alight. He began laying dry grasses and the tiniest twigs on the flame. He could not pick and choose, for he had to lift the fuel between the heels of his hands. Small pieces of rotten wood and green moss clung to the twigs, and he bit them off as well as he could with his teeth. He cherished the flame carefully and awkwardly. It meant life, and it must not perish. The withdrawal of blood from the surface of his body now made him begin to shiver, and he grew more awkward. A large piece of green moss fell squarely on the little fire. He tried to poke it out with his fingers, but his shivering frame made him poke too far, and he disrupted the nucleus of the little fire, the burning grasses and tiny twigs separating and scattering. He tried to poke them together again, but in spite of the tenseness of the effort, his shivering got away with him, and the twigs were hopelessly scattered. Each twig gushed a puff of smoke and went out. The fire-provider had failed. As he looked apathetically about him, his eyes chanced on the dog, sitting across the ruins of the fire from him, in the snow, making restless, hunching movements, slightly lifting one forefoot and then the other, shifting its weight back and forth on them with wistful eagerness.

The sight of the dog put a wild idea into his head. He remembered the tale of the man, caught in a blizzard, who killed a steer and crawled inside the carcass, and so was saved. He would kill the dog and bury his hands in the warm body until the numbness went out of them. Then he could build another fire. He spoke to the dog, calling it to him; but in his voice was a strange note of fear that frightened the animal, who had never known the man to speak in such way before. Something was the matter, and its suspicious nature sensed danger—it knew not what danger, but somewhere, somehow, in its brain arose an apprehension of the man. It flattened its ears down at the sound of the man's voice, and its restless, hunching movements and the liftings and shiftings of its forefeet became more pronounced; but it would not come to the man. He got on his hands and knees and crawled toward the dog. This unusual posture again excited suspicion, and the animal sidled mincingly away.

The man sat up in the snow for a moment and struggled for calmness. Then he pulled on his mittens, by means of his teeth, and got upon his feet. He glanced down at first in order to assure himself that he was really standing up, for the absence of sensation in his feet left him unrelated to the earth. His erect position in itself started to drive the webs of suspicion from the dog's mind; and when he spoke peremptorily,

with the sound of whiplashes in his voice, the dog rendered its customary allegiance and came to him. As it came within reaching distance, the man lost his control. His arms flashed out to the dog, and he experienced genuine surprise when he discovered that his hands could not clutch, that there was   5
neither bend nor feeling in the fingers. He had forgotten for the moment that they were frozen and that they were freezing more and more. All this happened quickly, and before the animal could get away, he encircled its body with his arms. He sat down in the snow, and in this fashion held the dog, 10
while it snarled and whined and struggled.

But it was all he could do, hold its body encircled in his arms and sit there. He realized that he could not kill the dog. There was no way to do it. With his helpless hands he could neither draw nor hold his sheath-knife nor throttle the animal. He re- 15
leased it, and it plunged wildly away, with tail between its legs, and still snarling. It halted forty feet away and surveyed him curiously, with ears sharply pricked forward. The man looked down at his hands in order to locate them, and found them hanging on the ends of his arms. It struck him as curious 20
that one should have to use his eyes in order to find out where his hands were. He began threshing his arms back and forth, beating the mittened hands against his sides. He did this for five minutes, violently, and his heart pumped enough blood up to the surface to put a stop to his shivering. But no sensa- 25
tion was aroused in the hands. He had an impression that they hung like weights on the ends of his arms, but when he tried to run the impression down, he could not find it.

A certain fear of death, dull and oppressive, came to him. This fear quickly became poignant as he realized that it was 30
no longer a mere matter of freezing his fingers and toes, or of losing his hands and feet, but that it was a matter of life and death with the chances against him. This threw him into a panic, and he turned and ran up the creek-bed along the old, dim trail. The dog joined in behind and kept up with him. He 35
ran blindly, without intention, in fear such as he had never known in his life. Slowly, as he plowed and floundered through

the snow, he began to see things again,—the banks of the creek, the old timber-jams, the leafless aspens, and the sky. The running made him feel better. He did not shiver. Maybe, if he ran on, his feet would thaw out; and, anyway, if he ran far enough, he would reach camp and the boys. Without doubt he would lose some fingers and toes and some of his face; but the boys would take care of him, and save the rest of him when he got there. And at the same time there was another thought in his mind that said he would never get to the camp and the boys; that it was too many miles away, that the freezing had too great a start on him, and that he would soon be stiff and dead. This thought he kept in the background and refused to consider. Sometimes it pushed itself forward and demanded to be heard, but he thrust it back and strove to think of other things.

It struck him as curious that he could run at all on feet so frozen that he could not feel them when they struck the earth and took the weight of his body. He seemed to himself to skim along above the surface, and to have no connection with the earth. Somewhere he had once seen a winged Mercury, and he wondered if Mercury felt as he felt when skimming over the earth.

His theory of running until he reached camp and the boys had one flaw in it: he lacked the endurance. Several times he stumbled, and finally he tottered, crumpled up, and fell. When he tried to rise, he failed. He must sit and rest, he decided, and next time he would merely walk and keep on going. As he sat and regained his breath, he noted that he was feeling quite warm and comfortable. He was not shivering, and it even seemed that a warm glow had come to his chest and trunk. And yet, when he touched his nose or cheeks, there was no sensation. Running would not thaw them out. Nor would it thaw out his hands and feet. Then the thought came to him that the frozen portions of his body must be extending. He tried to keep this thought down, to forget it, to think of something else; he was aware of the panicky feeling that it caused, and he was afraid of the panic. But the thought asserted itself,

and persisted, until it produced a vision of his body totally
frozen. This was too much, and he made another wild run
along the trail. Once he slowed down to a walk, but the
thought of the freezing extending itself made him run again.
And all the time the dog ran with him, at his heels. When
he fell down a second time, it curled its tail over its forefeet
and sat in front of him, facing him, curiously eager and intent.
The warmth and security of the animal angered him, and he
cursed it till it flattened down its ears appeasingly. This time
the shivering came more quickly upon the man. He was losing
in his battle with the frost. It was creeping into his body from
all sides. The thought of it drove him on, but he ran no more
than a hundred feet, when he staggered and pitched headlong. It was his last panic. When he had recovered his breath
and control, he sat up and entertained in his mind the conception of meeting death with dignity. However, the conception
did not come to him in such terms. His idea of it was that he
had been making a fool of himself, running around like a
chicken with its head cut off—such was the simile that occurred to him. Well, he was bound to freeze anyway, and he
might as well take it decently. With this new-found peace of
mind came the first glimmerings of drowsiness. A good idea,
he thought, to sleep off to death. It was like taking an anæs-
thetic. Freezing was not so bad as people thought. There were
lots worse ways to die.

He pictured the boys finding his body next day. Suddenly
he found himself with them, coming along the trail and looking for himself. And, still with them, he came around a turn
in the trail and found himself lying in the snow. He did not
belong with himself any more, for even then he was out of
himself, standing with the boys and looking at himself in the
snow. It certainly was cold, was his thought. When he got back
to the States he could tell the folks what real cold was. He
drifted on from this to a vision of the old-timer on Sulphur
Creek. He could see him quite clearly, warm and comfortable,
and smoking a pipe.

"You were right, old hoss; you were right," the man mumbled to the old-timer of Sulphur Creek.

Then the man drowsed off into what seemed to him the most comfortable and satisfying sleep he had ever known. The dog sat facing him and waiting. The brief day drew to a close in a long, slow twilight. There were no signs of a fire to be made, and, besides, never in the dog's experience had it known a man to sit like that in the snow and make no fire. As the twilight drew on, its eager yearning for the fire mastered it, and with a great lifting and shifting of forefeet, it whined softly, then flattened its ears down in anticipation of being chidden by the man. But the man remained silent. Later, the dog whined loudly. And still later it crept close to the man and caught the scent of death. This made the animal bristle and back away. A little longer it delayed, howling under the stars that leaped and danced and shone brightly in the cold sky. Then it turned and trotted up the trail in the direction of the camp it knew, where were the other food-providers and fire-providers.

Vocabulary

1. Does the author's term "an intangible pall" (p. 1, l. 9) mean the same thing as "subtle gloom" which is used in the same sentence to describe the day?

2. In the next paragraph (l. 19), the author describes the snow as "rolling in gentle undulations." What other words might he have used in describing the scene?

3. We read that the man's mind was empty of thoughts (p. 5, l. 11), yet in the preceding paragraph the author says that he had a "reiterated" thought. Is the author contradicting himself? What does the quoted word mean?

4. When the man spoke "peremptorily" (p. 14, l. 37) to his dog, how did he speak?

5. What was the man's fear like when the author says that it became "poignant" (p. 15, l. 30)?

Questions and Suggestions for Reading

ACTION

1. In this story the central figure is always doing something—either mentally or physically. In his first attempt to build a fire, after breaking through the ice, he fails because he has not looked sufficiently ahead at the possible consequences of his actions. What are the reasons for his other failures?

2. Notice that the man grows very calm after the first fire is extinguished. Does he remain calm? Why?

CONFLICT

1. At the beginning of this story, the man is master of himself, his dog, and his surroundings. He has no conflict. At what point does he become the victim of the elements? Trace the steps by which his conflict with the elements is intensified.

2. At what point do you know that the main character will die? At what point does he know?

3. The dog is not an element like the snow and cold, but he has a reason for being in the story. Is this animal in the story simply to provide the main character with another chance for life? Is he in the story to prove that man should be kind to four-footed beasts or that instinct is better than reason? When the man turns on the dog, do you realize that he will be unable to kill the animal, or do you feel that the author has tricked you into believing that the man has one more chance to live?

Richard Connell

THE MOST DANGEROUS GAME

Off there to the right—somewhere—is a large island," said Whitney. "It's rather a mystery—"

"What island is it?" Rainsford asked.

"The old charts call it 'Ship-Trap Island,'" Whitney replied.
"A suggestive name, isn't it? Sailors have a curious dread of   5
the place. I don't know why. Some superstition—"

"Can't see it," remarked Rainsford, trying to peer through the
dank tropical night that was palpable as it pressed its thick
warm blackness in upon the yacht.

"You've good eyes," said Whitney, with a laugh, "and I've   10
seen you pick off a moose moving in the brown fall bush at
four hundred yards, but even you can't see four miles or so
through a moonless Caribbean night."

"Nor four yards," admitted Rainsford. "Ugh! It's like moist
black velvet."   15

"It will be light in Rio," promised Whitney. "We should
make it in a few days. I hope the jaguar guns have come from
Purdey's. We should have some good hunting up the Amazon.
Great sport, hunting."

"The best sport in the world," agreed Rainsford.   20

"For the hunter," amended Whitney. "Not for the jaguar."

"Don't talk rot, Whitney," said Rainsford. "You're a big-game
hunter, not a philosopher. Who cares how a jaguar feels?"

"Perhaps the jaguar does," observed Whitney.

"Bah! They've no understanding."   25

"Even so, I rather think they understand one thing—fear.
The fear of pain and the fear of death."

"Nonsense," laughed Rainsford. "This hot weather is making you soft, Whitney. Be a realist. The world is made up of two classes—the hunters and the hunted. Luckily, you and I are hunters. Do you think we've passed that island yet?"

"I can't tell in the dark. I hope so."   5

"Why?" asked Rainsford.

"The place has a reputation—a bad one."

"Cannibals?" suggested Rainsford.

"Hardly. Even cannibals wouldn't live in such a God-forsaken place. But it's gotten into sailor lore, somehow. Didn't 10 you notice that the crew's nerves seemed a bit jumpy to-day?"

"They were a bit strange, now you mention it. Even Captain Nielsen—"

"Yes, even that tough-minded old Swede, who'd go up to the devil himself and ask him for a light. Those fishy blue eyes 15 held a look I never saw there before. All I could get out of him was: 'This place has an evil name among sea-faring men, sir.' Then he said to me, very gravely: 'Don't you feel anything?'— as if the air about us was actually poisonous. Now, you mustn't laugh when I tell you this—I did feel something like a sudden 20 chill.

"There was no breeze. The sea was as flat as a plate-glass window. We were drawing near the island then. What I felt was a—a mental chill; a sort of sudden dread."

"Pure imagination," said Rainsford. "One superstitious sailor 25 can taint the whole ship's company with his fear."

"Maybe. But sometimes I think sailors have an extra sense that tells them when they are in danger. Sometimes I think evil is a tangible thing—with wave lengths, just as sound and light have. An evil place can, so to speak, broadcast vibrations 30 of evil. Anyhow, I'm glad we're getting out of this zone. Well, I think I'll turn in now, Rainsford."

"I'm not sleepy," said Rainsford. "I'm going to smoke another pipe up on the afterdeck.

"Good night, then, Rainsford. See you at breakfast."   35

"Right. Good night, Whitney."

There was no sound in the night as Rainsford sat there, but the muffled throb of the engine that drove the yacht swiftly through the darkness, and the swish and ripple of the wash of the propeller.

Rainsford, reclining in a steamer chair, indolently puffed on his favorite brier. The sensuous drowsiness of the night was on him. "It's so dark," he thought, "that I could sleep without closing my eyes; the night would be my eyelids—"

An abrupt sound startled him. Off to the right he heard it, and his ears, expert in such matters, could not be mistaken. Again he heard the sound, and again. Somewhere, off in the blackness, some one had fired a gun three times.

Rainsford sprang up and moved quickly to the rail, mystified. He strained his eyes in the direction from which the reports had come, but it was like trying to see through a blanket. He leaped upon the rail and balanced himself there, to get greater elevation; his pipe, striking a rope, was knocked from his mouth. He lunged for it; a short, hoarse cry came from his lips as he realized he had reached too far and had lost his balance. The cry was pinched off short as the blood-warm waters of the Caribbean Sea closed over his head.

He struggled up to the surface and tried to cry out, but the wash from the speeding yacht slapped him in the face and the salt water in his open mouth made him gag and strangle. Desperately he struck out with strong strokes after the receding lights of the yacht, but he stopped before he had swum fifty feet. A certain cool-headedness had come to him; it was not the first time he had been in a tight place. There was a chance that his cries could be heard by some one aboard the yacht, but that chance was slender, and grew more slender as the yacht raced on. He wrestled himself out of his clothes, and shouted with all his power. The lights of the yacht became faint and ever-vanishing fireflies; then they were blotted out entirely by the night.

Rainsford remembered the shots. They had come from the right, and doggedly he swam in that direction, swimming with slow, deliberate strokes, conserving his strength. For a seemingly endless time he fought the sea. He began to count his strokes; he could do possibly a hundred more and then—

Rainsford heard a sound. It came out of the darkness, a high screaming sound, the sound of an animal in an extremity of anguish and terror. 5

He did not recognize the animal that made the sound; he did not try to; with fresh vitality he swam toward the sound. He heard it again; then it was cut short by another noise, crisp, staccato.

"Pistol shot," muttered Rainsford, swimming on. 10

Ten minutes of determined effort brought another sound to his ears—the most welcome he had ever heard—the muttering and growling of the sea breaking on a rocky shore. He was almost on the rocks before he saw them; on a night less calm he would have been shattered against them. With his remain- 15 ing strength he dragged himself from the swirling waters. Jagged crags appeared to jut into the opaqueness, he forced himself upward, hand over hand. Gasping, his hands raw, he reached a flat place at the top. Dense jungle came down to the very edge of the cliffs. What perils that tangle of trees and 20 underbrush might hold for him did not concern Rainsford just then. All he knew was that he was safe from his enemy, the sea, and that utter weariness was on him. He flung himself down at the jungle edge and tumbled headlong into the deep- est sleep of his life. 25

When he opened his eyes he knew from the position of the sun that it was late in the afternoon. Sleep had given him new vigor; a sharp hunger was picking at him. He looked about him, almost cheerfully.

"Where there are pistol shots, there are men. Where there 30 are men, there is food," he thought. But what kind of men, he wondered, in so forbidding a place? An unbroken front of snarled and ragged jungle fringed the shore.

He saw no sign of a trail through the closely knit web of weeds and trees; it was easier to go along the shore, and 35 Rainsford floundered along by the water. Not far from where he had landed, he stopped.

Some wounded thing, by the evidence a large animal, had thrashed about in the underbrush; the jungle weeds were crushed down and the moss was lacerated; one patch of weeds was stained crimson. A small, glittering object not far away caught Rainsford's eye and he picked it up. It was an empty cartridge.

"A twenty-two," he remarked. "That's odd. It must have been a fairly large animal too. The hunter had his nerve with him to tackle it with a light gun. It's clear that the brute put up a fight. I suppose the first three shots I heard was when the hunter flushed his quarry and wounded it. The last shot was when he trailed it here and finished it."

He examined the ground closely and found what he had hoped to find—the print of hunting boots. They pointed along the cliff in the direction he had been going. Eagerly he hurried along, now slipping on a rotten log or a loose stone, but making headway; night was beginning to settle down on the island.

Bleak darkness was blacking out the sea and jungle when Rainsford sighted the lights. He came upon them as he turned a crook in the coast line, and his first thought was that he had come upon a village, for there were many lights. But as he forged along he saw to his great astonishment that all the lights were in one enormous building—a lofty structure with pointed towers plunging upward into the gloom. His eyes made out the shadowy outlines of a palatial château; it was set on a high bluff, and on three sides of it cliffs dived down to where the sea licked greedy lips in the shadows.

"Mirage," thought Rainsford. But it was no mirage, he found, when he opened the tall spiked iron gate. The stone steps were real enough; the massive door with a leering gargoyle for a knocker was real enough; yet about it all hung an air of unreality.

He lifted the knocker, and it creaked up stiffly, as if it had never before been used. He let it fall, and it startled him with its booming loudness. He thought he heard steps within; the door remained closed. Again Rainsford lifted the heavy

knocker, and let it fall. The door opened then, opened as suddenly as if it were on a spring, and Rainsford stood blinking
in the river of glaring gold light that poured out. The first
thing Rainsford's eyes discerned was the largest man Rainsford had ever seen—a gigantic creature, solidly made and   5
black-bearded to the waist. In his hand the man held a long-
barreled revolver, and he was pointing it straight at Rainsford's heart.

Out of the snarl of beard two small eyes regarded Rainsford.   10

"Don't be alarmed," said Rainsford, with a smile which he
hoped was disarming. "I'm no robber. I fell off a yacht. My
name is Sanger Rainsford of New York City."

The menacing look in the eyes did not change. The revolver 15
pointed as rigidly as if the giant were a statue. He gave no
sign that he understood Rainsford's words, or that he had even
heard them. He was dressed in uniform, a black uniform
trimmed with gray astrakhan.

"I'm Sanger Rainsford of New York," Rainsford began again. 20
"I fell off a yacht. I am hungry."

The man's only answer was to raise with his thumb the
hammer of his revolver. Then Rainsford saw the man's free
hand go to his forehead in a military salute, and he saw him
click his heels together and stand at attention. Another man 25
was coming down the broad marble steps, an erect, slender
man in evening clothes. He advanced to Rainsford and held
out his hand.

In a cultivated voice marked by a slight accent that gave it
added precision and deliberateness, he said: "It is a very   30
great pleasure and honor to welcome Mr. Sanger Rainsford,
the celebrated hunter, to my home."

Automatically Rainsford shook the man's hand.

"I've read your book about hunting snow leopards in Tibet,
you see," explained the man. "I am General Zaroff."   35

Rainsford's first impression was that the man was singularly
handsome; his second was that there was an original, almost
bizarre quality about the general's face. He was a tall man

past middle age, for his hair was a vivid white; but his thick
eyebrows and pointed military mustache were as black as the
night from which Rainsford had come. His eyes, too, were
black and very bright. He had high cheek bones, a sharp-cut
nose, a spare, dark face, the face of a man used to giving or-   5
ders, the face of an aristocrat. Turning to the giant in uniform,
the general made a sign. The giant put away his pistol, sa-
luted, withdrew.

"Ivan is an incredibly strong fellow," remarked the general,
"but he has the misfortune to be deaf and dumb. A simple   10
fellow, but, I'm afraid, like all his race, a bit of a savage."

"Is he Russian?"

"He is a Cossack," said the general, and his smile showed
red lips and pointed teeth. "So am I."

"Come," he said, "we shouldn't be chatting here. We can   15
talk later. Now you want clothes, food, rest. You shall have
them. This is a most restful spot."

Ivan had reappeared, and the general spoke to him with
lips that moved but gave forth no sound.

"Follow Ivan, if you please, Mr. Rainsford," said the gen-   20
eral. "I was about to have my dinner when you came. I'll wait
for you. You'll find that my clothes will fit you, I think."

It was to a huge, beam-ceilinged bedroom with a canopied
bed big enough for six men that Rainsford followed the silent
giant. Ivan laid out an evening suit, and Rainsford, as he put   25
it on, noticed that it came from a London tailor who ordinarily
cut and sewed for none below the rank of duke.

The dining room to which Ivan conducted him was in
many ways remarkable. There was a medieval magnificence
about it; it suggested a baronial hall of feudal times with its   30
oaken panels, its high ceiling, its vast refectory table where
twoscore men could sit down to eat. About the hall were the
mounted heads of many animals—lions, tigers, elephants,
moose, bears; larger or more perfect specimens Rainsford had
never seen. At the great table the general was sitting, alone.   35

"You'll have a cocktail, Mr. Rainsford," he suggested. The
cocktail was surpassingly good; and, Rainsford noted, the

table appointments were of the finest—the linen, the crystal, the silver, the china.

They were eating *borsch*, the rich, red soup with whipped cream so dear to Russian palates. Half apologetically General Zaroff said: "We do our best to preserve the amenities of civilization here. Please forgive any lapses. We are well off the beaten track, you know. Do you think the champagne has suffered from its long ocean trip?"

"Not in the least," declared Rainsford. He was finding the general a most thoughtful and affable host, a true cosmopolite. But there was one small trait of the general's that made Rainsford uncomfortable. Whenever he looked up from his plate he found the general studying him, appraising him narrowly.

"Perhaps," said General Zaroff, "you were surprised that I recognized your name. You see, I read all books on hunting published in English, French, and Russian. I have but one passion in my life, Mr. Rainsford, and it is the hunt."

"You have some wonderful heads here," said Rainsford as he ate a particularly well cooked filet mignon. "That Cape buffalo is the largest I ever saw."

"Oh, that fellow. Yes, he was a monster."

"Did he charge you?"

"Hurled me against a tree," said the general. "Fractured my skull. But I got the brute."

"I've always thought," said Rainsford, "that the Cape buffalo is the most dangerous of all big game."

For a moment the general did not reply; he was smiling his curious red-lipped smile. Then he said slowly: "No. You are wrong, sir. The Cape buffalo is not the most dangerous big game." He sipped his wine. "Here in my preserve on this island," he said in the same slow tone, "I hunt more dangerous game."

Rainsford expressed his surprise. "Is there big game on this island?"

The general nodded. "The biggest."

"Really?"

"Oh, it isn't here naturally, of course. I have to stock the island."

"What have you imported, general?" Rainsford asked. "Tigers?"

The general smiled. "No," he said. "Hunting tigers ceased   5
to interest me some years ago. I exhausted their possibilities, you see. No thrill left in tigers, no real danger. I live for danger, Mr. Rainsford."

The general took from his pocket a gold cigaret case and offered his guest a long black cigaret with a silver tip; it was 10
perfumed and gave off a smell like incense.

"We will have some capital hunting, you and I," said the general. "I shall be most glad to have your society."

"But what game—" began Rainsford.

"I'll tell you," said the general. "You will be amused, I know. 15
I think I may say, in all modesty, that I have done a rare thing. I have invented a new sensation. May I pour you another glass of port, Mr. Rainsford?"

"Thank you, general."

The general filled both glasses, and said: "God makes some 20
men poets. Some He makes kings, some beggars. Me He made a hunter. My hand was made for the trigger, my father said. He was a very rich man with a quarter of a million acres in the Crimea, and he was an ardent sportsman. When I was only five years old he gave me a little gun, specially made in 25
Moscow for me, to shoot sparrows with. When I shot some of his prize turkeys with it, he did not punish me; he complimented me on my marksmanship. I killed my first bear in the Caucasus when I was ten. My whole life has been one prolonged hunt. I went into the army—it was expected of noble- 30
men's sons—and for a time commanded a division of Cossack cavalry, but my real interest was always the hunt. I have hunted every kind of game in every land. It would be impossible for me to tell you how many animals I have killed."

The general puffed at his cigaret.   35

"After the debacle in Russia I left the country, for it was imprudent for an officer of the Czar to stay there. Many noble Russians lost everything. I, luckily, had invested heavily in

American securities, so I shall never have to open a tea room in Monte Carlo or drive a taxi in Paris. Naturally, I continued to hunt—grizzlies in your Rockies, crocodiles in the Ganges, rhinoceroses in East Africa. It was in Africa that the Cape buffalo hit me and laid me up for six months. As soon as I recovered I started for the Amazon to hunt jaguars, for I had heard they were unusually cunning. They weren't." The Cossack sighed. "They were no match at all for a hunter with his wits about him, and a high-powered rifle. I was bitterly disappointed. I was lying in my tent with a splitting headache one night when a terrible thought pushed its way into my mind. Hunting was beginning to bore me! And hunting, remember, had been my life. I have heard that in America business men often go to pieces when they give up the business that has been their life."

"Yes, that's so," said Rainsford.

The general smiled. "I had no wish to go to pieces," he said. "I must do something. Now, mine is an analytical mind, Mr. Rainsford. Doubtless that is why I enjoy the problems of the chase."

"No doubt, General Zaroff."

"So," continued the general, "I asked myself why the hunt no longer fascinated me. You are much younger than I am, Mr. Rainsford, and have not hunted as much, but you perhaps can guess the answer."

"What was it?"

"Simply this: hunting had ceased to be what you call 'a sporting proposition.' It had become too easy. I always got my quarry. Always. There is no greater bore than perfection."

The general lit a fresh cigaret.

"No animal had a chance with me any more. That is no boast; it is a mathematical certainty. The animal had nothing but his legs and his instinct. Instinct is no match for reason. When I thought of this it was a tragic moment for me, I can tell you."

Rainsford leaned across the table, absorbed in what his host was saying.

"It came to me as an inspiration what I must do," the general went on.

"And that was?"

The general smiled the quiet smile of one who has faced an obstacle and surmounted it with success. "I had to invent 5
a new animal to hunt," he said.

"A new animal? You're joking."

"Not at all," said the general. "I never joke about hunting. I needed a new animal. I found one. So I bought this island, built this house, and here I do my hunting. The island is per- 10
fect for my purposes—there are jungles with a maze of trails in them, hills, swamps—"

"But the animal, General Zaroff?"

"Oh," said the general, "it supplies me with the most exciting hunting in the world. No other hunting compares with it 15
for an instant. Every day I hunt, and I never grow bored now, for I have a quarry with which I can match my wits."

Rainsford's bewilderment showed in his face.

"I wanted the ideal animal to hunt," explained the general. "So I said: 'What are the attributes of an ideal quarry?' And 20
the answer was, of course: 'It must have courage, cunning, and, above all, it must be able to reason.'"

"But no animal can reason," objected Rainsford.

"My dear fellow," said the general, "there is one that can."

"But you can't mean—" gasped Rainsford. 25

"And why not?"

"I can't believe you are serious, General Zaroff. This is a grisly joke."

"Why should I not be serious? I am speaking of hunting."

"Hunting? Good God, General Zaroff, what you speak of is 30
murder."

The general laughed with entire good nature. He regarded Rainsford quizzically. "I refuse to believe that so modern and civilized a young man as you seem to be harbors romantic 35
ideas about the value of human life. Surely your experiences in the war—"

"Did not make me condone cold-blooded murder," finished Rainsford stiffly.

Laughter shook the general. "How extraordinarily droll you are!" he said. "One does not expect nowadays to find a young man of the educated class, even in America, with such a naïve, and, if I may say so, mid-Victorian point of view. It's like finding a snuff-box in a limousine. Ah, well, doubtless you had Puritan ancestors. So many Americans appear to have had. I'll wager you'll forget your notions when you go hunting with me. You've a genuine new thrill in store for you, Mr. Rainsford."

"Thank you, I'm a hunter, not a murderer."

"Dear me," said the general, quite unruffled, "again that unpleasant word. But I think I can show you that your scruples are quite ill founded."

"Yes?"

"Life is for the strong, to be lived by the strong, and, if need be, taken by the strong. The weak of the world were put here to give the strong pleasure. I am strong. Why should I not use my gift? If I wish to hunt, why should I not? I hunt the scum of the earth—sailors from tramp ships—lascars, blacks, Chinese, whites, mongrels—a thorobred horse or hound is worth more than a score of them."

"But they are men," said Rainsford hotly.

"Precisely," said the general. "That is why I use them. It gives me pleasure. They can reason, after a fashion. So they are dangerous."

"But where do you get them?"

The general's left eyelid fluttered down in a wink. "This island is called Ship-Trap," he answered. "Sometimes an angry god of the high seas sends them to me. Sometimes, when Providence is not so kind, I help Providence a bit. Come to the window with me."

Rainsford went to the window and looked out toward the sea.

"Watch! Out there!" exclaimed the general, pointing into the night. Rainsford's eyes saw only blackness, and then, as the general pressed a button, far out to sea Rainsford saw the flash of lights.

The general chuckled. "They indicate a channel," he said, "where there's none: giant rocks with razor edges crouch like a sea monster with wide-open jaws. They can crush a ship as easily as I crush this nut." He dropped a walnut on the hardwood floor and brought his heel grinding down on it. "Oh, yes," he said, casually, as if in answer to a question, "I have electricity. We try to be civilized here."

"Civilized? And you shoot down men?"

A trace of anger was in the general's black eyes, but it was there for but a second, and he said, in his most pleasant manner: "Dear me, what a righteous young man you are! I assure you I do not do the thing you suggest. That would be barbarous. I treat these visitors with every consideration. They get plenty of good food and exercise. They get into splendid physical condition. You shall see for yourself to-morrow."

"What do you mean?"

"We'll visit my training school," smiled the general. "It's in the cellar. I have about a dozen pupils down there now. They're from the Spanish bark San Lucar that had the bad luck to go on the rocks out there. A very inferior lot, I regret to say. Poor specimens and more accustomed to the deck than to the jungle."

He raised his hand, and Ivan, who served as waiter, brought thick Turkish coffee. Rainsford, with an effort, held his tongue in check.

"It's a game, you see," pursued the general blandly. "I suggest to one of them that we go hunting. I give him a supply of food and an excellent hunting knife. I give him three hours' start. I am to follow, armed only with a pistol of the smallest caliber and range. If my quarry eludes me for three whole days, he wins the game. If I find him"—the general smiled—"he loses."

"Suppose he refuses to be hunted?"

"Oh," said the general, "I give him his option, of course. He need not play that game if he doesn't wish to. If he does not

wish to hunt, I turn him over to Ivan. Ivan once had the honor
of serving as official knouter to the Great White Czar, and he
has his own ideas of sport. Invariably, Mr. Rainsford, invariably they choose the hunt."

"And if they win?" 5

The smile on the general's face widened. "To date I have
not lost," he said.

Then he added, hastily: "I don't wish you to think me a
braggart, Mr. Rainsford. Many of them afford only the most
elementary sort of problem. Occasionally I strike a tartar. One 10
almost did win. I eventually had to use the dogs."

"The dogs?"

"This way, please. I'll show you."

The general steered Rainsford to a window. The lights from
the windows sent a flickering illumination that made gro- 15
tesque patterns on the courtyard below, and Rainsford could
see moving about there a dozen or so huge black shapes; as
they turned toward him, their eyes glittered greenly.

"A rather good lot, I think," observed the general. "They are
let out at seven every night. If anyone should try to get into 20
my house—or out of it—something extremely regrettable would
occur to him." He hummed a snatch of song from the Folies
Bergère.

"And now," said the general, "I want to show you my new
collection of heads. Will you come with me to the library?" 25

"I hope," said Rainsford, "that you will excuse me to-night,
General Zaroff. I'm really not feeling at all well."

"Ah, indeed?" the general inquired solicitously. "Well, I suppose that's only natural, after your long swim. You need a
good, restful night's sleep. To-morrow you'll feel like a new 30
man, I'll wager. Then we'll hunt, eh? I've one rather promising prospect—"

Rainsford was hurrying from the room.

"Sorry you can't go with me to-night," called the general.
"I expect rather fair sport—a big, strong black. He looks re- 35
sourceful—Well, good night, Mr. Rainsford; I hope you have
a good night's rest."

The bed was good, and the pajamas of the softest silk, and he was tired in every fiber of his being, but nevertheless Rainsford could not quiet his brain with the opiate of sleep. He lay, eyes wide open. Once he thought he heard stealthy steps in the corridor outside his room. He sought to throw open the door; it would not open. He went to the window and looked out. His room was high up in one of the towers. The lights of the château were out now, and it was dark and silent, but there was a fragment of sallow moon, and by its wan light he could see, dimly, the courtyard; there, weaving in and out in the pattern of shadow, were black, noiseless forms; the hounds heard him at the window and looked up, expectantly, with their green eyes. Rainsford went back to the bed and lay down. By many methods he tried to put himself to sleep. He had achieved a doze when, just as morning began to come, he heard, far off in the jungle, the faint report of a pistol.

General Zaroff did not appear until luncheon. He was dressed faultlessly in the tweeds of a country squire. He was solicitous about the state of Rainsford's health.

"As for me," sighed the general, "I do not feel so well. I am worried, Mr. Rainsford. Last night I detected traces of my old complaint."

To Rainsford's questioning glance the general said: "Ennui. Boredom."

Then, taking a second helping of Crêpes Suzette, the general explained: "The hunting was not good last night. The fellow lost his head. He made a straight trail that offered no problems at all. That's the trouble with these sailors; they have dull brains to begin with, and they do not know how to get about in the woods. They do excessively stupid and obvious things. It's most annoying. Will you have another glass of Chablis, Mr. Rainsford?"

"General," said Rainsford firmly, "I wish to leave this island at once."

The general raised his thickets of eyebrows; he seemed hurt. "But, my dear fellow," the general protested, "you've only just come. You've had no hunting—"

"I wish to go to-day," said Rainsford. He saw the dead black eyes of the general on him, studying him. General Zaroff's face suddenly brightened.

He filled Rainsford's glass with venerable Chablis from a dusty bottle.

"To-night," said the general, "we will hunt—you and I."

Rainsford shook his head. "No, general," he said. "I will not hunt."

The general shrugged his shoulders and delicately ate a hothouse grape. "As you wish, my friend," he said. "The choice rests entirely with you. But may I not venture to suggest that you will find my idea of sport more diverting than Ivan's?"

He nodded toward the corner to where the giant stood, scowling, his thick arms crossed on his hogshead of chest.

"You don't mean—" cried Rainsford.

"My dear fellow," said the general, "have I not told you I always mean what I say about hunting? This is really an inspiration. I drink to a foeman worthy of my steel—at last."

The general raised his glass, but Rainsford sat staring at him.

"You'll find this game worth playing," the general said enthusiastically. "Your brain against mine. Your woodcraft against mine. Your strength and stamina against mine. Outdoor chess! And the stake is not without value, eh?"

"And if I win—" began Rainsford huskily.

"I'll cheerfully acknowledge myself defeated if I do not find you by midnight of the third day," said General Zaroff. "My sloop will place you on the mainland near a town."

The general read what Rainsford was thinking.

"Oh, you can trust me," said the Cossack. "I will give you my word as a gentleman and a sportsman. Of course you, in turn, must agree to say nothing of your visit here."

"I'll agree to nothing of the kind," said Rainsford.

"Oh," said the general, "in that case— But why discuss that now? Three days hence we can discuss it over a bottle of Veuve Cliquot, unless—"

The general sipped his wine.

Then a businesslike air animated him. "Ivan," he said to

Rainsford, "will supply you with hunting clothes, food, a knife. I suggest you wear moccasins; they leave a poorer trail. I suggest too that you avoid the big swamp in the southeast corner of the island. We call it Death Swamp. There's quicksand there. One foolish fellow tried it. The deplorable part of it 5 was that Lazarus followed him. You can imagine my feelings, Mr. Rainsford. I loved Lazarus; he was the finest hound in my pack. Well, I must beg you to excuse me now. I always take a siesta after lunch. You'll hardly have time for a nap, I fear. You'll want to start, no doubt. I shall not follow till dusk. 10 Hunting at night is so much more exciting than by day, don't you think? Au revoir, Mr. Rainsford, au revoir."

General Zaroff, with a deep, courtly bow, strolled from the room.

From another door came Ivan. Under one arm he carried 15 khaki hunting clothes, a haversack of food, a leather sheath containing a long-bladed hunting knife; his right hand rested on a cocked revolver thrust in the crimson sash about his waist. . . .

20

Rainsford had fought his way through the bush for two hours. "I must keep my nerve. I must keep my nerve," he said through tight teeth.

He had not been entirely clear-headed when the château gates snapped shut behind him. His whole idea at first was to 25 put distance between himself and General Zaroff, and, to this end, he had plunged along, spurred on by the sharp rowels of something very like panic. Now he had got a grip on himself, had stopped, and was taking stock of himself and the situation. 30

He saw that straight flight was futile; inevitably it would bring him face to face with the sea. He was in a picture with a frame of water, and his operations, clearly, must take place within that frame.

"I'll give him a trail to follow," muttered Rainsford, and he 35 struck off from the rude paths he had been following into the trackless wilderness. He executed a series of intricate loops;

he doubled on his trail again and again, recalling all the lore
of the fox hunt, and all the dodges of the fox. Night found
him leg-weary, with hands and face lashed by the branches,
on a thickly wooded ridge. He knew it would be insane to
blunder on through the dark, even if he had the strength. His 5
need for rest was imperative and he thought: "I have played
the fox, now I must play the cat of the fable." A big tree with
a thick trunk and outspread branches was nearby, and, taking
care to leave not the slightest mark, he climbed up into the
crotch, and stretching out on one of the broad limbs, after a 10
fashion, rested. Rest brought him new confidence and almost
a feeling of security. Even so zealous a hunter as General
Zaroff could not trace him there, he told himself; only the
devil himself could follow that complicated trail through the
jungle after dark. But, perhaps, the general was a devil— 15

An apprehensive night crawled slowly by like a wounded
snake, and sleep did not visit Rainsford, altho the silence of a
dead world was on the jungle. Toward morning when a dingy
gray was varnishing the sky, the cry of some startled bird fo-
cused Rainsford's attention in that direction. Something was 20
coming through the bush, coming slowly, carefully, coming
by the same winding way Rainsford had come. He flattened
himself down on the limb, and through a screen of leaves almost as thick as tapestry, he watched. The thing that was approaching was a man. 25

It was General Zaroff. He made his way along with his eyes
fixed in utmost concentration on the ground before him. He
paused, almost beneath the tree, dropped to his knees and
studied the ground. Rainsford's impulse was to hurl himself
down like a panther, but he saw that the general's right hand 30
held something metallic—a small automatic pistol.

The hunter shook his head several times, as if he were
puzzled. Then he straightened up and took from his case one
of his black cigarets; its pungent incense-like smoke floated
up to Rainsford's nostrils. 35

Rainsford held his breath. The general's eyes had left the
ground and were traveling inch by inch up the tree. Rains-

ford froze there, every muscle tensed for a spring. But the
sharp eyes of the hunter stopped before they reached the
limb where Rainsford lay; a smile spread over his brown face.
Very deliberately he blew a smoke ring into the air; then he
turned his back on the tree and walked carelessly away, back   5
along the trail he had come. The swish of the underbrush
against his hunting boots grew fainter and fainter.

The pent-up air burst hotly from Rainsford's lungs. His first
thought made him feel sick and numb. The general could follow a trail through the woods at night; he could follow an ex-   10
tremely difficult trail; he must have uncanny powers; only by
the merest chance had the Cossack failed to see his quarry.

Rainsford's second thought was even more terrible. It sent
a shudder of cold horror through his whole being. Why had
the general smiled? Why had he turned back?   15

Rainsford did not want to believe what his reason told him
was true, but the truth was as evident as the sun that had by
now pushed through the morning mists. The general was
playing with him! The general was saving him for another
day's sport! The Cossack was the cat; he was the mouse. Then   20
it was that Rainsford knew the full meaning of terror.

"I will not lose my nerve. I will not."

He slid down from the tree, and struck off again into the
woods. His face was set and he forced the machinery of his
mind to function. Three hundred yards from his hiding place   25
he stopped where a huge dead tree leaned precariously on a
smaller, living one. Throwing off his sack of food, Rainsford
took his knife from its sheath and began to work with all his
energy.

The job was finished at last, and he threw himself down   30
behind a fallen log a hundred feet away. He did not have to
wait long. The cat was coming again to play with the mouse.

Following the trail with the sureness of a bloodhound, came
General Zaroff. Nothing escaped those searching black eyes, no
crushed blade of grass, no bent twig, no mark, no matter how   35
faint, in the moss. So intent was the Cossack on his stalking
that he was upon the thing Rainsford had made before he

saw it. His foot touched the protruding bough that was the trigger. Even as he touched it, the general sensed his danger and leaped back with the agility of an ape. But he was not quite quick enough; the dead tree, delicately adjusted to rest on the cut living one, crashed down and struck the general a glancing blow on the shoulder as it fell; but for his alertness, he must have been smashed beneath it. He staggered, but he did not fall; nor did he drop his revolver. He stood there, rubbing his injured shoulder, and Rainsford, with fear again gripping his heart, heard the general's mocking laugh ring through the jungle.

"Rainsford," called the general, "if you are within sound of my voice, as I suppose you are, let me congratulate you. Not many men know how to make a Malay man-catcher. Luckily, for me, I too have hunted in Malacca. You are proving interesting, Mr. Rainsford. I am going now to have my wound dressed; it's only a slight one. But I shall be back. I shall be back."

When the general, nursing his bruised shoulder, had gone, Rainsford took up his flight again. It was flight now, a desperate, hopeless flight, that carried him on for some hours. Dusk came, then darkness, and still he pressed on. The ground grew softer under his moccasins; the vegetation grew ranker, denser; insects bit him savagely. Then, as he stepped forward, his foot sank into the ooze. He tried to wrench it back, but the muck sucked viciously at his foot as if it were a giant leech. With a violent effort, he tore his foot loose. He knew where he was now. Death Swamp and its quicksand.

His hands were tight closed as if his nerve were something tangible that someone in the darkness was trying to tear from his grip. The softness of the earth had given him an idea. He stepped back from the quicksand a dozen feet or so and, like some huge prehistoric beaver, he began to dig.

Rainsford had dug himself in in France when a second's delay meant death. That had been a placid pastime compared to his digging now. The pit grew deeper; when it was above his shoulders, he climbed out and from some hard saplings cut stakes and sharpened them to a fine point. These stakes he planted in the bottom of the pit with the points sticking up. With flying fingers he wove a rough carpet of weeds and branches and with it he covered the mouth of the pit. Then, wet with sweat and aching with tiredness, he crouched be- 5 hind the stump of a lightning-charred tree.

He knew his pursuer was coming; he heard the padding sound of feet on the soft earth, and the night breeze brought him the perfume of the general's cigaret. It seemed to Rains- ford that the general was coming with unusual swiftness; he 10 was not feeling his way along, foot by foot. Rainsford, crouch- ing there, could not see the general, nor could he see the pit. He lived a year in a minute. Then he felt an impulse to cry aloud with joy, for he heard the sharp crackle of the breaking branches as the cover of the pit gave way; he heard the sharp 15 scream of pain as the pointed stakes found their mark. He leaped up from his place of concealment. Then he cowered back. Three feet from the pit a man was standing, with an electric torch in his hand.

"You've done well, Rainsford," the voice of the general 20 called. "Your Burmese tiger pit has claimed one of my best dogs. Again you score. I think, Mr. Rainsford, I'll see what you can do against my whole pack. I'm going home for a rest now. Thank you for a most amusing evening."

At daybreak Rainsford, lying near the swamp, was awak- ened by a sound that made him know that he had new things to learn about fear. It was a distant sound, faint and waver- ing, but he knew it. It was the baying of a pack of hounds.

Rainsford knew he could do one of two things. He could 30 stay where he was and wait. That was suicide. He could flee. That was postponing the inevitable. For a moment he stood there, thinking. An idea that held a wild chance came to him, and, tightening his belt, he headed away from the swamp.

The baying of the hounds drew nearer, then still nearer, 35 nearer, ever nearer. On a ridge Rainsford climbed a tree. Down a watercourse, not a quarter of a mile away, he could

see the bush moving. Straining his eyes, he saw the lean figure of General Zaroff; just ahead of him Rainsford made out
another figure whose wide shoulders surged through the tall
jungle weeds; it was the giant Ivan, and he seemed pulled
forward by some unseen force; Rainsford knew that Ivan must 5
be holding the pack in leash.

They would be on him any minute now. His mind worked
frantically. He thought of a native trick he had learned in
Uganda. He slid down the tree. He caught hold of a springy
young sapling and to it he fastened his hunting knife, with the 10
blade pointing down the trail; with a bit of wild grapevine he
tied back the sapling. Then he ran for his life. The hounds
raised their voices as they hit the fresh scent. Rainsford knew
now how an animal at bay feels.

He had to stop to get his breath. The baying of the hounds 15
stopped abruptly, and Rainsford's heart stopped too. They
must have reached the knife.

He shinned excitedly up a tree and looked back. His pursuers had stopped. But the hope that was in Rainsford's brain
when he climbed died, for he saw in the shallow valley that 20
General Zaroff was still on his feet. But Ivan was not. The
knife, driven by the recoil of the springing tree, had not wholly
failed.

Rainsford had hardly tumbled to the ground when the pack
took up the cry again. 25

"Nerve, nerve, nerve!" he panted, as he dashed along. A
blue gap showed between the trees dead ahead. Ever nearer
drew the hounds. Rainsford forced himself on toward that
gap. He reached it. It was the shore of the sea. Across a cove
he could see the gloomy gray stone of the château. Twenty 30
feet below him the sea rumbled and hissed. Rainsford hesitated. He heard the hounds. Then he leaped far out into the
sea. . . .

When the general and his pack reached the place by the
sea, the Cossack stopped. For some minutes he stood regard- 35
ing the blue-green expanse of water. He shrugged his shoulders. Then he sat down, took a drink of brandy from a silver

flask, lit a perfumed cigaret, and hummed a bit from "Madame Butterfly."

General Zaroff had an exceedingly good dinner in his great paneled dining hall that evening. With it he had a bottle of Pol Roger and half a bottle of Chambertin. Two slight annoy- 5 ances kept him from perfect enjoyment. One was the thought that it would be difficult to replace Ivan; the other was that his quarry had escaped him; of course the American hadn't played the game—so thought the general as he tasted his after-dinner liqueur. In his library he read, to soothe himself, 10 from the works of Marcus Aurelius. At ten he went up to his bedroom. He was deliciously tired, he said to himself, as he locked himself in. There was a little moonlight, so, before turning on his light, he went to the window and looked down at the courtyard. He could see the great hounds, and he 15 called: "Better luck another time," to them. Then he switched on the light.

A man, who had been hiding in the curtains of the bed, was standing there.

"Rainsford!" screamed the general. "How in God's name 20 did you get here?"

"Swam," said Rainsford. "I found it quicker than walking through the jungle."

The general sucked in his breath and smiled. "I congratu- late you," he said. "You have won the game." 25

Rainsford did not smile. "I am still a beast at bay," he said, in a low, hoarse voice. "Get ready, General Zaroff."

The general made one of his deepest bows. "I see," he said. "Splendid! One of us is to furnish a repast for the hounds. The other will sleep in this very excellent bed. On guard, 30 Rainsford. . . ."

He had never slept in a better bed, Rainsford decided.

Vocabulary

1. What does the word "palpable" mean (p. 20, l. 8)?

2. Suggest some similar words which the author might have used in place of "sensuous" (p. 22, l. 6).

3. How is the word "extremity," often used to designate an arm or leg, used in this story (p. 23, l. 4)?

4. The general says that he tries to "preserve the amenities of civilization"; in the next paragraph Rainsford thinks to himself that the general is "affable" but "appraising." After reading the story, you should know whether or not the general was telling the truth and whether or not Rainsford was right (p. 27, ll. 10 and 13).

5. Connell says the general "was solicitous about the state of Rainsford's health." What does he mean? How does this detail help to develop the general's character?

6. What does Rainsford mean (p. 36, l. 31) when he thinks that a straight flight is "futile"?

Questions and Suggestions for Reading

FORESHADOWING

1. At the beginning of the story Rainsford and Whitney talk about hunting the jaguar. What has this conversation to do with the events which follow?

2. What other hints does the author give which might indicate what is coming (don't forget the title of the story)?

3. What does General Zaroff's gesture of dropping a walnut on the floor and crushing it suggest?

SETTING

1. In many stories setting is unimportant. In a "boy meets girl" story, the place they meet is of very little consequence. The important thing in such stories is that they meet. However, in other stories, the setting permits the story to be. Where but on a re-

mote and "taboo" island could "The Dangerous Game" take place? Could it take place in New York, or Los Angeles, or Chicago?

2. If the story did take place in a city, what difficulties would both the hunter and the hunted be faced with? Would the hunter's weapon be the same?

SUSPENSE

1. Like Edgar Allan Poe, Connell is a master of suspense, for he deliberately keeps the reader guessing. It is interesting to see how he does this. If we look back at the story we see that the author manages to keep our interest and attention in the earlier "quieter" sections not through action but by creating a mysterious atmosphere, mentioning intriguing details, and by actually keeping information from us. The setting is important in the beginning, for it is a dark and foggy night; the reader suspects that something mysterious and frightening may be in the offing. Then he learns that the island is taboo and there are many superstitions about it, but there are no details. Later Rainsford hears a scream, but we never know who screamed or, until later, why. Even when the hero finds the cartridges, the author deliberately keeps us from knowing what their significance is. These details—the superstitions about the island, the scream, the empty cartridges —are naturally mysterious and interesting ones, even if they seem unrelated at the time. Connell has mentioned them in order to hold our interest until he has set his scene and described his characters. The fact that he is so successful is all a part of his careful craftsmanship.

2. In the last part of the story we discover very clearly the nature of the "most dangerous" game. At that point the author turns his full attention to Rainsford, guides us as readers along the paths he takes, and allows us to see the traps Rainsford sets for the General. Every time Rainsford leaves a new trail or sets a trap we wonder if he will succeed. We feel that he will, but we wonder. We don't find out until the very last sentence of the story.

3. After Rainsford dives into the water, the author turns to look at the General. We watch him eat his dinner, relax with a book, and move toward his bedroom. What happens next? Have you been expecting something more? What caused you to think that something more would happen?

William Saroyan

THE CIRCUS

Any time a circus used to come to town, that was all me and my old pal Joey Renna needed to make us run hog-wild, as the saying is. All we needed to do was see the signs on the fences and in the empty store windows to start going to the dogs and neglecting our educations. All we needed to know was that a circus was on its way to town for me and Joey to start wanting to know what good a little education ever did anybody anyway.

After the circus *reached* town we were just no good at all. We spent all our time down at the trains, watching them unload the animals, walking out Ventura Avenue with the wagons with lions and tigers in them and hanging around the grounds, trying to win the favor of the animal men, the workers, the acrobats, and the clowns.

The circus was everything everything else we knew wasn't. It was adventure, travel, danger, skill, grace, romance, comedy, peanuts, popcorn, chewing-gum and soda-water. We used to carry water to the elephants and stand around afterwards and try to seem associated with the whole magnificent affair, the putting up of the big tent, the getting everything in order, and the worldly-wise waiting for the people to come and spend their money.

One day Joey came tearing into the class room of the fifth grade at Emerson School ten minutes late, and without so much as removing his hat or trying to explain his being late, shouted, Hey, Aram, what the hell are you doing here? The circus is in town.

And sure enough I'd forgotten. I jumped up and ran out of the room with poor old Miss Flibety screaming after me, Aram Garoghlanian, you stay in this room. Do you hear me, Aram Garoghlanian?

I heard her all right and I knew what my not staying would 5 mean. It would mean another powerful strapping from old man Dawson. But I couldn't help it. I was just crazy about a circus.

I been looking all over for you, Joey said in the street. What happened?

I forgot, I said. I knew it was coming all right, but I forgot 10 it was today. How far along are they?

I was at the trains at five, Joey said. I been out at the grounds since seven. I had breakfast at the circus table. Boy, it was good.

Honest, Joey? I said. How were they?   15

They're all swell, Joey said. Couple more years, they told me, and I'll be ready to go away with them.

As what? I said. Lion-tamer, or something like that?

I guess maybe not as a lion-tamer, Joey said. I figure more like a workman till I learn about being a clown or something, 20 I guess. I don't figure I could work with lions right away.

We were out on Ventura Avenue, headed for the circus grounds, out near the County Fairgrounds, just north of the County Hospital.

Boy, what a breakfast, Joey said. Hot-cakes, ham and eggs, 25 sausages, coffee. Boy.

Why didn't you tell me? I said.

I thought you knew, Joey said. I thought you'd be down at the trains same as last year. I would have told you if I knew you'd forgotten. What made you forget?   30

I don't know, I said. Nothing, I guess.

I was wrong there, but I didn't know it at the time. I hadn't really forgotten. What I'd done was *remembered*. I'd gone to work and remembered the strapping Dawson gave me last year for staying out of school the day the circus was in town. 35 That was the thing that had kind of kept me sleeping after four-thirty in the morning when by rights I should have been up and dressing and on my way to the trains. It was the memory of that strapping old man Dawson had given me, but I didn't know it at the time. We used to take them strappings kind of for granted, me and Joey, on account of we wanted to be fair and square with the Board of Education and if it 5 was against the rules to stay out of school when you weren't sick, and if you were supposed to get strapped for doing it, well, there we were, we'd done it, so let the Board of Education balance things the best way they knew how. They did that with a strapping. They used to threaten to send me and 10 Joey to Reform School but they never did it.

Circus? old man Dawson used to say. I see. *Circus.* Well, bend down, boy.

So, first Joey, then me, would bend down and old man Dawson would get some powerful shoulder exercise while we 15 tried not to howl. We wouldn't howl for five or six licks, but after that we'd howl like Indians coming. They used to be able to hear us all over the school and old man Dawson, after our visits got to be kind of regular, urged us politely to try to make a little less noise, inasmuch as it was a school and people were 20 trying to study.

It ain't fair to the others, old man Dawson said. They're trying to learn something for themselves.

We can't help it, Joey said. It hurts.

That I know, old man Dawson said, but it seems to me 25 there's such a thing as modulation. I believe a lad can overdo his howling if he ain't thoughtful of others. Just try to modulate that awful howl a little. I think you can do it.

Then he gave Joey a strapping of twenty and Joey tried his best not to howl so loud. After the strapping his face was very 30 red and old man Dawson was very tired.

How was that? Joey said.

That was better, old man Dawson said. By far the most courteous you've managed yet.

I did my best, Joey said. 35

I'm grateful to you, old man Dawson said.

He was tired and out of breath. I moved up to the chair in

front of him that he furnished during these matters to help us
suffer the stinging pain. I got in the right position and he said,
Wait a minute, Aram. Give a man a chance to get his breath.
I'm not twenty-three years old. I'm *sixty*-three. Let me rest a
minute.   5

All right, I said, but I sure would like to get this over with.

Don't howl too loud, he said. Folks passing by in the street
are liable to think this is a veritable chamber of tortures. Does
it really hurt that much?

You can ask Joey, I said.   10

How about it, Joey? old man Dawson said. Aren't you lads
exaggerating just a little? Perhaps to impress someone in your
room? Some girl, perhaps?

We don't howl to impress anybody, Mr. Dawson, Joey
said. We wouldn't howl if we could help it. Howling makes us   15
feel ashamed, doesn't it, Aram?

It's awfully embarrassing to go back to our seats in our
room after howling that way, I said. We'd rather not howl if
we could help it.

Well, old man Dawson said, I'll not be unreasonable. I'll   20
only ask you to try to modulate it a little.

I'll do my best, Mr. Dawson, I said. Got your breath back?

Give me just a moment longer, Aram, he said.

When he got his breath back he gave me my twenty and I
howled a little louder than Joey and then we went back to   25
class. It was awfully embarrassing. Everybody was looking at
us.

Well, Joey said, what did you expect? The rest of you
would fall down and die if you got twenty. You wouldn't *howl
a little*, you'd die.   30

That'll be enough out of you, Miss Flibety said.

Well, it's true, Joey said. They're all scared. A circus comes
to town and what do they do? They come to school. They
don't go out to the circus.

That'll be enough, Miss Flibety said.   35

Who do they think they are, giving us dirty looks? Joey
said.

Miss Flibety lifted her hand, hushing Joey.

Now the circus was back in town, another year had gone by, it was April again, and we were on our way out to the grounds. Only this time it was worse than ever because they'd seen us at school and knew we were going out to the circus.

Do you think they'll send Stafford after us? I said.

Stafford was truant officer.

We can always run, Joey said. If he comes, I'll go one way, you go another. He can't chase *both* of us. At least one of us will get away.

All right, I said. Suppose one of us gets caught?

Well, let's see, Joey said. Should the one who isn't caught give himself up or should he wreck Stafford's Ford?

I vote for wreck, I said.

So do I, Joey said, so wreck it is.

When we got out to the grounds a couple of the little tents were up, and the big one was going up. We stood around and watched. It was great the way they did it. Just a handful of guys who looked like tramps doing work you'd think no less than a hundred men could do. Doing it with style, too.

All of a sudden a man everybody called Red hollered at me and Joey.

Here, you Arabs, he said, give us a hand.

Me and Joey ran over to him.

Yes, sir, I said.

He was a small man with very broad shoulders and very big hands. You didn't feel that he was small, because he seemed so powerful and because he had so much thick red hair on his head. You thought he was practically a giant.

He handed me and Joey a rope. The rope was attached to some canvas that was lying on the ground.

This is going to be easy, Red said. As the boys lift the pole and get it in place you keep pulling the rope, so the canvas will go up with the pole.

Yes, sir, Joey said.

Everybody was busy when we saw Stafford.

We can't run now, I said.

Let him come, Joey said. We told Red we'd give him a hand and we're going to do it.

I'll tell you what, I said. We'll tell him we'll go with him after we get the canvas up; then we'll run.

All right, Joey said.

Stafford was a big fellow in a business suit who had a beef-red face and looked as if he ought to be a lawyer or something. He came over and said, All right, you hooligans, come along with me.

We promised to give Red a hand, Joey said. We'll come just as soon as we get this canvas up.

We were pulling for all we were worth, slipping and falling. The men were all working hard. Red was hollering orders, and then the whole thing was over and we had done our part.

We didn't even get a chance to find out what Red was going to say to us, or if he was going to invite us to sit at the table for lunch, or what.

Joey busted loose and ran one way and I ran the other and Stafford came after *me*. I heard the circus men laughing and Red hollering, Run, boy, run. He can't catch *you*. He's soft. Give him a good run. He needs the exercise.

I could hear Stafford, too. He was very sore and he was cussing.

I got away, though, and stayed low until I saw him drive off in his Ford. Then I went back to the big tent and found Joey.

We'll get it this time, Joey said.

I guess it'll be Reform School this time, I said.

No, Joey said. I guess it'll be thirty. We're going to do some awful howling if it is. Thirty's a lot of whacks even if he *is* sixty-three years old. He ain't exactly a weakling.

Thirty? I said. Ouch. That's liable to make me cry.

Maybe, Joey said. Me too, maybe. Seems like ten can make you cry, then you hold off till it's eleven, then twelve, and you think you'll start crying on the next one, but you don't. We haven't so far, anyway. Maybe we will when it's thirty.

Oh, well, I said, that's tomorrow.

Red gave us some more work to do around the grounds and let us sit next to him at lunch. It was swell. We talked to some acrobats who were Spanish, and to a family of Italians who worked with horses. We saw both shows, the afternoon one and the evening one, and then we helped with the work, taking the circus to pieces again; then we went down to the trains, and then home. I got home real late. In the morning I was sleepy when I had to get up for school.

They were waiting for us. Miss Flibety didn't even let us sit down for the roll call. She just told us to go to the office. Old man Dawson was waiting for us, too. Stafford was there, too, and very sore.

I figured, Well, here's where we go to Reform School.

Here they are, Mr. Dawson said to Stafford. Take them away, if you like.

It was easy to tell they'd been talking for some time and hadn't been getting along any too well. Old man Dawson seemed irritated and Stafford seemed sore at him.

In *this* school, old man Dawson said, I do any punishing that's got to be done. Nobody else. I can't stop you from taking them to Reform School, though.

Stafford didn't say anything. He just left the office.

Well, lads, old man Dawson said. How was it?

We had lunch with them, Joey said.

Let's see now, old man Dawson said. What offense is this, the sixteenth or the seventeenth?

It ain't that many, Joey said. Must be eleven or twelve.

Well, old man Dawson said, I'm sure of one thing. This is the time I'm supposed to make it thirty.

I think the next one is the one you're supposed to make thirty, Joey said.

No, Mr. Dawson said, we've lost track somewhere, but I'm sure this is the time it goes up to thirty. Who's going to be first?

Me, I said.

All right, Aram, Mr. Dawson said. Take a good hold on the chair, brace yourself, and try to modulate your howl.

Yes, sir, I said. I'll do my best, but thirty's an awful lot.

Well, a funny thing happened. He gave me thirty all right and I howled all right, but it *was* a modulated howl. It was the most modulated howl I ever howled; because it was the *easiest* strapping I ever got. I counted them and there were 5 thirty all right, but they didn't hurt, so I didn't cry, as I was afraid I might.

It was the same with Joey. We stood together waiting to be dismissed.

I'm awfully grateful to you boys, old man Dawson said, for 10 modulating your howls so nicely this time. I don't want people to think I'm killing you.

We wanted to thank him for giving us such easy strappings, but we couldn't say it. I think he knew the way we felt, though, because he smiled in a way that gave us an idea he 15 knew.

Then we went back to class.

It was swell because we knew everything would be all right till the County Fair opened in September.

Vocabulary

1. Certainly there are no difficult words in this story, but the words which are used serve to give the reader a good picture of Aram's character. Notice that Aram always refers to himself and his friend as "me and Joey," and he comments that "Joey busted loose." At the end of the story Aram says "thirty's an *awful* lot," and old man Dawson says, "I'm *awfully* grateful to you boys. . . ." Obviously, Aram's grammar and diction are not always correct, but are they appropriate to the speaker and the situation?

Questions and Suggestions for Reading

SETTING

1. The boys live in a comparatively small community. How does this affect their attitudes toward the circus? How does the size of the community and school affect the punishment meted out by old man Dawson?

2. Time is a part of setting. Can you tell in which century or in which part of the century the action in this story takes place? When did circuses "make the circuit"?

DIALOGUE and POINT OF VIEW

1. Dialogue is effective when characters speak naturally. A small child will hardly have the vocabulary of an adult. If you weren't told that the boys are in the fifth grade, could you tell from the way they speak? How bright are they? Support your answer.

2. The point of view from which the story is told dictates simplicity or complexity of sentence structure. Notice the length of the sentences in this story. Even when the boys aren't speaking, the sentences are short. Why? Who is telling the story?

3. Why would old man Dawson, who is supposed to be an educated school administrator, say, "It ain't fair to the others ..."?

W. W. Jacobs

THE MONKEY'S PAW

Without, the night was cold and wet, but in the small parlor of Lakesnam Villa the blinds were drawn and the fire burned brightly. Father and son were at chess, the former, who possessed ideas about the game involving radical changes, putting his king into such sharp and unnecessary perils that it even provoked comment from the white-haired old lady knitting placidly by the fire.

"Hark at the wind," said Mr. White, who, having seen a fatal mistake after it was too late, was amiably desirous of preventing his son from seeing it.

"I'm listening," said the latter, grimly surveying the board as he stretched out his hand. "Check."

"I should hardly think that he'd come tonight," said his father, with his hand poised over the board.

"Mate," replied the son.

"That's the worst of living so far out," bawled Mr. White, with sudden and unlooked-for violence; "of all the beastly, slushy, out-of-the-way places to live in, this is the worst. Pathway's a bog, and the road's a torrent. I don't know what people are thinking about. I suppose because only two houses on the road are let, they think it doesn't matter."

"Never mind, dear," said his wife soothingly; "perhaps you'll win the next one."

Mr. White looked up sharply, just in time to intercept a knowing glance between mother and son. The words died away on his lips, and he hid a guilty grin in his thin gray beard.

"There he is," said Herbert White, as the gate banged to loudly and heavy footsteps came toward the door.

The old man rose with hospitable haste, and opening the door, was heard condoling with the new arrival. The new arrival also condoled with himself, so that Mrs. White said, "Tut, 5 tut!" and coughed gently as her husband entered the room, followed by a tall burly man, beady of eye and rubicund of visage.

"Sergeant-Major Morris," he said, introducing him.

The sergeant-major shook hands, and taking the proffered 10 seat by the fire, watched contentedly while his host got out whisky and tumblers and stood a small copper kettle on the fire.

At the third glass his eyes got brighter, and he began to talk, the little family circle regarding with eager interest this visi- 15 tor from distant parts, as he squared his broad shoulders in the chair and spoke of strange scenes and doughty deeds, of wars and plagues and strange peoples.

"Twenty-one years of it," said Mr. White, nodding at his wife and son. "When he went away he was a slip of a youth in the 20 warehouse. Now look at him."

"He don't look to have taken much harm," said Mrs. White politely.

"I'd like to go to India myself," said the old man, "just to look round a bit, you know." 25

"Better where you are," said the sergeant-major, shaking his head. He put down the empty glass and, sighing softly, shook it again.

"I should like to see those old temples and fakirs and jug-glers," said the old man. "What was that you started telling me 30 the other day about a monkey's paw or something, Morris?"

"Nothing," said the soldier hastily. "Leastways, nothing worth hearing."

"Monkey's paw?" said Mrs. White curiously.

"Well, it's just a bit of what you might call magic, perhaps," 35 said the sergeant-major off-handedly.

His three listeners leaned forward eagerly. The visitor absent-mindedly put his empty glass to his lips and then set it down again. His host filled it for him.

"To look at," said the sergeant-major, fumbling in his pocket, "it's just an ordinary little paw, dried to a mummy."

He took something out of his pocket and proffered it. Mrs. White drew back with a grimace, but her son, taking it, examined it curiously.

"And what is there special about it?" inquired Mr. White, as he took it from his son and, having examined it, placed it upon the table.

"It had a spell put on it by an old fakir," said the sergeant-major, "a very holy man. He wanted to show that fate ruled people's lives, and that those who interfered with it did so to their sorrow. He put a spell on it so that three separate men could each have three wishes from it."

His manner was so impressive that his hearers were conscious that their light laughter jarred somewhat.

"Well, why don't you have three, sir?" said Herbert White cleverly.

The soldier regarded him in the way that middle age is wont to regard presumptuous youth. "I have," he said quietly, and his blotchy face whitened.

"And did you really have the three wishes granted?" asked Mrs. White.

"I did," said the sergeant-major, and his glass tapped against his strong teeth.

"And has anybody else wished?" inquired the old lady.

"The first man had his three wishes, yes," was the reply. "I don't know what the first two were, but the third was for death. That's how I got the paw."

His tones were so grave that a hush fell upon the group. "If you've had your three wishes, it's no good to you now, then, Morris," said the old man at last. "What do you keep it for?"

The soldier shook his head. "Fancy, I suppose," he said slowly. "I did have some idea of selling it, but I don't think I will. It has caused enough mischief already. Besides, people won't buy. They think it's a fairy tale, some of them, and those who do think anything of it want to try it first and pay me afterward."

"If you could have another three wishes," said the old man, eyeing him keenly, "would you have them?"

"I don't know," said the other. "I don't know."   5

He took the paw, and dangling it between his front finger and thumb, suddenly threw it upon the fire. White, with a slight cry, stooped down and snatched it off.

"Better let it burn," said the soldier solemnly.

"If you don't want it, Morris," said the old man, "give it to   10
me."

"I won't," said his friend doggedly. "I threw it on the fire. If you keep it, don't blame me for what happens. Pitch it on the fire again, like a sensible man."

The other shook his head and examined his new possession   15
closely. "How do you do it?" he inquired.

"Hold it up in your right hand and wish aloud," said the sergeant-major, "but I warn you of the consequences."

"Sounds like the *Arabian Nights*," said Mrs. White, as she rose and began to set the supper. "Don't you think you might   20
wish for four pairs of hands for me?"

Her husband drew the talisman from his pocket and then all three burst into laughter as the sergeant-major, with a look of alarm on his face, caught him by the arm. "If you must wish," he said gruffly, "wish for something sensible."   25

Mr. White dropped it back into his pocket, and placing chairs, motioned his friend to the table. In the business of supper the talisman was partly forgotten, and afterward the three sat listening in an enthralled fashion to a second installment of the soldier's adventures in India.   30

"If the tale about the monkey paw is not more truthful than those he has been telling us," said Herbert, as the door closed behind their guest, just in time for him to catch the last train, "we shan't make much out of it."

"Did you give him anything for it, father?" inquired Mrs.   35
White, regarding her husband closely.

"A trifle," said he, coloring slightly. "He didn't want it, but

I made him take it. And he pressed me again to throw it away."

"Likely," said Herbert, with pretended horror. "Why, we're going to be rich, and famous, and happy. Wish to be an emperor, father, to begin with; then you can't be henpecked."

He darted round the table, pursued by the maligned Mrs. White armed with an antimacassar.

Mr. White took the paw from his pocket and eyed it dubiously. "I don't know what to wish for, and that's a fact," he said slowly. "It seems to me I've got all I want."

"If you only cleared the house, you'd be quite happy, wouldn't you?" said Herbert, with his hand on his shoulder. "Well, wish for two hundred pounds, then; that'll just do it."

His father, smiling shamefacedly at his own credulity, held up the talisman, as his son, with a solemn face somewhat marred by a wink at his mother, sat down at the piano and struck a few impressive chords.

"I wish for two hundred pounds," said the old man distinctly.

A fine crash from the piano greeted the words, interrupted by a shuddering cry from the old man. His wife and son ran toward him.

"It moved," he cried, with a glance of disgust at the object as it lay on the floor. "As I wished it twisted in my hands like a snake."

"Well, I don't see the money," said his son, as he picked it up and placed it on the table, "and I bet I never shall."

"It must have been your fancy, father," said his wife, regarding him anxiously.

He shook his head. "Never mind, though; there's no harm done, but it gave me a shock all the same."

They sat down by the fire again while the two men finished their pipes. Outside, the wind was higher than ever, and the old man started nervously at the sound of a door banging upstairs. A silence unusual and depressing settled upon all three, which lasted until the old couple rose to retire for the night.

"I expect you'll find the cash tied up in a big bag in the middle of your bed," said Herbert, as he bade them good night, "and something horrible squatting up on top of the wardrobe watching you as you pocket your ill-gotten gains."

II

In the brightness of the wintry sun next morning as it streamed over the breakfast table Herbert laughed at his fears. There was an air of prosaic wholesomeness about the room which it had lacked on the previous night, and the dirty, shriveled little paw was pitched on the sideboard with a carelessness which betokened no great belief in its virtues.

"I suppose all old soldiers are the same," said Mrs. White. "The idea of our listening to such nonsense! How could wishes be granted in these days? And if they could, how could two hundred pounds hurt you, father?"

"Might drop on his head from the sky," said the frivolous Herbert.

"Morris said the things happened so naturally," said his father, "that you might if you so wished attribute it to co-incidence."

"Well, don't break into the money before I come back," said Herbert, as he rose from the table. "I'm afraid it'll turn you into a mean, avaricious man, and we shall have to disown you."

His mother laughed, and followed him to the door, watched him down the road, and returning to the breakfast table, was very happy at the expense of her husband's credulity. All of which did not prevent her from scurrying to the door at the postman's knock, nor prevent her from referring somewhat shortly to retired sergeant-majors of bibulous habits when she found that the post brought a tailor's bill.

"Herbert will have some more of his funny remarks, I expect, when he comes home," she said, as they sat at dinner.

"I dare say," said Mr. White, pouring himself out some beer; "but for all that, the thing moved in my hand; that I'll swear to."

"You thought it did," said the old lady soothingly.

"I say it did," replied the other. "There was no thought about it. I had just— What's the matter?"

His wife made no reply. She was watching the mysterious movements of a man outside, who, peering in an undecided fashion at the house, appeared to be trying to make up his mind to enter. In mental connection with the two hundred pounds, she noticed that the stranger was well dressed and wore a silk hat of glossy newness. Three times he paused at the gate, and then walked on again. The fourth time he stood with his hand upon it, and then with sudden resolution flung it open and walked up the path. Mrs. White at the same moment placed her hands behind her, and hurriedly unfastening the strings of her apron, put that useful article of apparel beneath the cushion of her chair.

She brought the stranger, who seemed ill at ease, into the room. He gazed furtively at Mrs. White, and listened in a preoccupied fashion as the old lady apologized for the appearance of the room, and her husband's coat, a garment which he usually reserved for the garden. She then waited as patiently as her sex would permit for him to broach his business, but he was at first strangely silent.

"I—was asked to call," he said at last, and stooped and picked a piece of cotton from his trousers. "I came from Maw and Meggins."

The old lady started. "Is anything the matter?" she asked breathlessly. "Has anything happened to Herbert? What is it? What is it?"

Her husband interposed. "There, there, mother," he said hastily. "Sit down, and don't jump to conclusions. You've not brought bad news, I'm sure, sir," and he eyed the other wistfully.

"I'm sorry—" began the visitor.

"Is he hurt?" demanded the mother.

The visitor bowed in assent. "Badly hurt," he said quietly, "but he is not in any pain."

"Oh, thank God!" said the old woman, clasping her hands. "Thank God for that! Thank—"

She broke off suddenly as the sinister meaning of the assurance dawned upon her and she saw the awful confirmation of her fears in the other's averted face. She caught her breath, and turning to her slower-witted husband, laid her trembling old hand upon his. There was a long silence.

"He was caught in the machinery," said the visitor at length, in a low voice.

"Caught in the machinery," repeated Mr. White, in a dazed fashion, "yes."

He sat staring blankly out at the window, and taking his wife's hand between his own, pressed it as he had been wont to do in their old courting days nearly forty years before.

"He was the only one left to us," he said, turning gently to the visitor. "It is hard."

The other coughed, and rising, walked slowly to the window. "The firm wished me to convey their sincere sympathy with you in your great loss," he said, without looking around. "I beg that you will understand I am only their servant and merely obeying orders."

There was no reply; the old woman's face was white, her eyes staring, and her breath inaudible; on the husband's face was a look such as his friend the sergeant might have carried into his first action.

"I was to say that Maw and Meggins disclaim all responsibility," continued the other. "They admit no liability at all, but in consideration of your son's services they wish to present you with a certain sum as compensation."

Mr. White dropped his wife's hand, and rising to his feet, gazed with a look of horror at his visitor. His dry lips shaped the words, "How much?"

"Two hundred pounds," was the answer.

Unconscious of his wife's shriek, the old man smiled faintly, put out his hands like a sightless man, and dropped, a senseless heap to the floor.

III

In the huge new cemetery, some two miles distant, the old people buried their dead, and came back to a house steeped in shadow and silence. It was all over so quickly that at first they could hardly realize it, and remained in a state of expectation as though of something else to happen—something else which was to lighten this load, too heavy for old hearts to bear. But the days passed, and expectation gave place to resignation—the hopeless resignation of the old, sometimes miscalled apathy. Sometimes they hardly exchanged a word, for now they had nothing to talk about, and their days were long to weariness.

It was about a week after that that the old man, waking suddenly in the night, stretched out his hand and found himself alone. The room was in darkness, and the sound of subdued weeping came from the window. He raised himself in bed and listened.

"Come back," he said tenderly. "You will be cold."

"It is colder for my son," said the old woman, and wept afresh.

The sound of her sobs died away on his ears. The bed was warm, and his eyes heavy with sleep. He dozed fitfully, and then slept until a sudden wild cry from his wife awoke him with a start.

"The monkey's paw!" she cried wildly. "The monkey's paw!"

He started up in alarm. "Where? Where is it? What's the matter?"

She came stumbling across the room toward him. "I want it," she said quietly. "You've not destroyed it?"

"It's in the parlor, on the bracket," he replied, marvelling. "Why?"

She cried and laughed together, and bending over, kissed his cheek.

"I only just thought of it," she said hysterically. "Why didn't I think of it before? Why didn't you think of it?"

"Think of what?" he questioned.

"The other two wishes," she replied rapidly. "We've only had one."

"Was not that enough?" he demanded fiercely.

"No," she cried triumphantly; "we'll have one more. Go down and get it quickly, and wish our boy alive again."

The man sat up in bed and flung the bedclothes from his quaking limbs. "Good God, you are mad!" he cried, aghast.

"Get it," she panted; "get it quickly, and wish— Oh, my boy, my boy!"

Her husband struck a match and lit the candle. "Get back to bed," he said unsteadily. "You don't know what you are saying."

"We had the first wish granted," said the old woman feverishly; "why not the second?"

"A coincidence," stammered the old man.

"Go and get it and wish," cried the old woman, and dragged him toward the door.

He went down in the darkness, and felt his way to the parlor, and then to the mantelpiece. The talisman was in its place, and a horrible fear that the unspoken wish might bring his mutilated son before him ere he could escape from the room seized upon him, and he caught his breath as he found that he had lost the direction of the door. His brow cold with sweat, he felt his way round the table, and groped along the wall until he found himself in the small passage with the unwholesome thing in his hand.

Even his wife's face seemed changed as he entered the room. It was white and expectant, and to his fears seemed to have an unnatural look upon it. He was afraid of her.

"Wish!" she cried, in a strong voice.

"It is foolish and wicked," he faltered.

"Wish!" repeated his wife.

He raised his hand. "I wish my son alive again."

The talisman fell to the floor, and he regarded it shudderingly. Then he sank trembling into a chair as the old woman, with burning eyes, walked to the window and raised the blind.

He sat until he was chilled with the cold, glancing occasionally at the figure of the old woman peering through the window. The candle end, which had burnt below the rim of the china candlestick, was throwing pulsating shadows on the ceiling and walls, until, with a flicker larger than the rest, it expired. The old man, with an unspeakable sense of relief at the failure of the talisman, crept back to his bed, and a minute or two afterward the old woman came silently and apathetically beside him.

Neither spoke, but both lay silently listening to the ticking of the clock. A stair creaked, and a squeaky mouse scurried noisily through the wall. The darkness was oppressive, and after lying for some time screwing up his courage, the husband took the box of matches, and striking one, went down stairs for a candle.

At the foot of the stairs the match went out, and he paused to strike another, and at the same moment a knock, so quiet and stealthy as to be scarcely audible, sounded on the front door.

The matches fell from his hand. He stood motionless, his breath suspended until the knock was repeated. Then he turned and fled swiftly back to his room, and closed the door behind him. A third knock sounded through the house.

"*What's that?*" cried the old woman, starting up.

"A rat," said the old man, in shaking tones—"a rat. It passed me on the stairs."

His wife sat up in bed listening. A loud knock resounded through the house.

"It's Herbert!" she screamed. "It's Herbert!"

She ran to the door, but her husband was before her, and catching her by the arm, held her tightly.

"What are you going to do?" he whispered hoarsely.

"It's my boy; it's Herbert!" she cried, struggling mechanically. "I forgot it was two miles away. What are you holding me for? Let go. I must open the door."

"For God's sake don't let it in," cried the old man, trembling.

"You're afraid of your own son," she cried, struggling. "Let me go. I'm coming, Herbert; I'm coming."

There was another knock, and another. The old woman with a sudden wrench broke free and ran from the room. Her husband followed to the landing, and called after her appealingly as she hurried downstairs. He heard the chain rattle back and the bottom bolt drawn slowly and stiffly from the socket. Then the old woman's voice, strained and panting.

"The bolt," she cried loudly. "Come down. I can't reach it."

But her husband was on his hands and knees groping wildly

on the floor in search of the paw. If he could only find it before the thing outside got in. A perfect fusillade of knocks reverberated through the house, and he heard the scraping of a chair as his wife put it down in the passage against the door. He heard the creaking of the bolt as it came slowly back, and 5 at the same moment he found the monkey's paw, and frantically breathed his third and last wish.

The knocking ceased suddenly, although the echoes of it were still in the house. He heard the chair drawn back and the door opened. A cold wind rushed up the staircase, and a 10 long loud wail of disappointment and misery from his wife gave him courage to run down to her side, and then to the gate beyond. The street lamp flickering opposite shone on a quiet and deserted road.

Vocabulary

1. At the beginning of a story authors often describe characters and situations in a quiet and ordinary manner if moments of great upheaval or violent action are in the offing later. And, of course, these descriptive words always help to delineate character. Note that Mrs. White sits "placidly" (p. 54, l. 7) by the fire, while Mr. White is "amiably" (p. 54, l. 9) desirous of keeping his son from seeing the error at chess which will give the game to his son. He also is heard "condoling" (p. 55, l. 4) the Sergeant-Major, who is "rubicund of visage" (p. 55, ll. 7-8).

2. Twice within one page the author uses the word "proffered" (p. 55, l. 10 and p. 56 l. 5); and twice he uses a word in two different forms: "apathy" (p. 62, l. 2) and "apathetically" (p. 63, l. 35).

3. Mr. White smiles at his own "credulity" (p. 58, l. 13) when he thinks of his first wish, but he is later teased by his son Herbert, who says he is afraid Mr. White will turn into an "avari-

cious" man (p. 59, l. 18). From what you know of Mr. White, is this possible?

4. The author says that there is "an air of prosaic wholesomeness about the room . . ." (p. 59, l. 3). What does he mean?

Questions and Suggestions for Reading

STRUCTURE

1. This story is divided into three sections. Section one tells us how Mr. White gets the monkey's paw; section two tells us how the first wish is granted. The first two sections, in other words, prepare for the last. Why doesn't the author simply tell us that Mr. White made a wish which was granted and begin with section three, the most important section?

2. The author of this story plays on a very old superstition about multiples of numbers. He divides the story into three sections, states that three separate men can have three wishes granted by the paw, and arranges for three listeners to hear the Sergeant-Major tell his story—after his third glass of whisky. Notice other references to numbers in the story.

FORESHADOWING

1. Early in the story the sergeant-major states that a spell was put on the monkey's paw by an old fakir who "wanted to show that fate ruled people's lives, and that those who interfered with it did so to their sorrow." Does the rest of the story support his statement?

2. Herbert White says teasingly (p. 58, l. 24), "Well, I don't see the money and I bet I never shall." The remark seems inconsequential at the time it is made, but later the reader sees that the author was actually preparing him for developments to come. Are there other such hints?

3. What is the third wish? How do you know? Was the second wish granted? Does Mr. White really believe in the powers of the paw? How do you know?

4. Are you prepared for the end of the story? How else could it have ended? Recall that the sergeant-major said early in the story that the first man who had the paw wished for death.

Damon Runyon

BUTCH MINDS THE BABY

One evening along about seven o'clock I am sitting in Mindy's restaurant putting on the gefillte fish, which is a dish I am very fond of, when in comes three parties from Brooklyn wearing caps as follows: Harry the Horse, Little Isadore and Spanish John.

Now these parties are not such parties as I will care to have much truck with, because I often hear rumors about them that are very discreditable, even if the rumors are not true. In fact, I hear that many citizens of Brooklyn will be very glad indeed to see Harry the Horse, Little Isadore and Spanish John move away from there, as they are always doing something that is considered a knock to the community, such as robbing people, or maybe shooting or stabbing them, and throwing pineapples, and carrying on generally.

I am really much surprised to see these parties on Broadway, as it is well known that the Broadway coppers just naturally love to shove such parties around, but here they are in Mindy's, and there I am, so of course I give them a very large hello, as I never wish to seem inhospitable, even to Brooklyn parties. Right away they come over to my table and sit down, and Little Isadore reaches out and spears himself a big hunk of my gefillte fish with his fingers, but I overlook this, as I am using the only knife on the table.

Then they all sit there looking at me without saying anything, and the way they look at me makes me very nervous indeed. Finally I figure that maybe they are a little embar-

67

rassed being in a high-class spot such as Mindy's, with legitimate people around and about, so I say to them, very polite:

"It is a nice night."

"What is nice about it?" asks Harry the Horse, who is a
thin man with a sharp face and sharp eyes.

Well, now that it is put up to me in this way, I can see
there is nothing so nice about the night, at that, so I try to
think of something else jolly to say, while Little Isadore keeps
spearing at my gefillte fish with his fingers, and Spanish John
nabs one of my potatoes.

"Where does Big Butch live?" Harry the Horse asks.

"Big Butch?" I say, as if I never hear the name before in my
life, because in this man's town it is never a good idea to answer any question without thinking it over, as sometime you
may give the right answer to the wrong guy, or the wrong
answer to the right guy. "Where does Big Butch live?" I ask
them again.

"Yes, where does he live?" Harry the Horse says, very impatient. "We wish you to take us to him."

"Now wait a minute, Harry," I say, and I am now more
nervous than somewhat. "I am not sure I remember the exact
house Big Butch lives in, and furthermore I am not sure Big
Butch will care to have me bringing people to see him, especially three at a time, and especially from Brooklyn. You know
Big Butch has a very bad disposition, and there is no telling
what he may say to me if he does not like the idea of me taking you to him."

"Everything is very kosher," Harry the Horse says. "You need
not be afraid of anything whatever. We have a business proposition for Big Butch. It means a nice score for him, so you take
us to him at once, or the chances are I will have to put the
arm on somebody around here."

Well, as the only one around there for him to put the arm
on at this time seems to be me, I can see where it will be
good policy for me to take these parties to Big Butch, especially as the last of my gefillte fish is just going down Little
Isadore's gullet, and Spanish John is finishing up my potatoes,

and is donking a piece of rye bread in my coffee, so there is
nothing more for me to eat.

So I lead them over into West Forty-ninth Street, near
Tenth Avenue, where Big Butch lives on the ground floor of
an old brownstone-front house, and who is sitting out on the
stoop but Big Butch himself. In fact, everybody in the neighborhood is sitting out on the front stoops over there, including
women and children, because sitting out on the front stoops
is quite a custom in this section.

Big Butch is peeled down to his undershirt and pants, and
he has no shoes on his feet, as Big Butch is a guy who likes
his comfort. Furthermore, he is smoking a cigar, and laid out
on the stoop beside him on a blanket is a little baby with not
much clothes on. This baby seems to be asleep, and every
now and then Big Butch fans it with a folded newspaper to
shoo away the mosquitoes that wish to nibble on the baby.
These mosquitoes come across the river from the Jersey side
on hot nights and they seem to be very fond of babies.

"Hello, Butch," I say, as we stop in front of the stoop.

"Sh-h-h-h!" Butch says, pointing at the baby, and making
more noise with his shush than an engine blowing off steam.
Then he gets up and tiptoes down to the sidewalk where we
are standing, and I am hoping that Butch feels all right, because when Butch does not feel so good he is apt to be very
short with one and all. He is a guy of maybe six foot two and
a couple of feet wide, and he has big hairy hands and a mean
look.

In fact, Big Butch is known all over this man's town as a
guy you must not monkey with in any respect, so it takes
plenty of weight off of me when I see that he seems to know
the parties from Brooklyn, and nods at them very friendly,
especially at Harry the Horse. And right away Harry states
a most surprising proposition to Big Butch.

It seems that there is a big coal company which has an
office in an old building down in West Eighteenth Street, and
in this office is a safe, and in this safe is the company pay roll
of twenty thousand dollars cash money. Harry the Horse

knows the money is there because a personal friend of his who
is the paymaster for the company puts it there late this very
afternoon.

It seems that the paymaster enters into a dicker with Harry
the Horse and Little Isadore and Spanish John for them to   5
slug him while he is carrying the pay roll from the bank to the
office in the afternoon, but something happens that they miss
connections on the exact spot, so the paymaster has to carry
the sugar on to the office without being slugged, and there it
is now in two fat bundles.   10

Personally it seems to me as I listen to Harry's story that
the paymaster must be a very dishonest character to be making deals to hold still while he is being slugged and the company's sugar taken away from him, but of course it is none of
my business, so I take no part in the conversation.   15

Well, it seems that Harry the Horse and Little Isadore and
Spanish John wish to get the money out of the safe, but none
of them knows anything about opening safes, and while they
are standing around over in Brooklyn talking over what is to
be done in this emergency Harry suddenly remembers that   20
Big Butch is once in the business of opening safes for a living.

In fact, I hear afterwards that Big Butch is considered
the best safe opener east of the Mississippi River in his day,
but the law finally takes to sending him to Sing Sing for opening these safes, and after he is in and out of Sing Sing three 25
different times for opening safes Butch gets sick and tired of
the place, especially as they pass what is called the Baumes
Law in New York, which is a law that says if a guy is sent to
Sing Sing four times hand running, he must stay there the
rest of his life, without any argument about it.   30

So Big Butch gives up opening safes for a living, and goes
into business in a small way, such as running beer, and handling a little Scotch now and then, and becomes an honest
citizen. Furthermore, he marries one of the neighbor's children
over on the West Side by the name of Mary Murphy, and I   35
judge the baby on this stoop comes of this marriage between
Big Butch and Mary because I can see that it is a very homely

baby, indeed. Still, I never see many babies that I consider
rose geraniums for looks, anyway.

Well, it finally comes out that the idea of Harry the Horse
and Little Isadore and Spanish John is to get Big Butch to
open the coal company's safe and take the pay-roll money out,   5
and they are willing to give him fifty per cent of the money
for his bother, taking fifty per cent for themselves for finding
the plant, and paying all the overhead, such as the paymaster,
out of their bit, which strikes me as a pretty fair sort of deal
for Big Butch. But Butch only shakes his head.   10

"It is old-fashioned stuff," Butch says. "Nobody opens pete
boxes for a living any more. They make the boxes too good,
and they are all wired up with alarms and are a lot of trouble
generally. I am in a legitimate business now and going along.
You boys know I cannot stand another fall, what with being   15
away three times already, and in addition to this I must mind
the baby. My old lady goes to Mrs. Clancy's wake tonight up
in the Bronx, and the chances are she will be there all night,
as she is very fond of wakes, so I must mind little John Ignatius Junior."   20

"Listen, Butch," Harry the Horse says, "this is a very soft
pete. It is old-fashioned, and you can open it with a toothpick.
There are no wires on it, because they never put more than a
dime in it before in years. It just happens they have to put the
twenty G's in it tonight because my pal the paymaster makes   25
it a point not to get back from the jug with the scratch in time
to pay off today, especially after he sees we miss out on him.
It is the softest touch you will ever know, and where can a
guy pick up ten G's like this?"

I can see that Big Butch is thinking the ten G's over very   30
seriously, at that, because in these times nobody can afford to
pass up ten G's, especially a guy in the beer business, which
is very, very tough just now. But finally he shakes his head
again and says like this:

"No," he says, "I must let it go, because I must mind the   35
baby. My old lady is very, very particular about this, and I
dast not leave little John Ignatius Junior for a minute. If Mary

comes home and finds I am not minding the baby she will put
the blast on me plenty. I like to turn a few honest bobs now
and then as well as anybody, but," Butch says, "John Ignatius
Junior comes first with me."

Then he turns away and goes back to the stoop as much as   5
to say he is through arguing, and sits down beside John Ignatius Junior again just in time to keep a mosquito from carrying off one of John's legs. Anybody can see that Big Butch is
very fond of this baby, though personally I will not give you
a dime a dozen for babies, male and female.   10

Well, Harry the Horse and Little Isadore and Spanish John
are very much disappointed, and stand around talking among
themselves, and paying no attention to me, when all of a sudden Spanish John, who never has much to say up to this time,
seems to have a bright idea. He talks to Harry and Isadore,   15
and they get all pleasured up over what he has to say, and
finally Harry goes to Big Butch.

"Sh-h-h-h!" Big Butch says, pointing to the baby as Harry
opens his mouth.

"Listen, Butch," Harry says in a whisper, "we can take the   20
baby with us, and you can mind it and work, too."

"Why," Big Butch whispers back, "this is quite an idea indeed. Let us go into the house and talk things over."

So he picks up the baby and leads us into his joint, and gets
out some pretty fair beer, though it is needled a little, at that, 25
and we sit around the kitchen chewing the fat in whispers.
There is a crib in the kitchen, and Butch puts the baby in this
crib, and it keeps on snoozing away first rate while we are
talking. In fact, it is sleeping so sound that I am commencing
to figure that Butch must give it some of the needled beer he 30
is feeding us, because I am feeling a little dopey myself.

Finally Butch says that as long as he can take John Ignatius
Junior with him he sees no reason why he shall not go and
open the safe for them, only he says he must have five per cent
more to put in the baby's bank when he gets back, so as to   35
round himself up with his ever-loving wife in case of a beef
from her over keeping the baby out in the night air. Harry the
Horse says he considers this extra five per cent a little strong,

but Spanish John, who seems to be a very square guy, says that after all it is only fair to cut the baby in if it is to be with them when they are making the score, and Little Isadore seems to think this is all right, too. So Harry the Horse gives in, and says five per cent it is.   5

Well, as they do not wish to start out until after midnight, and as there is plenty of time, Big Butch gets out some more needled beer, and then he goes looking for the tools with which he opens safes, and which he says he does not see since the day John Ignatius Junior is born and he gets them out to   10 build the crib.

Now this is a good time for me to bid one and all farewell, and what keeps me there is something I cannot tell you to this day, because personally I never before have any idea of taking part in a safe opening, especially with a baby, as I con-   15 sider such actions very dishonorable. When I come to think things over afterwards, the only thing I can figure is the needled beer, but I wish to say I am really very much sur- prised at myself when I find myself in a taxicab along about one o'clock in the morning with these Brooklyn parties and   20 Big Butch and the baby.

Butch has John Ignatius Junior rolled up in a blanket and John is still pounding his ear. Butch has a satchel of tools, and what looks to me like a big flat book, and just before we leave the house Butch hands me a package and tells me to be very   25 careful with it. He gives Little Isadore a smaller package, which Isadore shoves into his pistol pocket, and when Isadore sits down in the taxi something goes wa-wa, like a sheep, and Big Butch becomes very indignant because it seems Isadore is sitting on John Ignatius Junior's doll, which says "Mamma"   30 when you squeeze it.

It seems Big Butch figures that John Ignatius Junior may wish something to play with in case he wakes up, and it is a good thing for Little Isadore that the mamma doll is not squashed so it cannot say "Mamma" any more, or the chances   35 are Little Isadore will get a good bust in the snoot.

We let the taxicab go a block away from the spot we are headed for in West Eighteenth Street, between Seventh and

Eighth Avenues, and walk the rest of the way two by two. I walk with Big Butch, carrying my package, and Butch is lugging the baby and his satchel and the flat thing that looks like a book. It is so quiet down in West Eighteenth Street at such an hour that you can hear yourself think, and in fact I hear myself thinking very plain that I am a big sap to be on a job like this, especially with a baby, but I keep going just the same, which shows you what a very big sap I am, indeed.

There are very few people in West Eighteenth Street when we get there, and one of them is a fat guy who is leaning against a building almost in the center of the block, and who takes a walk for himself as soon as he sees us. It seems that this fat guy is the watchman at the coal company's office and is also a personal friend of Harry the Horse, which is why he takes the walk when he sees us coming.

It is agreed before we leave Big Butch's house that Harry the Horse and Spanish John are to stay outside the place as lookouts, while Big Butch is inside opening the safe, and that Little Isadore is to go with Butch. Nothing whatever is said by anybody about where I am to be at any time, and I can see that, no matter where I am, I will still be an outsider, but, as Butch gives me the package to carry, I figure he wishes me to remain with him.

It is no bother at all getting into the office of the coal company, which is on the ground floor, because it seems the watchman leaves the front door open, this watchman being a most obliging guy, indeed. In fact he is so obliging that by and by he comes back and lets Harry the Horse and Spanish John tie him up good and tight, and stick a handkerchief in his mouth and chuck him in an areaway next to the office, so nobody will think he has anything to do with opening the safe in case anybody comes around asking.

The office looks out on the street, and the safe that Harry the Horse and Little Isadore and Spanish John wish Big Butch to open is standing up against the rear wall of the office facing the street windows. There is one little electric light burning very dim over the safe so that when anybody walks past the place outside, such as a watchman, they can look in through

the window and see the safe at all times, unless they are blind.
It is not a tall safe, and it is not a big safe, and I can see Big
Butch grins when he sees it, so I figure this safe is not much
of a safe, just as Harry the Horse claims.

Well, as soon as Big Butch and the baby and Little Isadore 5
and me get into the office, Big Butch steps over to the safe
and unfolds what I think is the big flat book, and what is it
but a sort of screen painted on one side to look exactly like
the front of a safe. Big Butch stands this screen up on the floor
in front of the real safe, leaving plenty of space in between, 10
the idea being that the screen will keep anyone passing in the
street outside from seeing Butch while he is opening the safe,
because when a man is opening a safe he needs all the privacy
he can get.

Big Butch lays John Ignatius Junior down on the floor on 15
the blanket behind the phony safe front and takes his tools
out of the satchel and starts to work opening the safe, while
Little Isadore and me get back in a corner where it is dark,
because there is not room for all of us back of the screen.
However, we can see what Big Butch is doing, and I wish to 20
say while I never before see a professional safe opener at work,
and never wish to see another, this Butch handles himself like
a real artist.

He starts drilling into the safe around the combination lock,
working very fast and very quiet, when all of a sudden what 25
happens but John Ignatius Junior sits up on the blanket and
lets out a squall. Naturally this is most disquieting to me, and
personally I am in favor of beaning John Ignatius Junior with
something to make him keep still, because I am nervous
enough as it is. But the squalling does not seem to bother Big 30
Butch. He lays down his tools and picks up John Ignatius Junior and starts whispering, "There, there, there, my itty od-
dleums. Da-dad is here."

Well, this sounds very nonsensical to me in such a situation
and it makes no impression whatever on John Ignatius Junior. 35
He keeps on squalling, and I judge he is squalling pretty loud
because I see Harry the Horse and Spanish John both walk
past the window and look in very anxious. Big Butch jiggles

John Ignatius Junior up and down and keeps whispering baby
talk to him, which sounds very undignified coming from a high-
class safe opener, and finally Butch whispers to me to hand
him the package I am carrying.

He opens the package, and what is in it,but a baby's nursing
bottle full of milk. Moreover, there is a little tin stew pan, and
Butch hands the pan to me and whispers to me to find a water
tap somewhere in the joint and fill the pan with water. So I
go stumbling around in the dark in a room behind the office
and bark my shins several times before I find a tap and fill the
pan. I take it back to Big Butch, and he squats there with the
baby on one arm, and gets a tin of what is called canned heat
out of the package and lights this canned heat with his cigar
lighter, and starts heating the pan of water with the nursing
bottle in it.

Big Butch keeps sticking his finger in the pan of water
while it is heating, and by and by he puts the rubber nipple
of the nursing bottle in his mouth and takes a pull at it to see
if the milk is warm enough, just like I see dolls who have babies do. Apparently the milk is okay, as Butch hands the bottle
to John Ignatius Junior, who grabs hold of it with both hands
and starts sucking on the business end. Naturally he has to
stop squalling, and Big Butch goes to work on the safe again,
with John Ignatius Junior sitting on the blanket, pulling on the
bottle and looking wiser than a treeful of owls.

It seems the safe is either a tougher job than anybody figures, or Big Butch's tools are not so good, what with being old
and rusty and used for building baby cribs, because he breaks
a couple of drills and works himself up into quite a sweat without getting anywhere. Butch afterwards explains to me that
he is one of the first guys in this country to open safes without
explosives, but he says to do this work properly you have to
know the safes so as to drill to the tumblers of the lock just
right, and it seems that this particular safe is a new type to
him, even if it is old, and he is out of practice.

Well, in the meantime John Ignatius Junior finishes his bottle and starts mumbling again, and Big Butch gives him a tool
to play with, and finally Butch needs this tool and tries to take

it away from John Ignatius Junior, and the baby lets out such a squawk that Butch has to let him keep it until he can sneak it away from him, and this causes more delay.

Finally Big Butch gives up trying to drill the safe open, and he whispers to us that he will have to put a little shot in it to loosen up the lock, which is all right with us, because we are getting tired of hanging around and listening to John Ignatius Junior's glug-glugging. As far as I am personally concerned, I am wishing I am home in bed.

Well, Butch starts pawing through his satchel looking for something and it seems that what he is looking for is a little bottle of some kind of explosive with which to shake the lock on the safe up some, and at first he cannot find this bottle, but finally he discovers that John Ignatius Junior has it and is gnawing at the cork, and Butch has quite a battle making John Ignatius Junior give it up.

Anyway, he fixes the explosive in one of the holes he drills near the combination lock on the safe, and then he puts in a fuse, and just before he touches off the fuse Butch picks up John Ignatius Junior and hands him to Little Isadore, and tells us to go into the room behind the office. John Ignatius Junior does not seem to care for Little Isadore, and I do not blame him, at that, because he starts to squirm around quite some in Isadore's arms and lets out a squall, but all of a sudden he becomes very quiet indeed, and, while I am not able to prove it, something tells me that Little Isadore has his hand over John Ignatius Junior's mouth.

Well, Big Butch joins us right away in the back room, and sound comes out of John Ignatius Junior again as Butch takes him from Little Isadore, and I am thinking that it is a good thing for Isadore that the baby cannot tell Big Butch what Isadore does to him.

"I put in just a little bit of a shot," Big Butch says, "and it will not make any more noise than snapping your fingers."

But a second later there is a big whoom from the office, and the whole joint shakes, and John Ignatius Junior laughs right out loud. The chances are he thinks it is the Fourth of July.

"I guess maybe I put in too big a charge," Big Butch says,

and then he rushes into the office with Little Isadore and me after him, and John Ignatius Junior still laughing very heartily for a small baby. The door of the safe is swinging loose, and the whole joint looks somewhat wrecked, but Big Butch loses no time in getting his dukes into the safe and grabbing out 5 two big bundles of cash money, which he sticks inside his shirt.

As we go into the street Harry the Horse and Spanish John come running up much excited, and Harry says to Big Butch like this:

"What are you trying to do," he says, "wake up the whole 10 town?"

"Well," Butch says, "I guess maybe the charge is too strong, at that, but nobody seems to be coming, so you and Spanish John walk over to Eighth Avenue, and the rest of us will walk to Seventh, and if you go along quiet, like people minding 15 their own business, it will be all right."

But I judge Little Isadore is tired of John Ignatius Junior's company by this time, because he says he will go with Harry the Horse and Spanish John, and this leaves Big Butch and John Ignatius Junior and me to go the other way. So we start 20 moving, and all of a sudden two cops come tearing around the corner toward which Harry and Isadore and Spanish John are going. The chances are the cops hear the earthquake Big Butch lets off and are coming to investigate.

But the chances are, too, that if Harry the Horse and the 25 other two keep on walking along very quietly like Butch tells them to, the coppers will pass them up entirely, because it is not likely that coppers will figure anybody to be opening safes with explosives in this neighborhood. But the minute Harry the Horse sees the coppers he loses his nut, and he outs with 30 the old equalizer and starts blasting away, and what does Spanish John do but get his out, too, and open up.

The next thing anybody knows, the two coppers are down on the ground with slugs in them, but other coppers are coming from every which direction, blowing whistles and doing a 35 little blasting themselves, and there is plenty of excitement, especially when the coppers who are not chasing Harry the

Horse and Little Isadore and Spanish John start poking around the neighborhood and find Harry's pal, the watchman, all tied up nice and tight where Harry leaves him, and the watchman explains that some scoundrels blow open the safe he is watching.

All this time Big Butch and me are walking in the other direction toward Seventh Avenue, and Big Butch has John Ignatius in his arms, and John Ignatius is now squalling very loud, indeed. The chances are he is still thinking of the big whoom back there which tickles him so and is wishing to hear some more whooms. Anyway, he is beating his own best record for squalling, and as we go walking along Big Butch says to me like this:

"I dast not run," he says, "because if any coppers see me running they will start popping at me and maybe hit John Ignatius Junior, and besides running will joggle the milk up in him and make him sick. My old lady always warns me never to joggle John Ignatius Junior when he is full of milk."

"Well, Butch," I say, "there is no milk in me, and I do not care if I am joggled up, so if you do not mind, I will start doing a piece of running at the next corner."

But just then around the corner of Seventh Avenue toward which we are headed comes two or three coppers, with a big fat sergeant with them, and one of the coppers, who is half out of breath as if he has been doing plenty of sprinting, is explaining to the sergeant that somebody blows a safe down the street and shoots a couple of coppers in the getaway.

And there is Big Butch, with John Ignatius Junior in his arms and twenty G's in his shirt front and a tough record behind him, walking right up to them.

I am feeling very sorry, indeed, for Big Butch, and very sorry for myself, too, and I am saying to myself that if I get out of this I will never associate with anyone but ministers of the gospel as long as I live. I can remember thinking that I am getting a better break than Butch, at that, because I will not have to go to Sing Sing for the rest of my life, like him, and I also remember wondering what they will give John Ignatius Junior, who is still tearing off these squalls, with Big Butch saying, "There, there, there, Daddy's itty woogleums." Then I hear one of the coppers say to the fat sergeant:

"We better nail these guys. They may be in on this."

Well, I can see it is good-by to Butch and John Ignatius Junior and me, as the fat sergeant steps up to Big Butch, but instead of putting the arm on Butch, the fat sergeant only points at John Ignatius Junior and asks very sympathetic:

"Teeth?"

"No," Big Butch says. "Not teeth. Colic. I just get the doctor here out of bed to do something for him, and we are going to a drug store to get some medicine."

Well, naturally I am very much surprised at this statement, because of course I am not a doctor, and if John Ignatius Junior has colic it serves him right, but I am only hoping they do not ask for my degree, when the fat sergeant says:

"Too bad. I know what it is. I got three of them at home. But," he says, "it acts more like it is teeth than colic."

Then as Big Butch and John Ignatius Junior and me go on about our business I hear the fat sergeant say to the copper, very sarcastic:

"Yea, of course a guy is out blowing safes with a baby in his arms! You will make a great detective, you will!"

I do not see Big Butch for several days after I learn that Harry the Horse and Little Isadore and Spanish John get back to Brooklyn all right, except they are a little nicked up here and there from the slugs the coppers toss at them, while the coppers they clip are not damaged so very much. Furthermore, the chances are I will not see Big Butch for several years, if it is left to me, but he comes looking for me one night, and he seems to be all pleasured up about something.

"Say," Big Butch says to me, "you know I never give a copper credit for knowing any too much about anything, but I wish to say that this fat sergeant we run into the other night is a very, very smart duck. He is right about it being teeth that is ailing John Ignatius Junior, for what happens yesterday but John cuts in his first tooth."

Vocabulary

1. Once more we find an author using words and sentence structure to characterize. Notice that the characters speak formally about very informal things: Butch never says, "I've got to mind Junior," but he says, "I've got to mind little John Ignatius Junior"; and the hoods say very formally, "We wish you to take us to him." On the other hand the narrator uses such terms as "needled beer" and "coppers," which are obviously slang expressions. Why is Runyon inconsistent?

Questions and Suggestions for Reading

POINT OF VIEW

1. This story is told in the first person. The narrator simply repeats the conversation held between the gangsters and himself and between the gangsters and Big Butch. He makes various observations and comments, and makes the reader feel as though he were the only one listening to the story. Runyon is certainly not the "I" character. He has made up a narrator to whom he entrusts the telling of his story. What do we learn about the "I" character from his observations, actions, and comments? What do we know about the people with whom he associates? How would the story differ if it were told in another person?

PLOT

1. Although a short story writer usually strives for realism, this story revolves around impossibilities, improbabilities, and coincidence. What are some of these improbabilities and coincidences? Has Runyon tried to create a real world, or is he simply trying to entertain us by creating an unreal world?

"Saki" (H. H. Munro)

THE OPEN WINDOW

"My aunt will be down presently, Mr. Nuttel,"
said a very self-possessed young lady of fifteen; "in the meantime you must try to put up with me."

Framton Nuttel endeavoured to say the correct something
which should duly flatter the niece of the moment without un- 5
duly discounting the aunt that was to come. Privately he
doubted more than ever whether these formal visits on a suc-
cession of total strangers would do much toward helping the
nerve cure which he was supposed to be undergoing.

"I know how it will be," his sister had said when he was 10
preparing to migrate to this rural retreat; "you will bury yourself down there and not speak to a living soul, and your nerves
will be worse than ever from moping. I shall just give you letters of introduction to all the people I know there. Some of
them, as far as I can remember, were quite nice." 15

Framton wondered whether Mrs. Sappleton, the lady to
whom he was presenting one of the letters of introduction,
came into the nice division.

"Do you know many of the people round here?" asked the
niece, when she judged that they had had sufficient silent 20
communion.

"Hardly a soul," said Framton. "My sister was staying here,
at the rectory, you know, some four years ago, and she gave
me letters of introduction to some of the people here."

He made the last statement in a tone of distinct regret. 25

"Then you know practically nothing about my aunt?" pursued the self-possessed young lady.

"Only her name and address," admitted the caller. He was wondering whether Mrs. Sappleton was in the married or widowed state. An indefinable something about the room seemed to suggest masculine habitation.

"Her great tragedy happened just three years ago," said the child; "that would be since your sister's time."

"Her tragedy?" asked Framton; somehow, in this restful country spot, tragedies seemed out of place.

"You may wonder why we keep that window wide open on an October afternoon," said the niece, indicating a large French window that opened on to a lawn.

"It is quite warm for the time of the year," said Framton; "but has that window got anything to do with the tragedy?"

"Out through that window, three years ago to a day, her husband and her two young brothers went off for their day's shooting. They never came back. In crossing the moor to their favourite snipe-shooting ground they were all three engulfed in a treacherous piece of bog. It had been that dreadful wet summer, you know, and places that were safe in other years gave way suddenly without warning. Their bodies were never recovered. That was the dreadful part of it." Here the child's voice lost its self-possessed note and became falteringly human. "Poor aunt always thinks that they will come back some day, they and the little brown spaniel that was lost with them, and walk in at that window just as they used to do. That is why the window is kept open every evening till it is quite dusk. Poor dear aunt, she has often told me how they went out, her husband with his white waterproof coat over his arm, and Ronnie, her youngest brother, singing 'Bertie, why do you bound?' as he always did to tease her, because she said it got on her nerves. Do you know, sometimes on still, quiet evenings like this, I almost get a creepy feeling that they will all walk in through that window—"

She broke off with a little shudder. It was a relief to Framton when the aunt bustled into the room with a whirl of apologies for being late in making her appearance.

"I hope Vera has been amusing you?" she said.

"She has been very interesting," said Framton.

"I hope you don't mind the open window," said Mrs. Sappleton briskly; "my husband and brothers will be home directly from shooting, and they always come in this way. They've been out for snipe in the marshes to-day, so they'll make a fine mess over my poor carpets. So like you menfolks, isn't it?"

She rattled on cheerfully about the shooting and the scarcity of birds and the prospects for duck in the winter. To Framton it was all purely horrible. He made a desperate but only partially successful effort to turn the talk on to a less ghastly topic; he was conscious that his hostess was giving him only a fragment of her attention, and her eyes were constantly straying past him to the open window and the lawn beyond. It was certainly an unfortunate coincidence that he should have paid his visit on this tragic anniversary.

"The doctors agree in ordering me complete rest, an absence of mental excitement, and avoidance of anything in the nature of violent physical exercise," announced Framton, who laboured under the tolerably wide-spread delusion that total strangers and chance acquaintances are hungry for the least detail of one's ailments and infirmities, their cause and cure. "On the matter of diet they are not so much in agreement," he continued.

"No?" said Mrs. Sappleton, in a voice which replaced a yawn only at the last moment. Then she suddenly brightened into alert attention—but not to what Framton was saying.

"Here they are at last!" she cried. "Just in time for tea, and don't they look as if they were muddy up to the eyes!"

Framton shivered slightly and turned toward the niece with a look intended to convey sympathetic comprehension. The child was staring out through the open window with dazed horror in her eyes. In a chill shock of nameless fear Framton swung round in his seat and looked in the same direction.

In the deepening twilight three figures were walking across the lawn toward the window; they all carried guns under their arms, and one of them was additionally burdened with a white coat hung over his shoulders. A tired brown spaniel kept close at their heels. Noiselessly they neared the house, and then a hoarse young voice chanted out of the dusk: "I said, Bertie, why do you bound?"

Framton grabbed wildly at his stick and hat; the hall-door, the gravel-drive, and the front gate were dimly-noted stages in his headlong retreat. A cyclist coming along the road had to run into the hedge to avoid imminent collision.

"Here we are, my dear," said the bearer of the white mackintosh, coming in through the window; "fairly muddy, but most of it's dry. Who was that who bolted out as we came up?"

"A most extraordinary man, a Mr. Nuttel," said Mrs. Sappleton; "could only talk about his illness, and dashed off without a word of good-bye or apology when you arrived. One would think he had seen a ghost."

"I expect it was the spaniel," said the niece calmly; "he told me he had a horror of dogs. He was once hunted into a cemetery somewhere on the banks of the Ganges by a pack of pariah dogs and had to spend the night in a newly dug grave with the creatures snarling and grinning and foaming just above him. Enough to make anyone lose their nerve."

Romance at short notice was her specialty.

Vocabulary

1. A great part of the characterization of Vera in this story lies in the word "self-possessed" used to describe her. Be sure you understand this term (p. 82, l. 2).

2. Which meaning is closest to the correct one for the word "endeavoured" (p. 82, l. 4): meant, hesitated, tried, or started?

3. What was Nuttel going to do when he was "preparing to migrate to this rural retreat" (p. 82, l. 11)?

4. Suggest what the "indefinable something" is that seems "to suggest masculine habitation" (p. 83, l. 3 and l. 4).

5. Would Framton's look which "intended to convey sympathetic comprehension" cause the girl to stare through the window "with dazed horror" (p. 84, ll. 31, 32, and 33)?

Questions and Suggestions for Reading

STOCK CHARACTERIZATION

1. Authors often use names which suggest the personalities or dominant traits of their characters. Chester Gould, the creator of the comic strip "Dick Tracy," is famous for his "tag names." Remember B. O. Plenty? Consider the names in this story. Describe the kind of character the name Framton Nuttel suggests. Mrs. Sappleton? Vera?

2. After having asked the seemingly innocent question, "Then you know practically nothing about my aunt?" the girl proceeds to tell a broad yarn about her aunt's husband and two brothers. What other story does she tell which is obviously a lie? Are you sure? Cite proof.

3. Vera must size up Nuttel very quickly, or else she would be afraid to tell such an outrageous lie. Nuttel might have mentioned the so-called tragedy to her aunt. Why doesn't he?

4. Why does Nuttel believe Vera? Is it because of a weakness in his character, because of her self-possession, or because of her name, which means "truth"?

5. Is the ending (Nuttel's hasty exit and Vera's explanation of it) necessary to the story? Does it add to your knowledge of Vera? Of Nuttel? Of her aunt? Of the other members of her family?

6. Is the last sentence really necessary? What is "romance"?

Leonard Q. Ross

MR. K*A*P*L*A*N
AND SHAKESPEARE

It was Miss Higby's idea in the first place. She
had suggested to Mr. Parkhill that the students came to her
class unaware of the *finer* side of English, of its beauty and,
as she put it, "the glorious heritage of our literature." She suggested that perhaps poetry might be worked into the exer-   5
cises of Mr. Parkhill's class. The beginners' grade had, after
all, been subjected to almost a year of English and might be
presumed to have achieved some linguistic sophistication. Poetry would make the students conscious of precise enunciation;
it would make them read with greater care and an ear for   10
sounds. Miss Higby, who had once begun a master's thesis on
Coventry Patmore, *loved* poetry. And, it should be said in all
justice, she argued her cause with considerable logic. Poetry
would be excellent for the enunciation of the students, thought
Mr. Parkhill.   15

So it was that when he faced the class the following Tues-
day night, Mr. Parkhill had a volume of Shakespeare on his
desk, and an eager, almost an expectant, look in his eye. The
love that Miss Higby bore for poetry in general was as nothing compared to the love that Mr. Parkhill bore for Shakes-   20
peare in particular. To Mr. Parkhill, poetry meant Shakespeare. Many years ago he had played Polonius in his senior
class play.

"Tonight, class," said Mr. Parkhill, "I am going to try an
experiment."   25

The class looked up dutifully. They had come to regard Mr.
Parkhill's pedagogical innovations as part of the natural order.

87

"I am going to introduce you to poetry—great poetry. You see—" Mr. Parkhill delivered a modest lecture on the beauty of poetry, its expression of the loftier thoughts of men, its economy of statement. He hoped it would be a relief from spelling and composition exercises to use poetry as the subject matter of the regular Recitation and Speech period. "I shall write a passage on the board and read it for you. Then, for Recitation and Speech, you will give short addresses, using the passage as the general topic, telling us what it has brought to your minds, what thoughts and ideas."

The class seemed quite pleased by the announcement. Miss Mitnick blushed happily. (This blush was different from most of Miss Mitnick's blushes; there was aspiration and idealism in it.) Mr. Norman Bloom sighed with a business-like air: you could tell that for him poetry was merely another assignment, like a speech on "What I Like to Eat Best" or a composition on "A Day at a Picnic." Mrs. Moskowitz, to whom any public performance was unpleasant, tried to look enthusiastic, without much success. And Mr. Hyman Kaplan, the heroic smile on his face as indelibly as ever, looked at Mr. Parkhill with admiration and whispered to himself: "Poyetry! Now is poyetry! My! Mus' be progriss ve makink awreddy!"

"The passage will be from Shakespeare," Mr. Parkhill announced, opening the volume.

An excited buzz ran through the class as the magic of that name fell upon them.

"Imachine!" murmured Mr. Kaplan. "Jakesbeer!"

"*Shake*speare, Mr. Kaplan!"

Mr. Parkhill took a piece of chalk and, with care and evident love, wrote the following passage on the board in large, clear letters:

> Tomorrow, and tomorrow, and tomorrow
> Creeps in this petty pace from day to day,
> To the last syllable of recorded time;
> And all our yesterdays have lighted fools
> The way to dusty death. Out, out, brief candle!

Life's but a walking shadow, a poor player
That struts and frets his hour upon the stage,
And then is heard no more; it is a tale
Told by an idiot, full of sound and fury,
Signifying nothing.   5

A reverent hush filled the classroom, as eyes gazed with
wonder on this passage from the Bard. Mr. Parkhill was
pleased at this.

"I shall read the passage first," he said. "Listen carefully to
my enunciation—and—er—let Shakespeare's thoughts sink into   10
your minds."

Mr. Parkhill read: " 'Tomorrow, and tomorrow, and tomorrow . . .' " Mr. Parkhill read very well and this night, as if
some special fire burned in him, he read with rare eloquence.
"Out, out, brief candle!" In Miss Mitnick's eyes there was in-   15
spiration and wonder. "Life's but a walking shadow . . ." Mrs.
Moskowitz sat with a heavy frown, indicating cerebration. "It
is a tale told by an idiot . . ." Mr. Kaplan's smile had taken on
something luminous; but his eyes were closed: it was not clear
whether Mr. Kaplan had surrendered to the spell of the Im-   20
mortal Bard or to that of Morpheus.

"I shall—er—read the passage again," said Mr. Parkhill, clearing his throat vociferously until he saw Mr. Kaplan's eyes open.
" 'Tomorrow, and tomorrow, and tomorrow. . . .' "

When Mr. Parkhill had read the passage for the second   25
time, he said: "That should be quite clear now. Are there any
questions?"

There were a few questions. Mr. Scymzak wanted to know
whether "frets" was "a little kind excitement." Miss Schneid-
erman asked about "struts." Mr. Kaplan wasn't sure about   30
"cripps." Mr. Parkhill explained the words carefully, with several illustrative uses of each word. "No more questions? Well,
I shall allow a few minutes for you all to—er—think over the
meaning of the passage. Then we shall begin Recitation and
Speech."   35

Mr. Kaplan promptly closed his eyes again, his smile beatific. The students sank into that revery miscalled thought, searching their souls for the symbols evoked by Shakespeare's immortal words.

"Miss Caravello, will you begin?" asked Mr. Parkhill at last.

Miss Caravello went to the front of the room. "Da poem isa gooda," she said slowly. "Itsa have—"

"It *has*."

"It hasa beautiful wordsa. Itsa lak Dante, Italian poet—"

"Ha!" cried Mr. Kaplan scornfully. "Shaksbeer you metchink mit Tante? *Shaksbeer?* Mein Gott!"

It was obvious that Mr. Kaplan had identified himself with Shakespeare and would tolerate no disparagement of his *alter ego*.

"Miss Caravello is merely expressing her own ideas," said Mr. Parkhill pacifically. (Actually, he felt completely sympathetic to Mr. Kaplan's point of view.)

"Hau Kay," agreed Mr. Kaplan, with a generous wave of the hand. "But to me is no comparink a high-cless man like Shaksbeer mit a Tante, dat's all."

Miss Caravello, her poise shattered, said a few more words and sat down.

Mrs. Yampolsky's contribution was brief. "This is full deep meanings," she said, her eyes on the floor. "Is hard for a person not so good in English to unnistand. But I like."

" '*Like!*' " cried Mr. Kaplan with fine impatience. " '*Like?*' " "Batter *love*, Yampolsky. Mit Shaksbeer mus' be *love!*"

Mr. Parkhill had to suggest that Mr. Kaplan control his aesthetic passions. He did understand how Mr. Kaplan felt, however, and sensed a new bond between them. Mrs. Yampolsky staggered through several nervous comments and retired.

Mr. Bloom was next. He gave a long declamation, ending: "So is passimistic ideas in the poem, and I am optimist. Life should be happy—so we should remember this is only a poem. Maybe is Shakespeare too passimistic."

"You wronk, Bloom!" cried Mr. Kaplan with prompt indignation. "Shaksbeer is passimist because is de *life* passimist also!"

Mr. Parkhill, impressed by this philosophical stroke, realized that Mr. Kaplan, afire with the glory of the Swan of Avon, could not be suppressed. Mr. Kaplan was the kind of man who brooked no criticism of his gods. The only solution was to call on Mr. Kaplan for his recitation at once. Mr. Parkhill was, indeed, curious about what fresh thoughts Mr. Kaplan would utter after his passionate defences of the Bard. When Mr. Parkhill had corrected certain parts of Mr. Bloom's speech, emphasizing Mr. Bloom's failure to use the indefinite article, he said: "Mr. Kaplan, will *you* speak next?"

Mr. Kaplan's face broke into a glow; his smile was like a rainbow. "Soitinly," he said, walking to the front of the room. Never had he seemed so dignified, so eager, so conscious of a great destiny.

"Er—Mr. Kaplan," added Mr. Parkhill, suddenly aware of the possibilities which the situation Kaplan on Shakespeare involved: "Speak *carefully*."

"*Spacially* careful vill I be," Mr. Kaplan reassured him. He cleared his throat, adjusted his tie, and began: "Ladies an' gantleman, you hoid all kinds minninks abot dis piece poyetry, an'—"

"*Po*etry."

"—abot dis piece *po*etry. But to me is a difference minnink altogadder. Ve mus' tink abot Julius Scissor an' how *he* falt!"

Mr. Parkhill moved nervously, puzzled.

"In dese exact voids is Julius Scissor sayink—"

"Er—Mr. Kaplan," said Mr. Parkhill once he grasped the full import of Mr. Kaplan's error. "The passage is from 'Macbeth.' "

Mr. Kaplan looked at Mr. Parkhill with injured surprise. "*Not* from 'Julius Scissor'?" There was pain in his voice.

"No. And it's—er—'Julius *Cae*sar.' "

Mr. Kaplan waited until the last echo of the name had permeated his soul. "Podden me, Mr. Pockheel. Isn't '*seez*or' vat you cuttink somting up mit?"

"That," said Mr. Parkhill quickly, "is 'scissor.' You have used 'Caesar' for 'scissor' and 'scissor' for 'Caesar.' "

Mr. Kaplan nodded, marvelling at his own virtuosity.

"But go on with your speech, please." Mr. Parkhill, to tell the truth, felt a little guilty that he had not announced at the very beginning that the passage was from "Macbeth." "Tell us *why* you thought the lines were from 'Julius Caesar.'"

"Vell," said Mr. Kaplan to the class, his smile assuming its 5 normal serenity. "I vas positif, becawss I can *see* de whole ting." He paused, debating how to explain this cryptic remark. Then his eyes filled with a strange enchantment. "I see de whole scinn. It's in a tant, on de night bafore dey makink Julius de Kink fromm Rome. So he is axcited an' ken't slip. He is 10 layink in bad, tinking: 'Tomorrow an' tomorrow an' tomorrow. How slow dey movink! Almost cripps! Soch a pity de pace!'"

Before Mr. Parkhill could explain that "petty pace" did not mean "Soch a pity de pace!" Mr. Kaplan had soared on.

"De days go slow, fromm day to day, like leetle tsyllables on 15 phonograph racords fromm time."

Anxiety and bewilderment invaded Mr. Parkhill's eyes.

"'An' vat abot yestidday?' tinks Julius Scissor. Ha! 'All our yestiddays are only makink a good light for fools to die in de dost!'" 20

"'Dusty death' doesn't mean—" There was no interrupting Mr. Kaplan.

"An' Julius Scissor is so tired, an' he vants to fallink aslip. So he hollers, mit fillink, 'Go ot! Go ot! Short candle!' So it goes ot." 25

Mr. Kaplan's voice dropped to a whisper. "But he ken't slip. Now is bodderink him de idea fromm life. 'Vat is de life altogadder?' tinks Julius Scissor. An' he gives enswer, de pot I like de bast. 'Life is like a bum actor, strottink an' hollerink arond de stage for only vun hour bafore he's kicked ot. Life is 30 a tale told by idjots, dat's all, full of fonny sonds an' phooey!'"

Mr. Parkhill could be silent no longer. "'Full of sound and fury!'" he cried desperately. But inspiration, like an irresistible force, swept Mr. Kaplan on.

"'Life is monkey business! It don' minn a ting. It signifies 35 nottink!' An' den Julius Scissor closes his ice fest—" Mr. Kaplan demonstrated the Consul's exact ocular process in closing his "ice"— "—an' falls dad!"

The class was hushed as Mr. Kaplan stopped. In the silence, a tribute to the fertility of Mr. Kaplan's imagination and the power of his oratory, Mr. Kaplan went to his seat. But just before he sat down, as if adding a postscript, he sighed: "Dat vas mine idea. But ufcawss is all wronk, becawss Mr. Pockheel said 5 de voids ain't abot Julius Scissor altogadder. It's all abot an Irishman by de name Macbat."

Then Mr. Kaplan sat down.

It was some time before Mr. Parkhill could bring himself to criticize Mr. Kaplan's pronunciation, enunciation, diction, 10 grammar, idiom, and sentence structure. For Mr. Parkhill discovered that he could not easily return to the world of reality. He was still trying to tear himself away from that tent outside Rome, where "Julius Scissor," cursed with insomnia, had thought of time and life—and philosophized himself to a strange 15 and sudden death.

Mr. Parkhill was distinctly annoyed with Miss Higby.

Vocabulary

1. The beginner's class is described as having "achieved some linguistic sophistication." Only by understanding the meaning of such a phrase can one realize why Mr. Parkhill became very annoyed, at the end of the story, with Miss Higby's suggestion that his class work on poetry.

2. How does the word "enunciation," used a number of times by Mr. Parkhill, differ from the word "pronunciation"?

3. Notice how the following descriptive words and phrases are used to characterize:

   a. What does the comment about Mr. Parkhill's "pedagogical innovations" tell us about the teacher (p. 87, l. 27)?

   b. Try describing, in other terms, Miss Mitnick's blush which has "aspiration and idealism in it" (p. 88, ll. 13-14).

   c. Mrs. Moskowitz has "a heavy frown, indicating cerebration." What does this tell us about her (p. 89, l. 17)?

d. Mr. Parkhill clears his throat "vociferously" in an attempt to get the attention of Mr. Kaplan (p. 89, ll. 22-23). This action tells us something about both characters. Later, when Mr. Kaplan is paying attention, the author observes that the student "would tolerate no disparagement of his *alter ego*" (p. 90, ll. 12-13). Does that mean the same as the comment (p. 91, ll. 3-4) that "Mr. Kaplan was the kind of man who brooked no criticism of his gods"?

Questions and Suggestions for Reading

CHARACTERIZATION and DIALOGUE

1. Understanding stories written in dialect is often very difficult. For this reason, it is best if these stories be read aloud and if the authors exaggerate the spelling of unusual words or sounds. The author of such a story must also present a true and not merely a stereotyped representation of the dialect. Is author Ross a clear dialect writer? Do Italians really add a final *a* as Mrs. Caravello does? Of what nationality is Mr. Kaplan? Certainly he has learned some of his English outside of the classroom. Can you tell where? In what city or section of the country does Mr. Kaplan live? What kind of people does he associate with? In other words, what is his environment?

2. The other characters' reaction to Mr. Kaplan helps reveal the type of person he is. How does the class as a whole respond to him? How does Mr. Parkhill respond?

3. Mr. Kaplan's interpretation of the passage from Shakespeare helps characterize him too. Notice his vivid imagination and his power to transport the whole group into a world of make-believe.

James Thurber

YOU COULD LOOK IT UP*

It all begun when we dropped down to C'lum-
bus, Ohio, from Pittsburgh to play a exhibition game on our
way out to St. Louis. It was gettin' on into September, and
though we'd been leadin' the league by six, seven games most
of the season, we was now in first place by a margin you could   5
'a' got it into the eye of a thimble, bein' only a half a game
ahead of St. Louis. Our slump had given the boys the leapin'
jumps, and they was like a bunch a old ladies at a lawn fete
with a thunderstorm comin' up, runnin' around snarlin' at each
other, eatin' bad and sleepin' worse, and battin' for a team av-   10
erage of maybe .186. Half the time nobody'd speak to nobody
else, without it was to bawl 'em out.

Squawks Magrew was managin' the boys at the time, and
he was darn near crazy. They called him "Squawks" 'cause
when things was goin' bad he lost his voice, or perty near lost   15
it, and squealed at you like a little girl you stepped on her doll
or somethin'. He yelled at everybody and wouldn't listen to nobody, without maybe it was me. I'd been trainin' the boys for
ten year, and he'd take more lip from me than from anybody
else. He knowed I was smarter'n him, anyways, like you're   20
goin' to hear.

This was thirty, thirty-one year ago; you could look it up,
'cause it was the same year C'lumbus decided to call itself the
Arch City, on account of a lot of iron arches with electric-light
bulbs into 'em which stretched acrost High Street. Thomas Al-   25
bert Edison sent 'em a telegram, and they was speeches and

* Reprinted by permission. Copyright, 1941, The Curtis Publishing
Company.

95

maybe even President Taft opened the celebration by pushin'
a button. It was a great week for the Buckeye capital, which
was why they got us out there for this exhibition game.

Well, we just lose a double-header to Pittsburgh, 11 to 5 and
7 to 3, so we snarled all the way to C'lumbus, where we put up
at the Chittaden Hotel, still snarlin'. Everybody was tetchy,
and when Billy Klinger took a sock at Whitey Cott at breakfast, Whitey throwed marmalade all over his face.

"Blind each other, whatta I care?" says Magrew. "You can't
see nothin' anyways."

C'lumbus win the exhibition game, 3 to 2, whilst Magrew
set in the dugout, mutterin' and cursin' like a fourteen-year-
old Scotty. He bad-mouthed everybody on the ball club and
he bad-mouthed everybody offa the ball club, includin' the
Wright brothers, who, he claimed, had yet to build a airship
big enough for any of our boys to hit it with a ball bat.

"I wisht I was dead," he says to me. "I wisht I was in heaven
with the angels."

I told him to pull hisself together, 'cause he was drivin' the
boys crazy, the way he was goin' on, sulkin' and bad-mouthin'
and whinin'. I was older'n he was and smarter'n he was, and
he knowed it. I was ten times smarter'n he was about this Pearl
du Monville, first time I ever laid eyes on the little guy, which
was one of the saddest days of my life.

Now, most people name of Pearl is girls, but this Pearl du
Monville was a man, if you could call a fella a man who was
only thirty-four, thirty-five inches high. Pearl du Monville was
a midget. He was part French and part Hungarian, and maybe
even part Bulgarian or somethin'. I can see him now, a sneer
on his little pushed-in pan, swingin' a bamboo cane and
smokin' a big cigar. He had a gray suit with a big black check
into it, and he had a gray felt hat with one of them rainbow-
colored hatbands onto it, like the young fellas wore in them
days. He talked like he was talkin' into a tin can, but he didn't
have no foreign accent. He might 'a' been fifteen or he might
'a' been a hundred, you couldn't tell. Pearl du Monville.

After the game with C'lumbus, Magrew headed straight

for the Chittaden bar—the train for St. Louis wasn't goin' for
three, four hours—and there he set, drinkin' rye and talkin' to
this bartender.

"How I pity me, brother," Magrew was tellin' this bartender.
"How I pity me." That was alwuz his favorite tune. So he was   5
settin' there, tellin' this bartender how heart-breakin' it was to
be manager of a bunch a blindfolded circus clowns, when up
pops this Pearl du Monville outa nowheres.

It give Magrew the leapin' jumps. He thought at first maybe
the D.T.'s had come back on him; he claimed he'd had 'em   10
once, and little guys had popped up all around him, wearin'
red, white and blue hats.

"Go on, now!" Magrew yells. "Get away from me!"

But the midget clumb up on a chair acrost the table from
Magrew and says, "I seen that game today, Junior, and you   15
ain't got no ball club. What you got there, Junior," he says, "is
a side show."

"Whatta ya mean, 'Junior'?" says Magrew, touchin' the little
guy to satisfy hisself he was real.

"Don't pay him no attention, mister," says the bartender.   20
"Pearl calls everybody 'Junior,' 'cause it alwuz turns out he's a
year older'n anybody else."

"Yeh?" says Magrew. "How old is he?"

"How old are you, Junior?" says the midget.

"Who, me? I'm fifty-three," says Magrew.   25

"Well, I'm fifty-four," says the midget.

Magrew grins and asts him what he'll have, and that was
the beginnin' of their beautiful friendship, if you don't care
what you say.

Pearl du Monville stood up on his chair and waved his cane   30
around and pretended like he was ballyhooin' for a circus.
"Right this way, folks!" he yells. "Come on in and see the
greatest collection of freaks in the world! See the armless
pitchers, see the eyeless batters, see the infielders with five
thumbs!" and on and on like that, feedin' Magrew gall and   35
handin' him a laugh at the same time, you might say.

You could hear him and Pearl du Monville hootin' and hol-

lerin' and singin' way up to the fourth floor of the Chittaden,
where the boys was packin' up. When it come time to go to
the station, you can imagine how disgusted we was when we
crowded into the doorway of that bar and seen them two
singin' and goin' on.   5

"Well, well, well," says Magrew, lookin' up and spottin' us.
"Look who's here. . . . Clowns, this is Pearl du Monville, a
monseer of the old, old school. . . . Don't shake hands with 'em,
Pearl, 'cause their fingers is made of chalk and would bust right
off in your paws," he says, and he starts guffawin' and Pearl   10
starts titterin' and we stand there givin' 'em the iron eye, it
bein' the lowest ebb a ball-club manager'd got hisself down to
since the national pastime was started.

Then the midget begun givin' us the ballyhoo. "Come on in!"
he says, wavin' his cane. "See the legless base runners, see the 15
outfielders with the butter fingers, see the southpaw with the
arm of a little chee-ild!"

Then him and Magrew begun to hoop and holler and nudge
each other till you'd of thought this little guy was the funniest
guy than even Charlie Chaplin. The fellas filed outa the bar   20
without a word and went on up to the Union Depot, leavin' me
to handle Magrew and his newfound crony.

Well, I got 'em outa there finely. I had to take the little guy
along, 'cause Magrew had a holt onto him like a vise and I
couldn't pry him loose.   25

"He's comin' along as masket," says Magrew, holdin' the
midget in the crouch of his arm like a football. And come along
he did, hollerin' and protestin' and beatin' at Magrew with his
little fists.

"Cut it out, will ya, Junior?" the little guy kept whinin'.   30
"Come on, leave a man loose, will ya, Junior?"

But Junior kept a holt onto him and begun yellin', "See the
guys with the glass arms, see the guys with the cast-iron brains,
see the fielders with the feet on their wrists!"

So it goes, right through the whole Union Depot, with peo-   35
ple starin' and catcallin', and he don't put the midget down till
he gets him through the gates.

"How'm I goin' to go along without no toothbrush?" the midget asts. "What'm I goin' to do without no other suit?" he says.

"Doc here," says Magrew, meanin' me—"doc here will look after you like you was his own son, won't you, doc?"

I give him the iron eye, and he finely got on the train and prob'ly went to sleep with his clothes on.

This left me alone with the midget. "Lookit," I says to him. "Why don't you go on home now? Come mornin', Magrew'll forget all about you. He'll prob'ly think you was somethin' he seen in a nightmare maybe. And he ain't goin' to laugh so easy in the mornin', neither," I says. "So why don't you go on home?"

"Nix," he says to me. "Skiddoo," he says, "twenty-three for you," and he tosses his cane up into the vestibule of the coach and clam'ers on up after it like a cat. So that's the way Pearl du Monville come to go to St. Louis with the ball club.

I seen 'em first at breakfast the next day, settin' opposite each other; the midget playin' Turkey in the Straw on a harmonium and Magrew starin' at his eggs and bacon like they was a uncooked bird with its feathers still on.

"Remember where you found this?" I says, jerkin' my thumb at the midget. "Or maybe you think they come with breakfast on these trains," I says, bein' a good hand at turnin' a sharp remark in them days.

The midget puts down the harmonium and turns on me. "Sneeze," he says; "your brains is dusty." Then he snaps a couple drops of water at me from a tumbler. "Drown," he says, tryin' to make his voice deep.

Now, both them cracks is Civil War cracks, but you'd of thought they was brand new and the funniest than any crack Magrew'd ever heard in his whole life. He started hoopin' and hollerin', and the midget started hoopin' and hollerin', so I walked on away and set down with Bugs Courtney and Hank Metters, payin' no attention to this weak-minded Damon and Phidias acrost the aisle.

Well, sir, the first game with St. Louis was rained out, and there we was facin' a double-header next day. Like maybe I told you, we lose the last three double-headers we play, makin' maybe twenty-five errors in the six games, which is all right for the intimates of a school for the blind, but is disgraceful for the world's champions. It was too wet to go to the zoo, and Magrew wouldn't let us go to the movies, 'cause they flickered 5 so bad in them days. So we just set around, stewin' and frettin'.

One of the newspaper boys come over to take a pitture of Billy Klinger and Whitey Cott shakin' hands—this reporter'd heard about the fight—and whilst they was standin' there, toe to toe, shakin' hands, Billy give a back lunge and a jerk, and 10 throwed Whitey over his shoulder into a corner of the room, like a sack a salt. Whitey come back at him with a chair, and Bethlehem broke loose in that there room. The camera was tromped to pieces like a berry basket. When we finely got 'em pulled apart, I heard a laugh, and there was Magrew and the 15 midget standin' in the doorway and givin' us the iron eye.

"Wrasslers," says Magrew, cold-like, "that's what I got for a ball club, Mr. Du Monville, wrasslers—and not very good wrasslers at that, you ast me."

"A man can't be good at everythin'," says Pearl, "but he 20 oughta be good at somethin'."

This sets Magrew guffawin' again, and away they go, the midget taggin' along by his side like a hound dog and handin' him a fast line of so-called comic cracks.

When we went out to face that battlin' St. Louis club in a 25 double-header the next afternoon, the boys was jumpy as tin toys with keys in their back. We lose the first game, 7 to 2, and are trailin', 4 to 0, when the second game ain't but ten minutes old. Magrew set there like a stone statue, speakin' to nobody. Then, in their half a the fourth, somebody singled to center 30 and knocked in two more runs for St. Louis.

That made Magrew squawk. "I wisht one thing," he says. "I wisht I was manager of a old ladies' sewin' circle 'stead of a ball club."

"You are, Junior, you are," says a familyer and disagreeable 35 voice.

It was that Pearl du Monville again, poppin' up outa no-

wheres, swingin' his bamboo cane and smokin' a cigar that's
three sizes too big for his face. By this time we'd finely got the
other side out, and Hank Metters slithered a bat acrost the
ground, and the midget had to jump to keep both his ankles
from bein' broke.   5

I thought Magrew'd bust a blood vessel. "You hurt Pearl
and I'll break your neck!" he yelled.

Hank muttered somethin' and went on up to the plate and
struck out.

We managed to get a couple runs acrost in our half a the   10
sixth, but they come back with three more in their half a the
seventh, and this was too much for Magrew.

"Come on, Pearl," he says. "We're gettin' outa here."

"Where you think you're goin'?" I ast him.

"To the lawyer's again," he says cryptly.   15

"I didn't know you'd been to the lawyer's once, yet," I says.

"Which that goes to show how much you don't know," he
says.

With that, they was gone, and I didn't see 'em the rest of
the day, nor know what they was up to, which was a God's   20
blessin'. We lose the nightcap, 9 to 3, and that puts us into second place plenty, and as low in our mind as a ball club can get.

The next day was a horrible day, like anybody that lived
through it can tell you. Practice was just over and the St. Louis
club was takin' the field, when I hears this strange sound from   25
the stands. It sounds like the nervous whickerin' a horse gives
when he smells somethin' funny on the wind. It was the fans
ketchin' sight of Pearl du Monville, like you have prob'ly
guessed. The midget had popped up onto the field all dressed
up in a minacher club uniform, sox, cap, little letters sewed   30
onto his chest, and all. He was swingin' a kid's bat and the only
thing kept him from lookin' like a real ballplayer seen through
the wrong end of a microscope was this cigar he was smokin'.

Bugs Courtney reached over and jerked it outa his mouth
and throwed it away. "You're wearin' that suit on the playin'   35
field," he says to him, severe as a judge. "You go insultin' it and
I'll take you out to the zoo and feed you to the bears."

Pearl blowed some smoke at him which he still has in his mouth.

Whilst Whitey was foulin' off four or five prior to strikin' out, I went on over to Magrew. "If I was as comic as you," I says, "I'd laugh myself to death," I says. "Is that any way to treat the uniform, makin' a mockery out of it?"

"It might surprise you to know I ain't makin' no mockery outa the uniform," says Magrew. "Pearl du Monville here has been made a bone-of-fida member of this so-called ball club. I fixed it up with the front office by long-distance phone."

"Yeh?" I says. "I can just hear Mr. Dillworth or Bart Jenkins agreein' to hire a midget for the ball club. I can just hear 'em." Mr. Dillworth was the owner of the club and Bart Jenkins was the secretary, and they never stood for no monkey business. "May I be so bold as to inquire," I says, "just what you told 'em?"

"I told 'em," he says, "I wanted to sign up a guy they ain't no pitcher in the league can strike him out."

"Uh-huh," I says, "and did you tell 'em what size of a man he is?"

"Never mind about that," he says. "I got papers on me, made out legal and proper, constitutin' one Pearl du Monville a bone-of-fida member of this former ball club. Maybe that'll shame them big babies into gettin' in there and swingin', knowin' I can replace any one of 'em with a midget, if I have a mind to. A St. Louis lawyer I seen twice tell me it's all legal and proper."

"A St. Louis lawyer would," I says, "seein' nothin' could make him happier than havin' you makin' a mockery outa this one-time baseball outfit," I says.

Well, sir, it'll all be there in the papers of thirty, thirty-one year ago, and you could look it up. The game went along without no scorin' for seven innings, and since they ain't nothin' much to watch but guys poppin' up or strikin' out, the fans pay most of their attention to the goin's-on of Pearl du Monville. He's out there in front a the dugout turnin' handsprings, balancin' his bat on his chin, walkin' a imaginary line, and so on. The fans clapped and laughed at him, and he ate it up.

So it went up to the last a the eighth, nothin' to nothin' not more'n seven, eight hits all told, and no errors on neither side. Our pitcher gets the first two men out easy in the eighth. Then up come a fella name of Porter or Billings, or some such name, and he lammed one up against the tobacco sign for three bases. 5 The next guy up slapped the first ball out into left for a base hit, and in come the fella from third for the only run of the ball game so far. The crowd yelled, the look a death come onto Magrew's face again, and even the midget quit his tomfoolin'. Their next man fouled out back a third, and we come up for 10 our last bats like a bunch a schoolgirls steppin' into a pool of cold water. I was lower in my mind than I'd been since the day in Nineteen-four when Chesbro throwed the wild pitch in the ninth inning with a man on third and lost the pennant for the Highlanders. I knowed something just as bad was goin' 15 to happen, which shows I'm a clairvoyun, or was then.

When Gordy Mills hit out to second, I just closed my eyes. I opened 'em up again to see Dutch Muller standin' on second, dustin' off his pants, him havin' got his first hit in maybe twenty times to the plate. Next up was Harry Loesing, battin' for our 20 pitcher, and he got a base on balls, walkin' on a fourth one you could 'a' combed your hair with.

Then up come Whitey Cott, our lead-off man. He crotches down in what was prob'ly the most fearsome stanch in organized ball, but all he can do is pop out to short. That brung up 25 Billy Klinger, with two down and a man on first and second. Billy took a cut at one you could 'a' knocked a plug hat offa this here Carnera with it, but then he gets sense enough to wait 'em out, and finely he walks, too, fillin' the bases.

Yes, sir, there you are; the tyin' run on third and the 30 winnin' run on second, first a the ninth, two men down, and Hank Metters comin' to the bat. Hank was built like a Pope-Hartford and he couldn't run no faster'n President Taft, but he had five home runs to his credit for the season, and that wasn't bad in them days. Hank was still hittin' better'n any- 35 body else on the ball club, and it was mighty heartenin', seein' him stridin' up towards the plate. But he never got there.

"Wait a minute!" yells Magrew, jumpin' to his feet. "I'm sendin' in a pinch hitter!" he yells.

You could 'a' heard a bomb drop. When a ball-club manager says he's sendin' in a pinch hitter for the best batter on the club, you know and I know and everybody knows he's lost his holt.

"They're goin' to be sendin' the funny wagon for you, if you don't watch out," I says, grabbin' a holt of his arm.

But he pulled away and run out towards the plate, yellin', "Du Monville battin' for Metters!"

All the fellas begun squawlin' at once, except Hank, and he just stood there starin' at Magrew like he'd gone crazy and was claimin' to be Ty Cobb's grandma or somethin'. Their pitcher stood out there with his hands on his hips and a disagreeable look on his face, and the plate umpire told Magrew to go on and get a batter up. Magrew told him again Du Monville was battin' for Metters, and the St. Louis manager finely got the idea. It brung him outa his dugout, howlin' and bawlin' like he'd lost a female dog and her seven pups.

Magrew pushed the midget towards the plate and he says to him, he says, "Just stand up there and hold that bat on your shoulder. They ain't a man in the world can throw three strikes in there 'fore he throws four balls!" he says.

"I get it, Junior!" says the midget. "He'll walk me and force in the tyin' run!" And he starts on up to the plate as cocky as if he was Willie Keeler.

I don't need to tell you Bethlehem broke loose on that there ball field. The fans got onto their hind legs, yellin' and whistlin', and everybody on the field begun wavin' their arms and hollerin' and shovin'. The plate umpire stalked over to Magrew like a traffic cop, waggin' his jaw and pointin' his finger, and the St. Louis manager kept yellin' like his house was on fire. When Pearl got up to the plate and stood there, the pitcher slammed his glove down onto the ground and started stompin' on it, and they ain't nobody can blame him. He's just walked two normal-sized human bein's, and now here's a guy up to the plate they ain't more'n twenty inches between his knees and his shoulders.

The plate umpire called in the field umpire, and they
talked a while, like a couple doctors seein' the bucolic plague
or somethin' for the first time. Then the plate umpire come
over to Magrew with his arms folded acrost his chest, and he
told him to go on and get a batter up, or he'd forfeit the game   5
to St. Louis. He pulled out his watch, but somebody batted it
outa his hand in the scufflin', and I thought there'd be a free-
for-all, with everybody yellin' and shovin' except Pearl du Monville, who stood up at the plate with his little bat on his shoulder, not movin' a muscle.   10

Then Magrew played his ace. I seen him pull some papers
outa his pocket and show 'em to the plate umpire. The umpire
begun lookin' at 'em like they was bills for somethin' he not
only never bought it, he never even heard of it. The other umpire studied 'em like they was a death warren, and all this time 15
the St. Louis manager and the fans and the players is yellin'
and hollerin'.

Well, sir, they fought about him bein' a midget, and they
fought about him usin' a kid's bat, and they fought about
where'd he been all season. They was eight or nine rule books   20
brung out and everybody was thumbin' through 'em, tryin' to
find out what it says about midgets, but it don't say nothin'
about midgets, 'cause this was somethin' never'd come up in
the history of the game before, and nobody'd ever dreamed
about it, even when they has nightmares. Maybe you can't   25
send no midgets in to bat nowadays, 'cause the old game's
changed a lot, mostly for the worst, but you could then, it
turned out.

The plate umpire finely decided the contrack papers was
all legal and proper, like Magrew said, so he waved the St.   30
Louis players back to their places and he pointed his finger
at their manager and told him to quit hollerin' and get on back
in the dugout. The manager says the game is percedin' under
protest, and the umpire bawls, "Play ball!" over 'n' above the
yellin' and booin', him havin' a voice like a hog-caller.   35

The St. Louis pitcher picked up his glove and beat at it with
his fist six or eight times, and then got set on the mound and
studied the situation. The fans realized he was really goin' to

pitch to the midget, and they went crazy, hoopin' and hollerin
louder'n ever, and throwin' pop bottles and hats and cushions
down onto the field. It took five, ten minutes to get the fans
quieted down again, whilst our fellas that was on base set
down on the bags and waited. And Pearl du Monville kept   5
standin' up there with the bat on his shoulder, like he'd been
told to.

So the pitcher starts studyin' the setup again, and you got
to admit it was the strangest setup in a ball game since the
players cut off their beards and begun wearin' gloves. I wisht 10
I could call the pitcher's name—it wasn't old Barney Pelty nor
Nig Jack Powell nor Harry Howell. He was a big right-hander,
but I can't call his name. You could look it up. Even in a
crotchin' position, the ketcher towers over the midget like the
Washington Monument.   15

The plate umpire tries standin' on his tiptoes, then he tries
crotchin' down, and he finely gets hisself into a stanch nobody'd
ever seen on a baseball field before, kinda squattin' down on
his hanches.

Well, the pitcher is sore as a old buggy horse in fly time.   20
He slams in the first pitch, hard and wild, and maybe two foot
higher'n the midget's head.

"Ball one!" hollers the umpire over 'n' above the racket,
'cause everybody is yellin' worsten ever.

The ketcher goes on out towards the mound and talks to   25
the pitcher and hands him the ball. This time the big right-
hander tries a undershoot, and it comes in a little closer, maybe
no higher'n a foot, foot and a half above Pearl's head. It would
'a' been a strike with a human bein' in there, but the umpire's
got to call it, and he does.   30

"Ball two!" he bellers.

The ketcher walks on out to the mound again, and the whole
infield comes over and gives advice to the pitcher about what
they'd do in a case like this, with two balls and no strikes on a
batter that oughta be in a bottle of alcohol 'stead of up there 35
at the plate in a big-league game between the teams that is
fightin' for first place.

For the third pitch, the pitcher stands there flat-footed and tosses up the ball like he's playin' ketch with a little girl.

Pearl stands there motionless as a hitchin' post, and the ball comes in big and slow and high—high for Pearl, that is, it bein' about on a level with his eyes, or a little higher'n a grown man's knees.

They ain't nothin' else for the umpire to do, so he calls, "Ball three!"

Everybody is onto their feet, hoopin' and hollerin', as the pitcher sets to throw ball four. The St. Louis manager is makin' signs and faces like he was a contorturer, and the infield is givin' the pitcher some more advice about what to do this time. Our boys who was on base stick right onto the bag, runnin' no risk of bein' nipped for the last out.

Well, the pitcher decides to give him a toss again, seein' he come closer with that than with a fast ball. They ain't nobody ever seen a slower ball throwed. It come in big as a balloon and slower'n any ball ever throwed before in the major leagues. It come right in over the plate in front of Pearl's chest, lookin' prob'ly big as a full moon to Pearl. They ain't never been a minute like the minute that followed since the United States was founded by the Pilgrim grandfathers.

Pearl du Monville took a cut at that ball, and he hit it! Magrew give a groan like a poleaxed steer as the ball rolls out in front a the plate into fair territory.

"Fair ball!" yells the umpire, and the midget starts runnin' for first, still carryin' that little bat, and makin' maybe ninety foot an hour. Bethlehem breaks loose on that ball field and in them stands. They ain't never been nothin' like it since creation was begun.

The ball's rollin' slow, on down towards third, goin' maybe eight, ten foot. The infield comes in fast and our boys break from their bases like hares in a brush fire. Everybody is standin' up, yellin' and hollerin', and Magrew is tearin' his hair outa his head, and the midget is scamperin' for first with all the speed of one of them little dash-hounds carryin' a satchel in his mouth.

The ketcher gets to the ball first, but he boots it on out past the pitcher's box, the pitcher fallin' on his face tryin' to stop it, the shortstop sprawlin' after it full length and zaggin' it on over towards the second baseman, whilst Muller is scorin' with the tyin' run and Loesing is roundin' third with the winnin' run. Ty Cobb could 'a' made a three-bagger outa that bunt, with everybody fallin' over theirself tryin' to pick the ball up. But Pearl is still maybe fifteen, twenty feet from the bag, toddlin' like a baby and yeepin' like a trapped rabbit, when the second baseman finely gets a holt of that ball and slams it over to first. The first baseman ketches it and stomps on the bag, the base umpire waves Pearl out, and there goes your old ball game, the craziest ball game ever played in the history of the organized world.

Their players start runnin' in, and then I see Magrew. He starts after Pearl, runnin' faster'n any man ever run before. Pearl sees him comin' and runs behind the base umpire's legs and gets a holt onto 'em. Magrew comes up, pantin' and roarin', and him and the midget plays ring-around-a-rosy with the umpire, who keeps shovin' at Magrew with one hand and tryin' to slap the midget loose from his legs with the other.

Finely Magrew ketches the midget, who is still yeepin' like a stuck sheep. He gets holt of that little guy by both his ankles and starts whirlin' him round and round his head like Magrew was a hammer thrower and Pearl was the hammer. Nobody can stop him without gettin' their head knocked off, so everybody just stands there and yells. Then Magrew lets the midget fly. He flies on out towards second, high and fast, like a human home run, headed for the soap sign in center field.

Their shortstop tries to get to him, but he can't make it, and I knowed the little fella was goin' to bust to pieces like a dollar watch on a asphalt street when he hit the ground. But it so happens their center fielder is just crossin' second, and he starts runnin' back, tryin' to get under the midget, who had took to spiralin' like a football 'stead of turnin' head over foot, which give him more speed and more distance.

I know you never seen a midget ketched, and you prob'ly

never even seen one throwed. To ketch a midget that's been throwed by a heavy-muscled man and is flyin' through the air, you got to run under him and with him and pull your hands and arms back and down when you ketch him, to break the compact of his body, or you'll bust him in two like a match- 5 stick. I seen Bill Lange and Willie Keeler and Tris Speaker make some wonderful ketches in my day, but I never seen nothin' like that center fielder. He goes back and back and still further back and he pulls that midget down outa the air like he was liftin' a sleepin' baby from a cradle. They wasn't a 10 bruise onto him, only his face was the color of cat's meat and he ain't got no air in his chest. In his excitement, the base um- pire, who was runnin' back with the center fielder when he ketched Pearl, yells, "Out!" and that give hysteries to the Beth- lehem which was ragin' like Niagry on that ball field. 15

Everybody was hoopin' and hollerin' and yellin' and runnin', with the fans swarmin' onto the field, and the cops tryin' to keep order, and some guys laughin' and some of the women fans cryin', and six or eight of us holdin' onto Magrew to keep him from gettin' at that midget and finishin' him off. Some of 20 the fans picks up the St. Louis pitcher and the center fielder, and starts carryin' 'em around on their shoulders, and they was the craziest goin's-on knowed to the history of organized ball on this side of the 'Lantic Ocean.

I seen Pearl du Monville strugglin' in the arms of a lady 25 fan with a ample bosom, who was laughin' and cryin' at the same time, and him beatin' at her with his little fists and bawlin' and yellin'. He clawed his way loose finely and disap- peared in the forest of legs which made that ball field look like it was Coney Island on a hot summer's day. 30

That was the last I ever seen of Pearl du Monville. I never seen hide nor hair of him from that day to this, and neither did nobody else. He just vanished into the thin of the air, as the fella says. He was ketched for the final out of the ball game and that was the end of him, just like it was the end of the 35 ball game, you might say, and also the end of our losin' streak, like I'm goin' to tell you.

That night we piled onto a train for Chicago, but we wasn't snarlin' and snappin' any more. No, sir, the ice was finely broke and a new spirit come into that ball club. The old zip come back with the disappearance of Pearl du Monville out back a second base. We got to laughin' and talkin' and kiddin' to- 5 gether, and 'fore long Magrew was laughin' with us. He got a human look onto his pan again, and he quit whinin' and com- plainin' and wishtin' he was in heaven with the angels.

Well, sir, we wiped up that Chicago series, winnin' all four games, and makin' seventeen hits in one of 'em. Funny thing 10 was, St. Louis was so shook up by that last game with us, they never did hit their stride again. Their center fielder took to misjudgin' everything that come his way, and the rest a the fellas followed suit, the way a club'll do when one guy blows up. 15

'Fore we left Chicago, I and some of the fellas went out and bought a pair of them little baby shoes, which we had 'em golded over and give 'em to Magrew for a souvenir, and he took it all in good spirit. Whitey Cott and Billy Klinger made up and was fast friends again, and we hit our home lot like a 20 ton of dynamite and they was nothin' could stop us from then on.

I don't recollect things as clear as I did thirty, forty year ago. I can't read no fine print no more, and the only person I got to check with on the golden days of the national pastime, as the 25 fella says, is my friend, old Milt Kline, over in Springfield, and his mind ain't as strong as it once was.

He gets Rube Waddell mixed up with Rube Marquard, for one thing, and anybody does that oughta be put away where he won't bother nobody. So I can't tell you the exact margin 30 we win the pennant by. Maybe it was two and a half games, or maybe it was three and a half. But it'll all be there in the newspapers and record books of thirty, thirty-one year ago and, like I was sayin', you could look it up.

Vocabulary

1. In this story the narrator often uses words which have different meanings from those intended, or he uses words which do not conform to standard English usage. Decide what he does mean in the following instances:

   a. ". . . we lose the last three double-headers we play, makin' maybe twenty-five errors in the six games, which is all right for the *intimates* of a school for the blind" (p. 100, ll. 1-3).

   b. "Whitey come back at him with a chair, and *Bethlehem* broke loose in that there room" (p. 100, ll. 12-13).

   c. "Pearl du Monville here has been made a *bone-of-fida* member of this so-called ball club' " (p. 102. ll. 8-9).

   d. "The other umpire studies 'em like they was a death *warren* . . ." (p. 105, ll. 14-15).

   e. "The manager says the game is *percedin'* under protest . . ." (p. 105, ll. 33-34).

   f. "The plate umpire tries standin' on his tiptoes, then he tries *crotchin'* down, and *finely* gets *hisself* into a *stanch,* nobody'd ever seen on a baseball field before, kinda squattin' down on his *hanches*" (p. 106, ll. 16-19).

Questions and Suggestions for Reading

MOTIVATION

1. As in "Butch Minds the Baby," the narrator is obviously not a well-educated man. But unlike the other narrator, this one uses much slang and many contractions. Why? Does this make his story more believable? Does it make the story more amusing?

2. Do you believe the narrator is telling the truth about the team? He says, "You could look it up," but he is extremely vague about the pennant scores. Why—if the race was such a memorable one?

3. The narrator feels that he is more intelligent than the manager, Squawks Magrew. Yet Squawks signs up Pearl du Monville and eventually puts the team back in the running. Why does Squawks sign up Pearl in the first place?

4. Why was the narrator so angry when Squawks hired Pearl? Did he wish he had thought of the idea himself? Did he think the team might be insulted?

Max Shulman

LOVE IS A FALLACY

Cool was I and logical. Keen, calculating, perspicacious, acute and astute—I was all of these. My brain was as powerful as a dynamo, as precise as a chemist's scales, as penetrating as a scalpel. And—think of it!—I was only eighteen.

It is not often that one so young has such a giant intellect. 5
Take, for example, Petey Bellows, my roommate at the university. Same age, same background, but dumb as an ox. A nice enough fellow, you understand, but nothing upstairs. Emotional type. Unstable. Impressionable. Worst of all, a faddist. Fads, I submit, are the very negation of reason. To be swept 10
up in every new craze that comes along, to surrender yourself to idiocy just because everybody else is doing it—this, to me, is the acme of mindlessness. Not, however, to Petey.

One afternoon I found Petey lying on his bed with an expression of such distress on his face that I immediately diagnosed 15
appendicitis. "Don't move," I said. "Don't take a laxative. I'll get a doctor."

"Raccoon," he mumbled thickly.

"Raccoon?" I said, pausing in my flight.

"I want a raccoon coat," he wailed. 20

I perceived that his trouble was not physical, but mental. "Why do you want a raccoon coat?"

"I should have known it," he cried, pounding his temples. "I should have known they'd come back when the Charleston came back. Like a fool I spent all my money for textbooks, and 25
now I can't get a raccoon coat."

"Can you mean," I said incredulously, "that people are actually wearing raccoon coats again?"

"All the Big Men on Campus are wearing them. Where've you been?"

"In the library," I said, naming a place not frequented by Big Men on Campus.

He leaped from the bed and paced the room. "I've got to have a raccoon coat," he said passionately. "I've got to!"

"Petey, why? Look at it rationally. Raccoon coats are unsanitary. They shed. They smell bad. They weigh too much. They're unsightly. They——"

"You don't understand," he interrupted impatiently. "It's the thing to do. Don't you want to be in the swim?"

"No," I said truthfully.

"Well, I do," he declared. "I'd give anything for a raccoon coat. Anything!"

My brain, that precision instrument, slipped into high gear. "Anything?" I asked, looking at him narrowly.

"Anything," he affirmed in ringing tones.

I stroked my chin thoughtfully. It so happened that I knew where to get my hands on a raccoon coat. My father had had one in his undergraduate days; it lay now in a trunk in the attic back home. It also happened that Petey had something I wanted. He didn't *have* it exactly, but at least he had first rights on it. I refer to his girl, Polly Espy.

I had long coveted Polly Espy. Let me emphasize that my desire for this young woman was not emotional in nature. She was, to be sure, a girl who excited the emotions, but I was not one to let my heart rule my head. I wanted Polly for a shrewdly calculated, entirely cerebral reason.

I was a freshman in law school. In a few years I would be out in practice. I was well aware of the importance of the right kind of wife in furthering a lawyer's career. The successful lawyers I had observed were, almost without exception, married to beautiful, gracious, intelligent women. With one omission, Polly fitted these specifications perfectly.

Beautiful she was. She was not yet of pin-up proportions,

but I felt sure that time would supply the lack. She already had the makings.

Gracious she was. By gracious I mean full of graces. She had an erectness of carriage, an ease of bearing, a poise that clearly indicated the best of breeding. At table her manners were exquisite. I had seen her at the Kozy Kampus Korner eating the specialty of the house—a sandwich that contained scraps of pot roast, gravy, chopped nuts, and a dipper of sauerkraut—without even getting her fingers moist.

Intelligent she was not. In fact, she veered in the opposite direction. But I believed that under my guidance she would smarten up. At my rate, it was worth a try. It is, after all, easier to make a beautiful dumb girl smart than to make an ugly smart girl beautiful.

"Petey," I said, "are you in love with Polly Espy?"

"I think she's a keen kid," he replied, "but I don't know if you'd call it love. Why?"

"Do you," I asked, "have any kind of formal arrangement with her? I mean are you going steady or anything like that?"

"No. We see each other quite a bit, but we both have other dates. Why?"

"Is there," I asked, "any other man for whom she has a particular fondness?"

"Not that I know of. Why?"

I nodded with satisfaction. "In other words, if you were out of the picture, the field would be open. Is that right?"

"I guess so. What are you getting at?"

"Nothing, nothing," I said innocently, and took my suitcase out of the closet.

"Where you going?" asked Petey.

"Home for the week end." I threw a few things into the bag.

"Listen," he said, clutching my arm eagerly, "while you're home, you couldn't get some money from your old man, could you, and lend it to me so I can buy a raccoon coat?"

"I may do better than that," I said with a mysterious wink and closed my bag and left.

"Look," I said to Petey when I got back Monday morning. I threw open the suitcase and revealed the huge, hairy, gamy object that my father had worn in his Stutz Bearcat in 1925.

"Holy Toledo!" said Petey reverently. He plunged his hands into the raccoon coat and then his face. "Holy Toledo!" he repeated fifteen or twenty times.

"Would you like it?" I asked.

"Oh, yes!" he cried, clutching the greasy pelt to him. Then a canny look came into his eyes. "What do you want for it?"

"Your girl," I said, mincing no words.

"Polly?" he said in a horrified whisper. "You want Polly?"

"That's right."

He flung the coat from him. "Never," he said stoutly.

I shrugged. "Okay. If you don't want to be in the swim, I guess it's your business."

I sat down in a chair and pretended to read a book, but out of the corner of my eye I kept watching Petey. He was a torn man. First he looked at the coat with the expression of a waif at a bakery window. Then he turned away and set his jaw resolutely. Then he looked back at the coat, with even more longing in his face. Then he turned away, but with not so much resolution this time. Back and forth his head swiveled, desire waxing, resolution waning. Finally he didn't turn away at all; he just stood and stared with mad lust at the coat.

"It isn't as though I was in love with Polly," he said thickly. "Or going steady or anything like that."

"That's right," I murmured.

"What's Polly to me, or me to Polly?"

"Not a thing," said I.

"It's just been a casual kick—just a few laughs, that's all."

"Try on the coat," said I.

He complied. The coat bunched high over his ears and dropped all the way down to his shoe tops. He looked like a mound of dead raccoons. "Fits fine," he said happily.

I rose from my chair. "Is it a deal?" I asked, extending my hand.

He swallowed. "It's a deal," he said and shook my hand.

I had my first date with Polly the following evening. This was in the nature of a survey; I wanted to find out just how much work I had to do to get her mind up to the standard I required. I took her first to dinner. "Gee, that was a delish dinner," she said as we left the restaurant. Then I took her to a movie. "Gee, that was a marvy movie," she said as we left the theater. And then I took her home. "Gee, I had a sensaysh time," she said as she bade me good night.

I went back to my room with a heavy heart. I had gravely underestimated the size of my task. This girl's lack of information was terrifying. Nor would it be enough merely to supply her with information. First she had to be taught to *think*. This loomed as a project of no small dimensions, and at first I was tempted to give her back to Petey. But then I got to thinking about her abundant physical charms and about the way she entered a room and the way she handled a knife and fork, and I decided to make an effort.

I went about it, as in all things, systematically. I gave her a course in logic. It happened that I, as a law student, was taking a course in logic myself, so I had all the facts at my finger tips. "Polly," I said to her when I picked her up on our next date, "tonight we are going over to the Knoll and talk."

"Oo, terrif," she replied. One thing I will say for this girl: you would go far to find another so agreeable.

We went to the Knoll, the campus trysting place, and we sat down under an old oak, and she looked at me expectantly. "What are we going to talk about?" she asked.

"Logic."

She thought this over for a minute and decided she liked it. "Magnif," she said.

"Logic," I said, clearing my throat, "is the science of thinking. Before we can think correctly, we must first learn to recognize the common fallacies of logic. These we will take up tonight."

"Wow-dow!" she cried, clapping her hands delightedly.

I winced, but went bravely on. "First let us examine the fallacy called Dicto Simpliciter."

"By all means," she urged, batting her lashes eagerly.

"Dicto Simpliciter means an argument based on an unqualified generalization. For example: Exercise is good. Therefore everybody should exercise."

"I agree," said Polly earnestly. "I mean exercise is wonderful. 5 I mean it builds the body and everything."

"Polly," I said gently, "the argument is a fallacy. *Exercise is good* is an unqualified generalization. For instance, if you have heart disease, exercise is bad, not good. Many people are ordered by their doctors *not* to exercise. You must *qualify* the 10 generalization. You must say exercise is *usually* good, or exercise is good *for most people*. Otherwise you have committed a Dicto Simpliciter. Do you see?"

"No," she confessed. "But this is marvy. Do more! Do more!"

"It will be better if you stop tugging at my sleeve," I told 15 her, and when she desisted, I continued. "Next we take up a fallacy called Hasty Generalization. Listen carefully: You can't speak French. I can't speak French. Petey Bellows can't speak French. I must therefore conclude that nobody at the University of Minnesota can speak French." 20

"Really?" said Polly, amazed. "*Nobody?*"

I hid my exasperation. "Polly, it's a fallacy. The generalization is reached too hastily. There are too few instances to support such a conclusion."

"Know any more fallacies?" she asked breathlessly. "This is 25 more fun than dancing even."

I fought off a wave of despair. I was getting nowhere with this girl, absolutely nowhere. Still, I am nothing if not persistent. I continued. "Next comes Post Hoc. Listen to this: Let's not take Bill on our picnic. Every time we take him out with 30 us, it rains."

"I know somebody just like that," she exclaimed. "A girl back home—Eula Becker, her name is. It never fails. Every single time we take her on a picnic—"

"Polly," I said sharply, "it's a fallacy. Eula Becker doesn't 35 *cause* the rain. She has no connection with the rain. You are guilty of Post Hoc if you blame Eula Becker."

"I'll never do it again," she promised contritely. "Are you mad at me?"

I sighed. "No, Polly, I'm not mad."

"Then tell me some more fallacies."

"All right. Let's try Contradictory Premises."

"Yes, let's," she chirped, blinking her eyes happily.

I frowned, but plunged ahead. "Here's an example of Contradictory Premises: If God can do anything, can He make a stone so heavy that He won't be able to lift it?"

"Of course," she replied promptly.

"But if He can do anything, He can lift the stone," I pointed out.

"Yah," she said thoughtfully. "Well, then I guess He can't make the stone."

"But He can do anything," I reminded her.

She scratched her pretty, empty head. "I'm all confused," she admitted.

"Of course you are. Because when the premises of an argument contradict each other, there can be no argument. If there is an irresistible force, there can be no immovable object. If there is an immovable object, there can be no irresistible force. Get it?"

"Tell me some more of this keen stuff," she said eagerly.

I consulted my watch. "I think we'd better call it a night. I'll take you home now, and you go over all the things you've learned. We'll have another session tomorrow night."

I deposited her at the girls' dormitory, where she assured me that she had had a perfectly terrif evening, and I went glumly home to my room. Petey lay snoring in his bed, the raccoon coat huddled like a great hairy beast at his feet. For a moment I considered waking him and telling him that he could have his girl back. It seemed clear that my project was doomed to failure. The girl simply had a logic-proof head.

But then I reconsidered. I had wasted one evening; I might as well waste another. Who knew? Maybe somewhere in the extinct crater of her mind a few embers still smoldered. Maybe somehow I could fan them into flame. Admittedly it was not a prospect fraught with hope, but I decided to give it one more try.

Seated under the oak the next evening I said, "Our first fallacy tonight is called Ad Misericordiam."

She quivered with delight.

"Listen closely," I said. "A man applies for a job. When the boss asks him what his qualifications are, he replies that he has a wife and six children at home, the wife is a helpless cripple, the children have nothing to eat, no clothes to wear, no shoes on their feet, there are no beds in the house, no coal in the cellar, and winter is coming."

A tear rolled down each of Polly's pink cheeks. "Oh, this is awful, awful," she sobbed.

"Yes, it's awful," I agreed, "but it's no argument. The man never answered the boss's question about his qualifications. Instead he appealed to the boss's sympathy. He committed the fallacy of Ad Misericordiam. Do you understand?"

"Have you got a handkerchief?" she blubbered.

I handed her a handkerchief and tried to keep from screaming while she wiped her eyes. "Next," I said in a carefully controlled tone, "we will discuss False Analogy. Here is an example: Students should be allowed to look at their textbooks during examinations. After all, surgeons have X-rays to guide them during an operation, lawyers have briefs to guide them during a trial, carpenters have blueprints to guide them when they are building a house. Why, then, shouldn't students be allowed to look at their textbooks during an examination?"

"There now," she said enthusiastically, "is the most marvy idea I've heard in years."

"Polly," I said testily, "the argument is all wrong. Doctors, lawyers, and carpenters aren't taking a test to see how much they have learned, but students are. The situations are altogether different, and you can't make an analogy between them."

"I still think it's a good idea," said Polly.

"Nuts," I muttered. Doggedly I pressed on. "Next we'll try Hypothesis Contrary to Fact."

"Sounds yummy," was Polly's reaction.

"Listen: If Madame Curie had not happened to leave a photographic plate in a drawer with a chunk of pitchblende, the world today would not know about radium."

"True, true," said Polly, nodding her head. "Did you see the   5
movie? Oh, it just knocked me out. That Walter Pidgeon is so dreamy. I mean he fractures me."

"If you can forget Mr. Pidgeon for a moment," I said coldly, "I would like to point out that the statement is a fallacy. Maybe Madame Curie would have discovered radium at some   10
later date. Maybe somebody else would have discovered it. Maybe any number of things would have happened. You can't start with a hypothesis that is not true and then draw any supportable conclusions from it."

"They ought to put Walter Pidgeon in more pictures," said   15
Polly. "I hardly ever see him any more."

One more chance, I decided. But just one more. There is a limit to what flesh and blood can bear. "The next fallacy is called Poisoning the Well."

"How cute!" she gurgled.   20

"Two men are having a debate. The first one gets up and says, 'My opponent is a notorious liar. You can't believe a word that he is going to say.' . . . Now, Polly, think. Think hard. What's wrong?"

I watched her closely as she knit her creamy brow in con-   25
centration. Suddenly a glimmer of intelligence—the first I had seen—came into her eyes. "It's not fair," she said with indignation. "It's not a bit fair. What chance has the second man got if the first man calls him a liar before he even begins talking?"

"Right!" I cried exultantly. "One hundred per cent right. It's   30
not fair. The first man has *poisoned the well* before anybody could drink from it. He has hamstrung his opponent before he could even start. . . . Polly, I'm proud of you."

"Pshaw," she murmured, blushing with pleasure.

"You see, my dear, these things aren't so hard. All you have   35
to do is concentrate. Think—examine—evaluate. Come now, let's review everything we have learned."

"Fire away," she said with an airy wave of her hand.

Heartened by the knowledge that Polly was not altogether a cretin, I began a long, patient review of all I had told her. Over and over and over again I cited instances, pointed out flaws, kept hammering away without letup. It was like digging a tunnel. At first everything was work, sweat, and darkness. I had no idea when I would reach the light, or even *if* I would. But I persisted. I pounded and clawed and scraped, and finally I was rewarded. I saw a chink of light. And then the chink got bigger and the sun came pouring in and all was bright.

Five grueling nights this took, but it was worth it. I had made a logician out of Polly; I had taught her to think. My job was done. She was worthy of me at last. She was a fit wife for me, a proper hostess for my many mansions, a suitable mother for my well-heeled children.

It must not be thought that I was without love for this girl. Quite the contrary. Just as Pygmalion loved the perfect woman he had fashioned, so I loved mine. I decided to acquaint her with my feelings at our very next meeting. The time had come to change our relationship from academic to romantic.

"Polly," I said when next we sat beneath our oak, "tonight we will not discuss fallacies."

"Aw, gee," she said, disappointed.

"My dear," I said, favoring her with a smile, "we have now spent five evenings together. We have gotten along splendidly. It is clear that we are well matched."

"Hasty Generalization," said Polly brightly.

"I beg your pardon," said I.

"Hasty Generalization," she repeated. "How can you say that we are well matched on the basis of only five dates?"

I chuckled with amusement. The dear child had learned her lessons well. "My dear," I said, patting her hand in a tolerant manner, "five dates is plenty. After all, you don't have to eat a whole cake to know that it's good."

"False Analogy," said Polly promptly. "I'm not a cake. I'm a girl."

I chuckled with somewhat less amusement. The dear child

had learned her lessons perhaps too well. I decided to change tactics. Obviously the best approach was a simple, strong, direct declaration of love. I paused for a moment while my massive brain chose the proper words. Then I began:

"Polly, I love you. You are the whole world to me, and the   5
moon and the stars and the constellations of outer space. Please, my darling, say that you will go steady with me, for if you will not, life will be meaningless. I will languish. I will refuse my meals. I will wander the face of the earth, a shambling hollow-eyed hulk."   10

There, I thought, folding my arms, that ought to do it.

"Ad Misericordiam," said Polly.

I ground my teeth. I was not Pygmalion; I was Frankenstein, and my monster had me by the throat. Frantically I fought back the tide of panic surging through me. At all costs   15
I had to keep cool.

"Well, Polly," I said, forcing a smile, "you certainly have learned your fallacies."

"You're darn right," she said with a vigorous nod.

"And who taught them to you, Polly?"   20

"You did."

"That's right. So you do owe me something, don't you, my dear? If I hadn't come along you never would have learned about fallacies."

"Hypothesis Contrary to Fact," she said instantly.   25

I dashed perspiration from my brow. "Polly," I croaked, "you mustn't take all these things so literally. I mean this is just classroom stuff. You know that the things you learn in school don't have anything to do with life."

"Dicto Simpliciter," she said, wagging her finger at me play- 30
fully.

That did it. I leaped to my feet, bellowing like a bull. "Will you or will you not go steady with me?"

"I will not," she replied.

"Why not?" I demanded.   35

"Because this afternoon I promised Petey Bellows that I would go steady with him."

I reeled back, overcome with the infamy of it. After he promised, after he made a deal, after he shook my hand! "The rat!" I shrieked, kicking up great chunks of turf. "You can't go with him, Polly. He's a liar. He's a cheat. He's a rat."

"Poisoning the Well," said Polly, "and stop shouting. I think 5 shouting must be a fallacy too."

With an immense effort of will, I modulated my voice. "All right," I said. "You're a logician. Let's look at this thing logically. How could you choose Petey Bellows over me? Look at me—a brilliant student, a tremendous intellectual, a man with 10 an assured future. Look at Petey—a knothead, a jitterbug, a guy who'll never know where his next meal is coming from. Can you give me one logical reason why you should go steady with Petey Bellows?"

"I certainly can," declared Polly. "He's got a raccoon coat." 15

Vocabulary

1. The narrator describes himself as "calculating, perspicacious, acute, and astute." Do these adjectives give us a good picture of him? What about the terms "negation of reason," "acme of mindlessness," and "cerebral reason"? Do they give us an even more complete picture of him?

2. There are many difficult words and terms in this amusing story. Even one word in the title, "fallacy," needs defining; on the other hand, some of the terms, such as "Dicto Simpliciter," "Hasty Generalization," and "Post Hoc" are defined by the examples following each of them.

Questions and Suggestions for Reading

IRONY and CHARACTER

1. Because of his "ambitions" for Polly, the narrator tricks himself. He teaches her logic (in five nights!) and then decides to

change their relationship into what he terms is a "logical" one. Is his approach to going steady logical? Is her answer logical?

2. Is Petey Bellows logical in wanting a raccoon coat? Are the narrator's objections to Petey's desire rational?

3. Can the narrator understand why he has failed in his attempt to win the girl?

4. Was the narrator cheated more by Polly or by Petey or by himself?

5. Early in the story (p. 112) the narrator says that he does not want to be "in the swim"; however, he does want to be a successful lawyer and all the successful lawyers he knows have "beautiful, gracious, intelligent women" for their wives. Thus he does, so to speak, want to be "in the swim." Does he realize the irony of his desires? Support your answer.

6. After describing himself as he does, do you feel that the narrator has presented a true or a biased view of himself? Why?

W. Somerset Maugham

THE FACTS OF LIFE

It was Henry Garnet's habit on leaving the city of an afternoon to drop in at his club and play bridge before going home to dinner. He was a pleasant man to play with. He knew the game well, and you could be sure that he would make the best of his cards. He was a good loser; and when he won was more inclined to ascribe his success to his luck than to his skill. He was indulgent, and if his partner made a mistake, could be trusted to find an excuse for him. It was surprising then on this occasion to hear him telling his partner with unnecessary sharpness that he had never seen a hand worse played; and it was more surprising still to see him not only make a grave error himself, an error of which you would never have thought him capable, but when his partner, not unwilling to get a little of his own back, pointed it out, insist against all reason and with considerable heat that he was perfectly right. But they were all old friends, the men he was playing with, and none of them took his ill humour very seriously. Henry Garnet was a broker, a partner in a firm of repute, and it occurred to one of them that something had gone wrong with some stock he was interested in.

"How's the market today?" he asked.

"Booming. Even the suckers are making money."

It was evident that stocks and shares had nothing to do with Henry Garnet's vexation; but something was the matter; that was evident, too. He was a hearty fellow who enjoyed excellent health; he had plenty of money; he was fond of his wife and devoted to his children. As a rule he had high spirits, and he laughed easily at the nonsense they were apt to talk while they played; but today he sat glum and silent. His brows were crossly puckered, and there was a sulky look about his mouth. Presently, to ease the tension, one of the others mentioned a 5 subject upon which they all knew Henry Garnet was glad to speak.

"How's your boy, Henry? I see he's done pretty well in the tournament."

Henry Garnet's frown grew darker. 10

"He's done no better than I expected him to."

"When does he come back from Monte?"

"He got back last night."

"Did he enjoy himself?"

"I suppose so; all I know is that he made a damned fool of 15 himself."

"Oh. How?"

"I'd rather not talk about it if you don't mind."

The three men looked at him with curiosity. Henry Garnet scowled at the green baize. 20

"Sorry, old boy. Your call."

The game proceeded in a strained silence. Garnet got his bid, and when he played his cards so badly that he went three down not a word was said. Another rubber was begun, and in the second game Garnet denied a suit. 25

"Having none?" his partner asked him.

Garnet's irritability was such that he did not even reply, and when at the end of the hand it appeared that he had revoked, and that his revoke cost the rubber, it was not to be expected that his partner should let his carelessness go with- 30 out remark.

"What the devil's the matter with you, Henry?" he said. "You're playing like a fool."

Garnet was disconcerted. He did not so much mind losing a big rubber himself, but he was sore that his inattention should 35 have made his partner lose too. He pulled himself together.

"I'd better not play any more. I thought a few rubbers

would calm me, but the fact is I can't give my mind to the game. To tell you the truth I'm in a hell of a temper."

They all burst out laughing.

"You don't have to tell us that, old boy. It's obvious."

Garnet gave them a rueful smile.   5

"Well, I bet you'd be in a temper if what's happened to me had happened to you. As a matter of fact I'm in a damned awkward situation, and if any of you fellows can give me any advice how to deal with it I'd be grateful."

"Let's have a drink and you tell us all about it. With a K.C.,   10
a Home Office official and an eminent surgeon—if we can't tell you how to deal with a situation, nobody can."

The K.C. got up and rang the bell for a waiter.

"It's about that damned boy of mine," said Henry Garnet.

Drinks were ordered and brought. And this is the story that   15
Henry Garnet told them.

The boy of whom he spoke was his only son. His name was Nicholas, and of course he was called Nicky. He was eighteen. The Garnets had two daughters besides, one of sixteen and the other of twelve, but however unreasonable it seemed, for a   20
father is generally supposed to like his daughters best, and though he did all he could not to show his preference, there was no doubt that the greater share of Henry Garnet's affection was given to his son. He was kind, in a chaffing, casual way, to his daughters, and gave them handsome presents on their birth- 25
days and at Christmas; but he doted on Nicky. Nothing was too good for him. He thought the world of him. He could hardly take his eyes off him. You could not blame him, for Nicky was a son that any parent might have been proud of. He was six foot two, lithe but muscular, with broad shoulders and a slim   30
waist, and he held himself gallantly erect; he had a charming head, well placed on the shoulders, with pale brown hair that waved slightly, blue eyes with long dark lashes under well-marked eyebrows, a full red mouth and a tanned, clean skin. When he smiled he showed very regular and very white teeth.   35
He was not shy, but there was a modesty in his demeanour that was attractive. In social intercourse he was easy, polite

and quietly gay. He was the offspring of nice, healthy, decent parents, he had been well brought up in a good home, he had been sent to a good school, and the general result was as engaging a specimen of young manhood as you were likely to find in a long time. You felt that he was as honest, open and virtuous as he looked. He had never given his parents a moment's uneasiness. As a child he was seldom ill and never naughty. As a boy he did everything that was expected of him. His school reports were excellent. He was wonderfully popular, and he ended his career, with a creditable number of prizes, as head of the school and captain of the football team. But this was not all. At the age of fourteen Nicky had developed an unexpected gift for lawn tennis. This was a game that his father not only was fond of, but played very well, and when he discerned in the boy the promise of a tennis player he fostered it. During the holidays he had him taught by the best professionals, and by the time he was sixteen he had won a number of tournaments for boys of his age. He could beat his father so badly that only parental affection reconciled the older player to the poor show he put up. At eighteen Nicky went to Cambridge and Henry Garnet conceived the ambition that before he was through with the university he should play for it. Nicky had all the qualifications for becoming a great tennis player. He was tall, he had a long reach, he was quick on his feet and his timing was perfect. He realized instinctively where the ball was coming and, seemingly without hurry, was there to take it. He had a powerful serve, with a nasty break that made it difficult to return, and his forehand drive, low, long and accurate, was deadly. He was not so good on the backhand and his volleying was wild, but all through the summer before he went to Cambridge Henry Garnet made him work on these points under the best teacher in England. At the back of his mind, though he did not even mention it to Nicky, he cherished a further ambition, to see his son play at Wimbledon, and who could tell, perhaps be chosen to represent his country in the Davis Cup. A great lump came into Henry Garnet's throat as he saw in fancy his son leap over the net to shake hands with the American champion whom he had just defeated, and walk off the court to the deafening plaudits of the multitude.

As an assiduous frequenter of Wimbledon, Henry Garnet had a good many friends in the tennis world, and one evening he found himself at a city dinner sitting next to one of them, a Colonel Brabazon, and in due course began talking to him of Nicky and what chance there might be of his being chosen to play for his university during the following season.

"Why don't you let him go down to Monte Carlo and play in the spring tournament there?" said the Colonel suddenly.

"Oh, I don't think he's good enough for that. He's not nineteen yet, he only went up to Cambridge last October; he wouldn't stand a chance against all those cracks."

"Of course, Austin and Von Cramm and so on would knock spots off him, but he might snatch a game or two; and if he got up against some of the smaller fry there's no reason why he shouldn't win two or three matches. He's never been up against any of the first-rate players, and it would be wonderful practice for him. He'd learn a lot more than he'll ever learn in the seaside tournaments you enter him for."

"I wouldn't dream of it. I'm not going to let him leave Cambridge in the middle of a term. I've always impressed upon him that tennis is only a game and it mustn't interfere with work."

Colonel Brabazon asked Garnet when the term ended.

"That's all right. He'd only have to cut about three days. Surely that could be arranged. You see, two of the men we were depending on have let us down, and we're in a hole. We want to send as good a team as we can. The Germans are sending their best players, and so are the Americans."

"Nothing doing, old boy. In the first place Nicky's not good enough, and secondly, I don't fancy the idea of sending a kid like that to Monte Carlo without anyone to look after him. If I could get away myself I might think of it, but that's out of the question."

"I shall be there. I'm going as the nonplaying captain of the English team. I'll keep an eye on him."

"You'll be busy, and besides, it's not a responsibility I'd like to ask you to take. He's never been abroad in his life, and to tell you the truth, I shouldn't have a moment's peace all the time he was there."

They left it at that, and presently Henry Garnet went home. He was so flattered by Colonel Brabazon's suggestion that he could not help telling his wife.

"Fancy his thinking Nicky's as good as that. He told me he'd seen him play and his style was fine. He only wants more practice to get into the first flight. We shall see the kid playing in the semifinals at Wimbledon yet, old girl."

To his surprise Mrs. Garnet was not so much opposed to the notion as he would have expected.

"After all the boy's eighteen. Nicky's never got into mischief yet, and there's no reason to suppose he will now."

"There's his work to be considered; don't forget that. I think it would be a very bad precedent to let him cut the end of term."

"But what can three days matter? It seems a shame to rob him of a chance like that. I'm sure he'd jump at it if you asked him."

"Well, I'm not going to. I haven't sent him to Cambridge just to play tennis. I know he's steady, but it's silly to put temptation in his way. He's much too young to go to Monte Carlo by himself."

"You say he won't have a chance against these crack players, but you can't tell."

Henry Garnet sighed a little. On the way home in the car it had struck him that Austin's health was uncertain and that Von Cramm had his off days. Supposing, just for the sake of argument, that Nicky had a bit of luck like that—then there would be no doubt that he would be chosen to play for Cambridge. But of course that was all nonsense.

"Nothing doing, my dear. I've made up my mind, and I'm not going to change it."

Mrs. Garnet held her peace. But next day she wrote to Nicky, telling him what had happened, and suggested to him what she would do in his place if, wanting to go, he wished to get his father's consent. A day or two later Henry Garnet received a letter from his son. He was bubbling over with excitement. He had seen his tutor, who was a tennis player himself, and the Provost of his college, who happened to know Colonel Brabazon, and no objection would be made to his leaving before the end of term; they both thought it an opportunity that shouldn't be missed. He didn't see what harm he could come to, and if only, just this once, his father would stretch a point, well, next term, he promised faithfully, he'd work like blazes. It was a very pretty letter. Mrs. Garnet watched her husband read it at the breakfast table; she was undisturbed by the frown on his face. He threw it over to her.

"I don't know why you thought it necessary to tell Nicky something I told you in confidence. It's too bad of you. Now you've thoroughly unsettled him."

"I'm so sorry. I thought it would please him to know that Colonel Brabazon had such a high opinion of him. I don't see why one should only tell people the disagreeable things that are said about them. Of course I made it quite clear that there could be no question of his going."

"You've put me in an odious position. If there's anything I hate it's for the boy to look upon me as a spoilsport and a tyrant."

"Oh, he'll never do that. He may think you rather silly and unreasonable, but I'm sure he'll understand that it's only for his own good that you're being so unkind."

"Christ," said Henry Garnet.

His wife had a great inclination to laugh. She knew the battle was won. Dear, oh dear, how easy it was to get men to do what you wanted. For appearance' sake Henry Garnet held out for forty-eight hours, but then he yielded, and a fortnight later Nicky came to London. He was to start for Monte Carlo next morning, and after dinner, when Mrs. Garnet and her elder daughter had left them, Henry took the opportunity to give his son some good advice.

"I don't feel quite comfortable about letting you go off to a place like Monte Carlo at your age practically by yourself," he finished, "but there it is, and I can only hope you'll be sensible. I don't want to play the heavy father, but there are three things especially that I want to warn you against: one is gambling, don't gamble; the second is money, don't lend anyone money;   5 and the third is women, don't have anything to do with women. If you don't do any of those three things you can't come to much harm, so remember them well."

"All right, Father," Nicky smiled.

"That's my last word to you. I know the world pretty well,   10 and believe me, my advice is sound."

"I won't forget it. I promise you."

"That's a good chap. Now let's go up and join the ladies."

Nicky beat neither Austin nor Von Cramm in the Monte Carlo tournament, but he did not disgrace himself. He snatched   15 an unexpected victory over a Spanish player and gave one of the Austrians a closer match than anyone had thought possible. In the mixed doubles he got into the semifinals. His charm conquered everyone, and he vastly enjoyed himself. It was generally allowed that he showed promise, and Colonel Brabazon   20 told him that when he was a little older and had had more practice with first-class players he would be a credit to his father. The tournament came to an end, and the day following he was to fly back to London. Anxious to play his best, he had lived very carefully, smoking little and drinking nothing, and   25 going to bed early; but on his last evening he thought he would like to see something of the life in Monte Carlo of which he had heard so much. An official dinner was given to the tennis players, and after dinner with the rest of them he went into the Sporting Club. It was the first time he had been there.   30 Monte Carlo was very full, and the rooms were crowded. Nicky had never before seen roulette played except in the pictures; in a maze he stopped at the first table he came to; chips of different sizes were scattered over the green cloth in what looked like a hopeless muddle; the croupier gave the wheel a sharp   35 turn and with a flick threw in the little white ball. After what seemed an endless time the ball stopped and another croupier with a broad, indifferent gesture raked in the chips of those who had lost.

Presently Nicky wandered over to where they were playing *trente et quarante,* but he couldn't understand what it was all about, and he thought it dull. He saw a crowd in another room and sauntered in. A big game of baccara was in progress, and he was immediately conscious of the tension. The players were protected from the thronging bystanders by a brass rail; they sat round the table, nine on each side, with the dealer in the middle and the croupier facing him. Big money was changing hands. The dealer was a member of the Greek Syndicate. Nicky looked at his impassive face. His eyes were watchful, but his expression never changed whether he won or lost. It was a terrifying, strangely impressive sight. It gave Nicky, who had been thriftily brought up, a peculiar thrill to see someone risk a thousand pounds on the turn of a card and when he lost make a little joke and laugh. It was all terribly exciting. An acquaintance came up to him.

"Been doing any good?" he asked.

"I haven't been playing."

"Wise of you. Rotten game. Come and have a drink."

"All right."

While they were having it Nicky told his friend that this was the first time he had ever been in the rooms.

"Oh, but you must have one little flutter before you go. It's idiotic to leave Monte without having tried your luck. After all it won't hurt you to lose a hundred francs or so."

"I don't suppose it will, but my father wasn't any too keen on my coming at all, and one of the three things he particularly advised me not to do was to gamble."

But when Nicky left his companion he strolled back to one of the tables where they were playing roulette. He stood for a while looking at the losers' money being raked in by the croupier and the money that was won paid out to the winners. It was impossible to deny that it was thrilling. His friend was right, it did seem silly to leave Monte without putting something on the table just once. It would be an experience, and at

his age you have to have all the experience you could get. He
reflected that he hadn't promised his father not to gamble, he'd
promised him not to forget his advice. It wasn't quite the same,
was it? He took a hundred-franc note out of his pocket and
rather shyly put it on number eighteen. He chose it because   5
that was his age. With a wildly beating heart he watched the
wheel turn; the little white ball whizzed about like a small demon of mischief; the wheel went round more slowly, the little
white ball hesitated, it seemed about to stop, it went on again;
Nicky could hardly believe his eyes when it fell into number   10
eighteen. A lot of chips were passed over to him, and his hands
trembled as he took them. It seemed to amount to a lot of
money. He was so confused that he never thought of putting
anything on the following round; in fact he had no intention of
playing any more, once was enough; and he was surprised   15
when eighteen again came up. There was only one chip on it.
   "By George, you've won again," said a man who was standing near to him.
   "Me? I hadn't got anything on."
   "Yes, you had. Your original stake. They always leave it on 20
unless you ask for it back. Didn't you know?"
   Another packet of chips was handed over to him. Nicky's
head reeled. He counted his gains: seven thousand francs. A
queer sense of power seized him; he felt wonderfully clever.
This was the easiest way of making money that he had ever   25
heard of. His frank, charming face was wreathed in smiles. His
bright eyes met those of a woman standing by his side. She
smiled.
   "You're in luck," she said.
   She spoke English, but with a foreign accent.   30
   "I can hardly believe it. It's the first time I've ever played."
   "That explains it. Lend me a thousand francs, will you? I've
lost everything I've got. I'll give it you back in half an hour."
   "All right."
   She took a large red chip from his pile and with a word of   35
thanks disappeared. The man who had spoken to him before
grunted.

"You'll never see that again."

Nicky was dashed. His father had particularly advised him not to lend anyone money. What a silly thing to do! And to somebody he'd never seen in his life. But the fact was, he felt at that moment such a love for the human race that it had never occurred to him to refuse. And that big red chip, it was almost impossible to realize that it had any value. Oh, well, it didn't matter, he still had six thousand francs, he'd just try his luck once or twice more, and if he didn't win he'd go home. He put a chip on sixteen, which was his elder sister's age, but it didn't come up; then on twelve, which was his younger sister's, and that didn't come up either; he tried various numbers at random, but without success. It was funny, he seemed to have lost his knack. He thought he would try just once more and then stop; he won. He had made up all his losses and had something over. At the end of an hour, after various ups and downs, having experienced such thrills as he had never known in his life, he found himself with so many chips that they would hardly go in his pockets. He decided to go. He went to the changers' office, and he gasped when twenty thousand-franc notes were spread out before him. He had never had so much money in his life. He put it in his pocket and was turning away when the woman to whom he had lent the thousand francs came up to him.

"I've been looking for you everywhere," she said. "I was afraid you'd gone. I was in a fever, I didn't know what you'd think of me. Here's your thousand francs and thank you so much for the loan."

Nicky, blushing scarlet, stared at her with amazement. How he had misjudged her! His father had said, don't gamble; well, he had, and he'd made twenty thousand francs; and his father had said, don't lend anyone money; well, he had, he'd lent quite a lot to a total stranger, and she'd returned it. The fact was that he wasn't nearly such a fool as his father thought: he'd had an instinct that he could lend her the money with safety, and you see, his instinct was right. But he was so obviously taken aback that the little lady was forced to laugh.

"What is the matter with you?" she asked.

"To tell you the truth I never expected to see the money back."

"What did you take me for? Did you think I was a—cocotte?"

Nicky reddened to the roots of his wavy hair.

"No, of course not."

"Do I look like one?"

"Not a bit."

She was dressed very quietly, in black, with a string of gold beads round her neck; her simple frock showed off a neat, slight figure; she had a pretty little face and a trim head. She was made up, but not excessively, and Nicky supposed that she was not more than three or four years older than himself. She gave him a friendly smile.

"My husband is in the administration in Morocco, and I've come to Monte Carlo for a few weeks because he thought I wanted a change."

"I was just going," said Nicky because he couldn't think of anything else to say.

"Already!"

"Well, I've got to get up early tomorrow. I'm going back to London by air."

"Of course. The tournament ended today, didn't it? I saw you play, you know, two or three times."

"Did you? I don't know why you should have noticed me."

"You've got a beautiful style. And you looked very sweet in your shorts."

Nicky was not an immodest youth, but it did cross his mind that perhaps she had borrowed that thousand francs in order to scrape acquaintance with him.

"Do you ever go to the Knickerbocker?" she asked.

"No. I never have."

"Oh, but you mustn't leave Monte without having been there. Why don't you come and dance a little? To tell you the truth, I'm starving with hunger, and I should adore some bacon and eggs."

Nicky remembered his father's advice not to have anything

to do with women, but this was different; you had only to look
at the pretty little thing to know at once that she was perfectly
respectable. Her husband was in what corresponded, he supposed, to the civil service. His father and mother had friends
who were civil servants, and they and their wives sometimes
came to dinner. It was true that the wives were neither so
young nor so pretty as this one, but she was just as ladylike as
they were. And after winning twenty thousand francs he
thought it wouldn't be a bad idea to have a little fun.

"I'd love to go with you," he said. "But you won't mind if I
don't stay very long. I've left instructions at my hotel that I'm
to be called at seven."

"We'll leave as soon as ever you like."

Nicky found it very pleasant at the Knickerbocker. He ate
his bacon and eggs with appetite. They shared a bottle of
champagne. They danced, and the little lady told him he
danced beautifully. He knew he danced pretty well, and of
course she was easy to dance with. As light as a feather. She
laid her cheek against his and when their eyes met there was
in hers a smile that made his heart go pit-a-pat. A coloured
woman sang in a throaty, sensual voice. The floor was crowded.

"Have you ever been told that you're very good-looking?"
she asked.

"I don't think so," he laughed. "Gosh," he thought, "I believe
she's fallen for me."

Nicky was not such a fool as to be unaware that women often
liked him, and when she made that remark he pressed her to
him a little more closely. She closed her eyes, and a faint sigh
escaped her lips.

"I suppose it wouldn't be quite nice if I kissed you before
all these people," he said.

"What do you think they would take me for?"

It began to grow late, and Nicky said that really he thought
he ought to be going.

"I shall go too," she said. "Will you drop me at my hotel on
your way?"

Nicky paid the bill. He was rather surprised at its amount,

but with all that money he had in his pocket he could afford not to care, and they got into a taxi. She snuggled up to him, and he kissed her. She seemed to like it.

"By Jove," he thought, "I wonder if there's anything doing."

It was true that she was a married woman, but her husband was in Morocco, and it certainly did look as if she'd fallen for him. Good and proper. It was true also that his father had warned him to have nothing to do with women, but, he reflected again, he hadn't actually promised he wouldn't, he'd only promised not to forget his advice. Well, he hadn't; he was bearing it in mind that very minute. But circumstances alter cases. She was a sweet little thing; it seemed silly to miss the chance of an adventure when it was handed to you like that on a tray. When they reached the hotel he paid off the taxi.

"I'll walk home," he said. "The air will do me good after the stuffy atmosphere of that place."

"Come up a moment," she said. "I'd like to show you the photo of my little boy."

"Oh, have you got a little boy?" he exclaimed, a trifle dashed.

"Yes, a sweet little boy."

He walked upstairs after her. He didn't in the least want to see the photograph of her little boy, but he thought it only civil to pretend he did. He was afraid he'd made a fool of himself; it occurred to him that she was taking him up to look at the photograph in order to show him in a nice way that he'd made a mistake. He'd told her he was eighteen.

"I suppose she thinks I'm just a kid."

He began to wish he hadn't spent all that money on champagne at the night club.

But she didn't show him the photograph of her little boy after all. They had no sooner got into her room than she turned to him, flung her arms round his neck, and kissed him full on the lips. He had never in all his life been kissed so passionately.

"Darling," she said.

For a brief moment his father's advice once more crossed Nicky's mind, and then he forgot it.

Nicky was a light sleeper, and the least sound was apt to wake him. Two or three hours later he awoke and for a moment could not imagine where he was. The room was not quite dark, for the door of the bathroom was ajar, and the light in it had been left on. Suddenly he was conscious that someone was moving about the room. Then he remembered. He saw that it was his little friend, and he was on the point of speaking when something in the way she was behaving stopped him. She was walking very cautiously, as though she were afraid of waking him; she stopped once or twice and looked over at the bed. He wondered what she was after. He soon saw. She went over to the chair on which he had placed his clothes and once more looked in his direction. She waited for what seemed to him an interminable time. The silence was so intense that Nicky thought he could hear his own heart beating. Then, very slowly, very quietly, she took up his coat, slipped her hand into the inside pocket and drew out all those beautiful thousand-franc notes that Nicky had been so proud to win. She put the coat back and placed some other clothes on it so that it should look as though it had not been disturbed, then, with the bundle of notes in her hand, for an appreciable time stood once more stock-still. Nicky had repressed an instinctive impulse to jump up and grab her; it was partly surprise that had kept him quiet, partly the notion that he was in a strange hotel, in a foreign country, and if he made a row he didn't know what might happen. She looked at him. His eyes were partly closed, and he was sure that she thought he was asleep. In the silence she could hardly fail to hear his regular breathing. When she had reassured herself that her movements had not disturbed him, she stepped, with infinite caution, across the room. On a small table in the window a cineraria was growing in a pot. Nicky watched her now with his eyes wide open. The plant was evidently placed quite loosely in the pot, for, taking it by the stalks, she lifted it out; she put the bank notes in the bottom of the pot and replaced the plant. It was an excellent hiding place. No one could have guessed that anything was concealed under that richly flowering plant. She pressed the earth down with her fingers and then, very slowly, taking care not to make the smallest noise, crept across the room and slipped back into bed.

"Chéri," she said, in a caressing voice.

Nicky breathed steadily, like a man immersed in deep sleep. The little lady turned over on her side and disposed herself to 5 slumber. But though Nicky lay so still, his thoughts worked busily. He was extremely indignant at the scene he had just witnessed, and to himself he spoke his thoughts with vigour.

"She's nothing but a damned tart. She and her dear little boy and her husband in Morocco. My eye! She's a rotten thief, 10 that's what she is. Took me for a mug. If she thinks she's going to get away with anything like that, she's mistaken."

He had already made up his mind what he was going to do with the money he had so cleverly won. He had long wanted a car of his own and had thought it rather mean of his father not 15 to have given him one. After all, a feller doesn't always want to drive about in the family bus. Well, he'd just teach the old man a lesson and buy one himself. For twenty thousand francs, two hundred pounds roughly, he could get a very decent second-hand car. He meant to get the money back, but just then 20 he didn't quite know how. He didn't like the idea of kicking up a row, he was a stranger, in a hotel he knew nothing of; it might very well be that the beastly woman had friends there; he didn't mind facing anyone in a fair fight, but he'd look pretty foolish if someone pulled a gun on him. He reflected besides, 25 very sensibly, that he had no proof the money was his. If it came to a showdown and she swore it was hers, he might very easily find himself hauled off to a police station. He really didn't know what to do. Presently by her regular breathing he knew that the little lady was asleep. She must have fallen 30 asleep with an easy mind, for she had done her job without a hitch. It infuriated Nicky that she should rest so peacefully while he lay awake, worried to death. Suddenly an idea occurred to him. It was such a good one that it was only by the exercise of all his self-control that he prevented himself from 35 jumping out of bed and carrying it out at once. Two could play at her game. She'd stolen his money; well, he'd steal it back

again, and they'd be all square. He made up his mind to wait
quite quietly until he was sure that deceitful woman was sound
asleep. He waited for what seemed to him a very long time.
She did not stir. Her breathing was as regular as a child's.

"Darling," he said at last.   5

No answer. No movement. She was dead to the world. Very
slowly, pausing after every movement, very silently, he slipped
out of bed. He stood still for a while, looking at her to see
whether he had disturbed her. Her breathing was as regular
as before. During the time he was waiting he had taken note   10
carefully of the furniture in the room so that in crossing it he
should not knock against a chair or a table and make a noise.
He took a couple of steps and waited; he took a couple of steps
more; he was very light on his feet and made no sound as he
walked; he took fully five minutes to get to the window, and   15
here he waited again. He started, for the bed slightly creaked,
but it was only because the sleeper turned in her sleep. He
forced himself to wait till he had counted one hundred. She
was sleeping like a log. With infinite care he seized the cineraria by the stalks and gently pulled it out of the pot; he put   20
his other hand in, his heart beat nineteen to the dozen as his
fingers touched the notes, his hand closed on them and he
slowly drew them out. He replaced the plant and in his turn
carefully pressed down the earth. While he was doing all this
he had kept one eye on the form lying in the bed. It remained   25
still. After another pause he crept softly to the chair on which
his clothes were lying. He first put the bundle of notes in his
coat pocket and then proceeded to dress. It took him a good
quarter of an hour, because he could afford to make no sound.
He had been wearing a soft shirt with his dinner jacket, and   30
he congratulated himself on this because it was easier to put
on silently than a stiff one. He had some difficulty in tying his
tie without a looking glass, but he very wisely reflected that it
didn't really matter if it wasn't tied very well. His spirits were
rising. The whole thing now began to seem rather a lark. At   35
length he was completely dressed except for his shoes, which
he took in his hand; he thought he would put them on when he

got into the passage. Now he had to cross the room to get to
the door. He reached it so quietly that he could not have disturbed the lightest sleeper. But the door had to be unlocked.
He turned the key very slowly; it creaked.

"Who's that?"   5

The little woman suddenly sat up in bed. Nicky's heart
jumped to his mouth. He made a great effort to keep his head.

"It's only me. It's six o'clock and I've got to go. I was trying
not to wake you."

"Oh, I forgot."   10

She sank back onto the pillow.

"Now that you're awake I'll put on my shoes."

He sat down on the edge of the bed and did this.

"Don't make a noise when you go out. The hotel people
don't like it. Oh, I'm so sleepy."   15

"You go right off to sleep again."

"Kiss me before you go." He bent down and kissed her.
"You're a sweet boy and a wonderful lover. *Bon voyage.*"

Nicky did not feel quite safe till he got out of the hotel. The
dawn had broken. The sky was unclouded, and in the harbour   20
the yachts and the fishing boats lay motionless on the still water. On the quay fishermen were getting ready to start on their
day's work. The streets were deserted. Nicky took a long
breath of the sweet morning air. He felt alert and well. He
also felt as pleased as Punch. With a swinging stride, his   25
shoulders well thrown back, he walked up the hill and along
the gardens in front of the Casino—the flowers in that clear
light had a dewy brilliance that was delicious—till he came to
his hotel. Here the day had already begun. In the hall porters
with mufflers round their necks and berets on their heads were 30
busy sweeping. Nicky went up to his room and had a hot bath.
He lay in it and thought with satisfaction that he was not such
a mug as some people might think. After his bath he did his
exercises, dressed, packed and went down to breakfast. He
had a grand appetite. No continental breakfast for him! He   35
had grapefruit, porridge, bacon and eggs, rolls fresh from the
oven, so crisp and delicious they melted in your mouth, mar-

malade and three cups of coffee. Though feeling perfectly well
before, he felt better after that. He lit the pipe he had recently
learnt to smoke, paid his bill and stepped into the car that was
waiting to take him to the aerodrome on the other side of
Cannes. The road as far as Nice ran over the hills, and below
him was the blue sea and the coast line. He couldn't help thinking it damned pretty. They passed through Nice, so gay and
friendly in the early morning, and presently they came to a
long stretch of straight road that ran by the sea. Nicky had paid
his bill, not with the money he had won the night before, but
with the money his father had given him; he had changed a
thousand francs to pay for supper at the Knickerbocker, but
that deceitful little woman had returned him the thousand
francs he had lent her, so that he still had twenty thousand-
franc notes in his pocket. He thought he would like to have a
look at them. He had so nearly lost them that they had a dou-
ble value for him. He took them out of his hip pocket into
which for safety's sake he had stuffed them when he put on
the suit he was travelling in, and counted them one by one.
Something very strange had happened to them. Instead of
there being twenty notes, as there should have been, there
were twenty-six. He couldn't understand it at all. He counted
them twice more. There was no doubt about it; somehow or
other he had twenty-six thousand francs instead of the twenty
he should have had. He couldn't make it out. He asked himself if it was possible that he had won more at the Sporting
Club than he had realized. But no, that was out of the question; he distinctly remembered the man at the desk laying the
notes out in four rows of five, and he had counted them himself. Suddenly the explanation occurred to him; when he had
put his hand into the flower pot, after taking out the cineraria,
he had grabbed everything he felt there. The flower pot was
the little hussy's money box, and he had taken out not only his
own money, but her savings as well. Nicky leant back in the
car and burst into a roar of laughter. It was the funniest thing
he had ever heard in his life. And when he thought of her going to the flower pot sometime later in the morning when she

awoke, expecting to find the money she had so cleverly got away with, and finding, not only that it wasn't there, but that her own had gone too, he laughed more than ever. And so far as he was concerned there was nothing to do about it, he knew neither her name nor the name of the hotel to which she had taken him. He couldn't return her money even if he wanted to.

"It serves her damned well right," he said.

This then was the story that Henry Garnet told his friends over the bridge table, for the night before. after dinner when his wife and daughter had left them to their port, Nicky had narrated it in full.

"And you know what infuriated me is that he's so damned pleased with himself. Talk of a cat swallowing a canary. And d'you know what he said to me when he'd finished? He looked at me with those innocent eyes of his and said: 'You know, Father, I can't help thinking there was something wrong about the advice you gave me. You said, don't gamble; well, I did, and I made a packet; you said, don't lend money; well, I did, and I got it back; and you said, don't have anything to do with women; well, I did, and I made six thousand francs on the deal.' "

It didn't make it any better for Henry Garnet that his three companions burst out laughing.

"It's all very well for you fellows to laugh, but you know, I'm in a damned awkward position. The boy looked up to me, he respected me, he took whatever I said as gospel truth, and now, I saw it in his eyes, he just looks upon me as a drivelling old fool. It's no good my saying one swallow doesn't make a summer; he doesn't see that it was just a fluke, he thinks the whole thing was due to his own cleverness. It may ruin him."

"You do look a bit of a damned fool, old man," said one of the others. "There's no denying that, is there?"

"I know I do, and I don't like it. It's so dashed unfair. Fate has no right to play one tricks like that. After all, you must admit that my advice was good."

"Very good."

"And the wretched boy ought to have burnt his fingers. Well, he hasn't. You're all men of the world, you tell me how I'm to deal with the situation now."

But they none of them could.

"Well, Henry, if I were you I wouldn't worry," said the law- 5
yer. "My belief is that your boy's born lucky, and in the long run that's better than to be born clever or rich."

Vocabulary

1. Do not confuse the word "describe" with "ascribe" (p. 125, l. 6).

2. What is Mr. Garnet's reaction when his bridge partners try to discover the cause of his "vexation" (p. 125, l. 24)?

3. Is Mr. Garnet angry when he is "disconcerted" (p. 126, l. 34)?

4. Mr. Garnet paid for professional tennis lessons for Nicky when he "discerned" the promise of a tennis player in the boy. What had he found?

5. Does the word "precedent," used in the sentence, "I think it would be a very bad precedent to let him cut the end of the term," mean "practice" (p. 130, ll. 16-18)?

6. In what position is Mr. Garnet placed when his wife puts him in an "odious position" (p. 131, l. 22)?

7. The author sometimes makes a statement and then in following paragraphs explains what he means. Does he do so (p. 133, l. 12) when describing the dealer's face as "impassive"?

8. How long is "an interminable time" (p. 139, ll. 13-14)?

Questions and Suggestions for Reading

PLOT

1. Maugham deliberately creates an incident which makes a father's wise advice look poor. First Mr. Garnet objects to Nicky's going to Monte Carlo because his son is too inexperienced in

tennis. Then he objects because he doesn't believe Nicky will be able to deal with situations the boy is likely to find there. However, Mr. Garnet tricks himself. After agreeing to allow Nicky to go to the Riveria, Mr. Garnet gives his advice and makes the boy promise to remember it—but he does not make his son promise not to do any of the things he warns him against. The rest of the story simply shows what happens when Nicky remembers but doesn't take his father's advice. Notice the stages through which Nicky passes.

2. Maugham frames this story with a bridge game. We see the players at the beginning, are aware of them throughout the whole course of Mr. Garnet's narrative, and return to them at the end. But in addition to this structural device, Mr. Garnet's story of Nicky is broken into two parts. What does the break signify?

POINT OF VIEW

1. In a number of Maugham's stories he allows someone to tell his story for him. In this case he puts four men around a bridge table and has one of them tell the story to the others. What person is used? First? Second? Third? A combination? Remember that Mr. Garnet does not start telling his story until page 127.

H. G. Wells

THE MAN WHO COULD WORK MIRACLES
A Pantoum in Prose

It is doubtful whether the gift was innate. For
my own part, I think it came to him suddenly. Indeed, until he
was thirty he was a sceptic, and did not believe in miraculous
powers. And here, since it is the most convenient place, I must
mention that he was a little man, and had eyes of a hot brown, 5
very erect red hair, a moustache with ends that he twisted up,
and freckles. His name was George McWhirter Fotheringay—
not the sort of name by any means to lead to any expectation
of miracles—and he was a clerk at Gomshott's. He was greatly
addicted to assertive argument. It was while he was asserting 10
the impossibility of miracles that he had his first intimation of
his extraordinary powers. This particular argument was being
held in the bar of the Long Dragon, and Toddy Beamish was
conducting the opposition by a monotonous but effective "So
you say," that drove Mr. Fotheringay to the very limit of his 15
patience.

There were present, besides these two, a very dusty cyclist,
landlord Cox, and Miss Maybridge, the perfectly respectable
and rather portly barmaid of the Dragon. Miss Maybridge was
standing with her back to Mr. Fotheringay, washing glasses; 20
the others were watching him, more or less amused by the
present ineffectiveness of the assertive method. Goaded by the
Torres Vedras tactics of Mr. Beamish, Mr. Fotheringay determined to make an unusual rhetorical effort. "Looky here, Mr.

Beamish," said Mr. Fotheringay. "Let us clearly understand what a miracle is. It's something contrariwise to the course of nature done by power of Will, something what couldn't happen without being specially willed."

"So *you* say," said Mr. Beamish, repulsing him.   5

Mr. Fotheringay appealed to the cyclist, who had hitherto been a silent auditor, and received his assent—given with a hesitating cough and a glance at Mr. Beamish. The landlord would express no opinion, and Mr. Fotheringay, returning to Mr. Beamish, received the unexpected concession of a quali-   10
fied assent to his definition of a miracle.

"For instance," said Mr. Fotheringay, greatly encouraged. "Here would be a miracle. That lamp, in the natural course of nature, couldn't burn like that upsy-down, could it, Beamish?"

"*You* say it couldn't," said Beamish.   15

"And you?" said Fotheringay. "You don't mean to say—eh?"

"No," said Beamish reluctantly. "No, it couldn't."

"Very well," said Mr. Fotheringay. "Then here comes someone, as it might be me, along here, and stands as it might be here, and says to that lamp, as I might do, collecting all my   20
will—'Turn upsy-down without breaking, and go on burning steady,' and——Hullo!"

It was enough to make anyone say "Hullo!" The impossible, the incredible, was visible to them all. The lamp hung inverted in the air, burning quietly with its flame pointing down. It was   25
as solid, as indisputable as ever a lamp was, the prosaic common lamp of the Long Dragon bar.

Mr. Fotheringay stood with an extended forefinger and the knitted brows of one anticipating a catastrophic smash. The cyclist, who was sitting next the lamp, ducked and jumped   30
across the bar. Everybody jumped, more or less. Miss Maybridge turned and screamed. For nearly three seconds the lamp remained still. A faint cry of mental distress came from Mr. Fotheringay. "I can't keep it up," he said, "any longer." He staggered back, and the inverted lamp suddenly flared, fell   35
against the corner of the bar, bounced aside, smashed upon the floor, and went out.

It was lucky it had a metal receiver, or the whole place would have been in a blaze. Mr. Cox was the first to speak, and his remark, shorn of needless excrescences, was to the effect that Fotheringay was a fool. Fotheringay was beyond disputing even so fundamental a proposition as that! He was astonished beyond measure at the thing that had occurred. The subsequent conversation threw absolutely no light on the matter so far as Fotheringay was concerned; the general opinion not only followed Mr. Cox very closely but very vehemently. Everyone accused Fotheringay of a silly trick, and presented him to himself as a foolish destroyer of comfort and security. His mind was a tornado of perplexity, he was himself inclined to agree with them, and he made a remarkably ineffectual opposition to the proposal of his departure.

He went home flushed and heated, coat-collar crumpled, eyes smarting, and ears red. He watched each of the ten street lamps nervously as he passed it. It was only when he found himself alone in his little bedroom in Church Row that he was able to grapple seriously with his memories of the occurrence, and ask, "What on earth happened?"

He had removed his coat and boots, and was sitting on the bed with his hands in his pockets repeating the text of his defence for the seventeenth time, "I didn't want the confounded thing to upset," when it occurred to him that at the precise moment he had said the commanding words he had inadvertently willed the thing he said, and that when he had seen the lamp in the air he had felt that it depended on him to maintain it there without being clear how this was to be done. He had not a particularly complex mind, or he might have stuck for a time at that "inadvertently willed," embracing, as it does, the abstrusest problems of voluntary action; but as it was, the idea came to him with a quite acceptable haziness. And from that, following, as I must admit, no clear logical path, he came to the test of experiment.

He pointed resolutely to his candle and collected his mind, though he felt he did a foolish thing. "Be raised up," he said. But in a second that feeling vanished. The candle was raised,

hung in the air one giddy moment, and as Mr. Fotheringay
gasped, fell with a smash on his toilet-table, leaving him in
darkness save for the expiring glow of its wick.

For a time Mr. Fotheringay sat in the darkness, perfectly
still. "It did happen, after all," he said. "And 'ow I'm to explain
it I *don't* know." He sighed heavily, and began feeling in his
pockets for a match. He could find none, and he rose and
groped about the toilet-table. "I wish I had a match," he said.
He resorted to his coat, and there were none there, and then
it dawned upon him that miracles were possible even with
matches. He extended a hand and scowled at it in the dark.
"Let there be a match in that hand," he said. He felt some light
object fall across his palm, and his fingers closed upon a match.

After several ineffectual attempts to light this, he discovered
it was a safety-match. He threw it down, and then it occurred
to him that he might have willed it lit. He did, and perceived
it burning in the midst of his toilet-table mat. He caught it up
hastily, and it went out. His perception of possibilities en-
larged, and he felt for and replaced the candle in its candlestick. "Here! *you* be lit," said Mr. Fotheringay, and forthwith
the candle was flaring, and he saw a little black hole in the
toilet-cover, with a wisp of smoke rising from it. For a time he
stared from this to the little flame and back, and then looked
up and met his own gaze in the looking-glass. By this help he
communed with himself in silence for a time.

"How about miracles now?" said Mr. Fotheringay at last,
addressing his reflection.

The subsequent meditations of Mr. Fotheringay were of a
severe but confused description. So far as he could see, it was
a case of pure willing with him. The nature of his first experiences disinclined him for any further experiments except of
the most cautious type. But he lifted a sheet of paper, and
turned a glass of water pink and then green, and he created a
snail, which he miraculously annihilated, and got himself a
miraculous new toothbrush. Somewhere in the small hours he
had reached the fact that his will-power must be of a particularly rare and pungent quality, a fact of which he had certainly

had inklings before, but no certain assurance. The scare and perplexity of his first discovery were now qualified by pride in this evidence of singularity and by vague intimations of advantage. He became aware that the church clock was striking one, and as it did not occur to him that his daily duties at Gomshott's might be miraculously dispensed with, he resumed undressing, in order to get to bed without further delay. As he struggled to get his shirt over his head he was struck with a brilliant idea. "Let me be in bed," he said, and found himself so. "Undressed," he stipulated; and, finding the sheets cold, added hastily, "and in my nightshirt—no, in a nice soft woollen nightshirt. Ah!" he said with immense enjoyment. "And now let me be comfortably asleep . . ."

He awoke at his usual hour and was pensive all through breakfast-time, wondering whether his overnight experience might not be a particularly vivid dream. At length his mind turned again to cautious experiments. For instance, he had three eggs for breakfast; two his landlady had supplied, good, but shoppy, and one was a delicious fresh goose-egg, laid, cooked, and served by his extraordinary will. He hurried off to Gomshott's in a state of profound but carefully concealed excitement, and only remembered the shell of the third egg when his landlady spoke of it that night. All day he could do no work because of this astonishing new self-knowledge, but this caused him no inconvenience, because he made up for it miraculously in his last ten minutes.

As the day wore on his state of mind passed from wonder to elation, albeit the circumstances of his dismissal from the Long Dragon were still disagreeable to recall, and a garbled account of the matter that had reached his colleagues led to some badinage. It was evident he must be careful how he lifted frangible articles, but in other ways his gift promised more and more as he turned it over in his mind. He intended among other things to increase his personal property by unostentatious acts of creation. He called into existence a pair of very splendid diamond studs, and hastily annihilated them again as young Gomshott came across the counting-house to his desk.

He was afraid young Gomshott might wonder how he came by them. He saw quite clearly the gift required caution and watchfulness in its exercise, but so far as he could judge the difficulties attending its mastery would be no greater than those he had already faced in the study of cycling. It was that analogy, perhaps, quite as much as the feeling that he would be unwelcome in the Long Dragon, that drove him out after supper into the lane beyond the gas-works, to rehearse a few miracles in private.

There was possibly a certain want of originality in his attempts, for apart from his will-power Mr. Fotheringay was not a very exceptional man. The miracle of Moses' rod came to his mind, but the night was dark and unfavourable to the proper control of large miraculous snakes. Then he recollected the story of "Tannhäuser" that he had read on the back of the Philharmonic programme. That seemed to him singularly attractive and harmless. He stuck his walking-stick—a very nice Poona-Penang lawyer—into the turf that edged the footpath, and commanded the dry wood to blossom. The air was immediately full of the scent of roses, and by means of a match he saw for himself that this beautiful miracle was indeed accomplished. His satisfaction was ended by advancing footsteps. Afraid of a premature discovery of his powers, he addressed the blossoming stick hastily: "Go back." What he meant was "Change back"; but of course he was confused. The stick receded at a considerable velocity, and incontinently came a cry of anger and a bad word from the approaching person. "Who are you throwing brambles at, you fool?" cried a voice. "That got me on the shin."

"I'm sorry, old chap," said Mr. Fotheringay, and then, realising the awkward nature of the explanation, caught nervously at his moustache. He saw Winch, one of the three Immering constables, advancing.

"What d'yer mean by it?" asked the constable. "Hullo! It's you, is it? The gent that broke the lamp at the Long Dragon!"

"I don't mean anything by it," said Mr. Fotheringay. "Nothing at all."

"What d'yer do it for then?"

"Oh bother!" said Mr. Fotheringay.

"Bother, indeed? D'yer know that stick hurt? What d'yer do it for, eh?"

For the moment Mr. Fotheringay could not think what he had done it for. His silence seemed to irritate Mr. Winch. "You've been assaulting the police, young man, this time. That's what *you* done!"

"Look here, Mr. Winch," said Mr. Fotheringay, annoyed and confused, "I'm very sorry. The fact is——"

"Well!"

He could think of no way but the truth. "I was working a miracle." He tried to speak in an off-hand way, but try as he would he couldn't.

"Working a ——! 'Ere, don't you talk rot. Working a miracle, indeed! Miracle! Well, that's downright funny! Why, you's the chap that don't believe in miracles. . . . Fact is, this is another of your silly conjuring tricks—that's what this is. Now, I tell you——"

But Mr. Fotheringay never heard what Mr. Winch was going to tell him. He realised he had given himself away, flung his valuable secret to all the winds of heaven. A violent gust of irritation swept him to action. He turned on the constable swiftly and fiercely. "Here," he said, "I've had enough of this, I have! I'll show you a silly conjuring trick, I will. Go to Hades! Go, now!"

He was alone!

Mr. Fotheringay performed no more miracles that night nor did he trouble to see what had become of his flowering stick. He returned to the town, scared and very quiet, and went to his bedroom. "Lord!" he said, "it's a powerful gift—an extremely powerful gift! I didn't hardly mean as much as that. Not really. . . . I wonder what Hades is like!"

He sat on the bed taking off his boots. Struck by a happy thought he transferred the constable to San Francisco, and without any more interference with normal causation went soberly to bed. In the night he dreamt of the anger of Winch.

The next day Mr. Fotheringay heard two interesting items of news. Someone had planted a most beautiful climbing rose against the elder Mr. Gomshott's private house in the Lulla-borough Road, and the river as far as Rawling's Mill was to be dragged for Constable Winch.

Mr. Fotheringay was abstracted and thoughtful all that day, and performed no miracles except certain provisions for Winch,   5
and the miracle of completing his day's work with punctual perfection in spite of all the bee-swarm of thoughts that hummed through his mind. And the extraordinary abstraction and meekness of his manner was remarked by several people, and made a matter for jesting. For the most part he was think-   10
ing of Winch.

On Sunday evening he went to chapel, and oddly enough, Mr. Maydig, who took a certain interest in occult matters, preached about "things that are not lawful." Mr. Fotheringay was not a regular chapel goer, but the system of assertive scep-   15
ticism, to which I have already alluded, was now very much shaken. The tenor of the sermon threw an entirely new light on these novel gifts, and he suddenly decided to consult Mr. Maydig immediately after the service. So soon as that was de-termined, he found himself wondering why he had not done   20
so before.

Mr. Maydig, a lean, excitable man with quite remarkably long wrists and neck, was gratified at a request for a private conversation from a young man whose carelessness in religious matters was a subject for general remark in the town. After a   25
few necessary delays, he conducted him to the study of the Manse, which was contiguous to the chapel, seated him com-fortably, and, standing in front of a cheerful fire—his legs threw a Rhodian arch of shadow on the opposite wall—requested Mr. Fotheringay to state his business.   30

At first Mr. Fotheringay was a little abashed, and found some difficulty in opening the matter. "You will scarcely be-lieve me, Mr. Maydig, I am afraid"—and so forth for some time. He tried a question at last, and asked Mr. Maydig his opinion of miracles.   35

Mr. Maydig was still saying "Well" in an extremely judicial tone, when Mr. Fotheringay interrupted again: "You don't be-lieve, I suppose, that some common sort of person—like myself, for instance—as it might be sitting here now, might have some sort of twist inside him that made him able to do things by his will."

"It's possible," said Mr. Maydig. "Something of the sort, perhaps, is possible."

"If I might make free with something here, I think I might show you a sort of experiment," said Mr. Fotheringay. "Now, take that tobacco-jar on the table, for instance. What I want to know is whether what I am going to do with it is a miracle or not. Just half a minute, Mr. Maydig, please."

He knitted his brows, pointed to the tobacco-jar and said: "Be a bowl of vi'lets."

The tobacco-jar did as it was ordered.

Mr. Maydig started violently at the change, and stood looking from the thaumaturgist to the bowl of flowers. He said nothing. Presently he ventured to lean over the table and smell the violets; they were fresh-picked and very fine ones. Then he stared at Mr. Fotheringay again.

"How did you do that?" he asked.

Mr. Fotheringay pulled his moustache. "Just told it—and there you are. Is that a miracle, or is it black art, or what is it? And what do you think's the matter with me? That's what I want to ask."

"It's a most extraordinary occurrence."

"And this day last week I knew no more that I could do things like that than you did. It came quite sudden. It's something odd about my will, I suppose, and that's as far as I can see."

"Is *that*—the only thing? Could you do other things besides that?"

"Lord, yes!" said Mr. Fotheringay. "Just anything." He thought, and suddenly recalled a conjuring entertainment he had seen. "Here!" He pointed. "Change into a bowl of fish—no, not that—change into a glass bowl full of water with goldfish swimming in it. That's better! You see that, Mr. Maydig?"

"It's astonishing. It's incredible. You are either a most extraordinary . . . But no——"

"I could change it into anything," said Mr. Fotheringay.

"Just anything. Here! be a pigeon, will you?"

In another moment a blue pigeon was fluttering round the room and making Mr. Maydig duck every time it came near him. "Stop there, will you," said Mr. Fotheringay; and the pigeon hung motionless in the air. "I could change it back to 5 a bowl of flowers," he said, and after replacing the pigeon on the table worked that miracle. "I expect you will want your pipe in a bit," he said, and restored the tobacco-jar.

Mr. Maydig had followed all these later changes in a sort of ejaculatory silence. He stared at Mr. Fotheringay and, in a 10 very gingerly manner, picked up the tobacco-jar, examined it, replaced it on the table, "*Well!*" was the only expression of his feelings.

"Now, after that it's easier to explain what I came about," said Mr. Fotheringay; and proceeded to a lengthy and involved 15 narrative of his strange experiences, beginning with the affair of the lamp in the Long Dragon and complicated by persistent allusions to Winch. As he went on, the transient pride Mr. Maydig's consternation had caused passed away; he became the very ordinary Mr. Fotheringay of everyday intercourse 20 again. Mr. Maydig listened intently, the tobacco-jar in his hand, and his bearing changed also with the course of the narrative. Presently, while Mr. Fotheringay was dealing with the miracle of the third egg, the minister interrupted with a fluttering extended hand— 25

"It is possible," he said. "It is credible. It is amazing, of course, but it reconciles a number of difficulties. The power to work miracles is a gift—a peculiar quality like genius or second sight—hitherto it has come very rarely and to exceptional people. But in this case . . . I have always wondered at the miracles 30 of Mahomet, and at Yogi's miracles, and the miracles of Madame Blavatsky. But, of course! Yes, it is simply a gift! It carries out so beautifully the arguments of that great thinker"—Mr. Maydig's voice sank—"his Grace the Duke of Argyll. Here we plumb some profounder law—deeper than the ordinary laws of 35 nature. Yes—yes. Go on. Go on!"

Mr. Fotheringay proceeded to tell of his misadventure with Winch, and Mr. Maydig, no longer overawed or scared, began to jerk his limbs about and interject astonishment. "It's this what troubled me most," proceeded Mr. Fotheringay; "it's this I'm most mightly in want of advice for; of course he's at San Francisco—wherever San Francisco may be—but of course it's awkward for both of us, as you'll see, Mr. Maydig. I don't see 5 how he can understand what has happened, and I dare say he's scared and exasperated something tremendous, and trying to get at me. I dare say he keeps on starting off to come here. I send him back, by a miracle every few hours, when I think of it. And of course, that's a thing he won't be able to 10 understand, and it's bound to annoy him; and, of course, if he takes a ticket every time it will cost him a lot of money. I done the best I could for him, but of course it's difficult for him to put himself in my place. I thought afterwards that his clothes might have got scorched, you know—if Hades is all it's sup- 15 posed to be—before I shifted him. In that case I suppose they'd have locked him up in San Francisco. Of course I willed him a new suit of clothes on him directly I thought of it. But, you see, I'm already in a deuce of a tangle——"

Mr. Maydig looked serious. "I see you are in a tangle. Yes, 20 it's a difficult position. How you are to end it . . ." He became diffuse and inconclusive.

"However, we'll leave Winch for a little and discuss the larger question. I don't think this is a case of the black art or anything of the sort. I don't think there is any taint of criminality about 25 it at all, Mr. Fotheringay—none whatever, unless you are suppressing material facts. No, it's miracles—pure miracles—miracles, if I may say so, of the very highest class."

He began to pace the hearthrug and gesticulate, while Mr. Fotheringay sat with his arm on the table and his head on his 30 arm, looking worried. "I don't see how I'm to manage about Winch," he said.

"A gift of working miracles—apparently a very powerful gift," said Mr. Maydig, "will find a way about Winch—never fear. My dear sir, you are a most important man—a man of the 35 most astonishing possibilities. As evidence, for example! And in other ways, the things you may do. . . ."

"Yes, I've thought of a thing or two," said Mr. Fotheringay.

"But—some of the things came a bit twisty. You saw that fish at first? Wrong sort of bowl and wrong sort of fish. And I thought I'd ask someone."

"A proper course," said Mr. Maydig, "a very proper course—altogether the proper course." He stopped and looked at Mr. 5 Fotheringay. "It's practically an unlimited gift. Let us test your powers, for instance. If they really *are* . . . If they really are all they seem to be."

And so, incredible as it may seem, in the study of the little house behind the Congregational Chapel, on the evening of 10 Sunday, Nov. 10, 1896, Mr. Fotheringay, egged on and inspired by Mr. Maydig, began to work miracles. The reader's attention is specially and definitely called to that date. He will object, probably has already objected, that certain points in this story are improbable, that if any things of the sort already described 15 had indeed occurred, they would have been in all the papers a year ago. The details immediately following he will find particularly hard to accept, because among other things they involve the conclusion that he or she, the reader in question, must have been killed in a violent and unprecedented manner 20 more than a year ago. Now a miracle is nothing if not improbable, and as a matter of fact the reader *was* killed in a violent and unprecedented manner a year ago. In the subsequent course of this story it will become perfectly clear and credible, as every right-minded and reasonable reader will admit. But 25 this is not the place for the end of the story, being but little beyond the hither side of the middle. And at first the miracles worked by Mr. Fotheringay were timid little miracles—little things with the cups and parlour fitments, as feeble as the miracles of Theosophists, and, feeble as they were, they were re- 30 ceived with awe by his collaborator. He would have preferred to settle the Winch business out of hand, but Mr. Maydig would not let him. But after they had worked a dozen of these domestic trivialities, their sense of power grew, their imagination began to show signs of stimulation, and their ambition en- 35 larged. Their first larger enterprise was due to hunger and the negligence of Mrs. Minchin, Mr. Maydig's housekeeper. The meal to which the minister conducted Mr. Fotheringay was

certainly ill-laid and uninviting as refreshment for two indus-
trious miracle-workers; but they were seated, and Mr. Maydig
was descanting in sorrow rather than in anger upon his housekeeper's shortcomings, before it occurred to Mr. Fotheringay
that an opportunity lay before him. "Don't you think, Mr. Maydig," he said, "if it isn't a liberty, I——"

"My dear Mr. Fotheringay! Of course! No—I didn't think."

Mr. Fotheringay waved his hand. "What shall we have?" he
said, in a large, inclusive spirit, and, at Mr. Maydig's order, re-
vised the supper very thoroughly. "As for me," he said, eyeing
Mr. Maydig's selection, "I am always particularly fond of a
tankard of stout and a nice Welsh rarebit, and I'll order that. I
ain't much given to Burgundy," and forthwith stout and Welsh
rarebit promptly appeared at his command. They sat long at
their supper, talking like equals, as Mr. Fotheringay presently
perceived with a glow of surprise and gratification, of all the
miracles they would presently do. "And, by the bye, Mr. Maydig," said Mr. Fotheringay, "I might perhaps be able to help
you—in a domestic way."

"Don't quite follow," said Mr. Maydig, pouring out a glass
of miraculous old Burgundy.

Mr. Fotheringay helped himself to a second Welsh rarebit
out of vacancy, and took a mouthful. "I was thinking," he said,
"I might be able (*chum, chum*) to work (*chum, chum*) a miracle with Mrs. Minchin (*chum, chum*)—make her a better
woman."

Mr. Maydig put down the glass and looked doubtful.
"She's——She strongly objects to interference, you know, Mr.
Fotheringay. And—as a matter of fact—it's well past eleven
and she's probably in bed and asleep. Do you think, on the
whole——"

Mr. Fotheringay considered these objections. "I don't see
that it shouldn't be done in her sleep."

For a time Mr. Maydig opposed the idea, and then he
yielded. Mr. Fotheringay issued his orders, and a little less at
their ease, perhaps, the two gentlemen proceeded with their
repast. Mr. Maydig was enlarging on the changes he might
expect in his housekeeper next day, with an optimism that

seemed even to Mr. Fotheringay's super senses a little forced
and hectic, when a series of confused noises from upstairs began. Their eyes exchanged interrogations, and Mr. Maydig left
the room hastily. Mr. Fotheringay heard him calling up to his
housekeeper and then his footsteps going softly up to her.   5

In a minute or so the minister returned, his step light, his
face radiant. "Wonderful!" he said, "and touching! Most touching!"

He began pacing the hearthrug. "A repentance—a most
touching repentance—through the crack of the door. Poor   10
woman! A most wonderful change! She had got up. She must
have got up at once. She had got up out of her sleep to smash
a private bottle of brandy in her box. And to confess it, too!
. . . But this gives us—it opens—a most amazing vista of possibilities. If we can work this miraculous change in *her* . . ."   15

"The thing's unlimited seemingly," said Mr. Fotheringay.
"And about Mr. Winch——"

"Altogether unlimited." And from the hearthrug Mr. Maydig, waving the Winch difficulty aside, unfolded a series of
wonderful proposals—proposals he invented as he went along.   20

Now what those proposals were does not concern the essen-
tials of this story. Suffice it that they were designed in a spirit
of infinite benevolence, the sort of benevolence that used to be
called post-prandial. Suffice it, too, that the problem of Winch
remained unsolved. Nor is it necessary to describe how far   25
that series got to its fulfillment. There were astonishing
changes. The small hours found Mr. Maydig and Mr. Fotheringay careering across the chilly market-square under the still
moon, in a sort of ecstasy of thaumaturgy, Mr. Maydig all flap
and gesture, Mr. Fotheringay short and bristling, and no longer 30
abashed at his greatness. They had reformed every drunkard
in the Parliamentary division, changed all the beer and alcohol
to water (Mr. Maydig had overruled Mr. Fotheringay on this
point), they had, further, greatly improved the railway communication of the place, drained Flinder's swamp, improved   35
the soil of One Tree Hill, and cured the Vicar's wart. And they
were going to see what could be done with the injured pier at
South Bridge. "The place," gasped Mr. Maydig, "won't be the

same place tomorrow. How surprised and thankful everyone will be!" And just at that moment the church clock struck three.

"I say," said Mr. Fotheringay, "that's three o'clock! I must be getting back. I've got to be at business by eight. And besides, Mrs. Wimms——"

"We're only beginning," said Mr. Maydig, full of the sweetness of unlimited power. "We're only beginning. Think of all the good we're doing. When people wake——"

"But——" said Mr. Fotheringay.

Mr. Maydig gripped his arm suddenly. His eyes were bright and wild. "My dear chap," he said, "there's no hurry. Look"—he pointed to the moon at the zenith—"Joshua!"

"Joshua?" said Mr. Fotheringay.

"Joshua," said Mr. Maydig. "Why not? Stop it."

Mr. Fotheringay looked at the moon.

"That's a bit tall," he said after a pause.

"Why not?" said Mr. Maydig. "Of course it doesn't stop. You stop the rotation of the earth, you know. Time stops. It isn't as if we were doing harm."

"H'm!" said Mr. Fotheringay. "Well." He sighed. "I'll try. Here——"

He buttoned up his jacket and addressed himself to the habitable globe, with as good an assumption of confidence as lay in his power. "Jest stop rotating, will you?" said Mr. Fotheringay.

Incontinently he was flying head over heels through the air at the rate of dozens of miles a minute. In spite of the innumerable circles he was describing per second, he thought; for thought is wonderful—sometimes as sluggish as flowing pitch, sometimes as instantaneous as light. He thought in a second, and willed. "Let me come down safe and sound. Whatever else happens, let me down safe and sound."

He willed it only just in time, for his clothes, heated by his rapid flight through the air, were already beginning to singe. He came down with a forcible but by no means injurious bump in what appeared to be a mound of fresh-turned earth. A large mass of metal and masonry, extraordinarily like the clock-tower in the middle of the market-square, hit the earth near him,

ricochetted over him, and flew into stonework, bricks, and masonry, like a bursting bomb. A hurtling cow hit one of the larger
blocks and smashed like an egg. There was a crash that made
all the most violent crashes of his past life seem like the sound
of falling dust, and this was followed by a descending series of   5
lesser crashes. A vast wind roared throughout earth and
heaven, so that he could scarcely lift his head to look. For a
while he was too breathless and astonished even to see where
he was or what had happened. And his first movement was to
feel his head and reassure himself that his streaming hair was   10
still his own.

"Lord!" gasped Mr. Fotheringay, scarce able to speak for
the gale. "I've had a squeak! What's gone wrong? Storms and
thunder. And only a minute ago a fine night. It's Maydig set
me on to this sort of thing. *What* a wind! If I go on fooling in   15
this way I'm bound to have a thundering accident!

"Where's Maydig?

"What a confounded mess everything's in!"

He looked about him so far as his flapping jacket would permit. The appearance of things was really extremely strange.   20
"The sky's all right anyhow," said Mr. Fotheringay. "And that's
about all that is all right. And even there it looks like a terrific
gale coming up. But there's the moon overhead. Just as it was
just now. Bright as midday. But as for the rest—Where's the
village? Where's—where's anything? And what on earth set this   25
wind a-blowing? *I* didn't order no wind."

Mr. Fotheringay struggled to get to his feet in vain, and
after one failure, remained on all fours, holding on. He surveyed the moonlit world to leeward, with the tails of his jacket
streaming over his head. "There's something seriously wrong,"   30
said Mr. Fotheringay. "And what it is—goodness knows."

Far and wide nothing was visible in the white glare through
the haze of dust that drove before a screaming gale but tumbled masses of earth and heaps of inchoate ruins, no trees, no
houses, no familiar shapes, only a wilderness of disorder van-   35
ishing at last into the darkness beneath the whirling columns
and streamers, the lightnings and thunderings of a swiftly rising storm. Near him in the livid glare was something that might

once have been an elm-tree, a smashed mass of splinters, shivered from boughs to base, and further a twisted mass of iron girders—only too evidently the viaduct—rose out of the piled confusion.

You see, when Mr. Fotheringay had arrested the rotation of the solid globe, he had made no stipulation concerning the trifling movables upon its surface. And the earth spins so fast that the surface at its equator is traveling at rather more than a thousand miles an hour, and in these latitudes at more than half that pace. So that the village, and Mr. Maydig, and Mr. Fotheringay, and everybody and everything had been jerked violently forward at about nine miles per second—that is to say, much more violently than if they had been fired out of a cannon. And every human being, every living creature, every house, and every tree—all the world as we know it—had been so jerked and smashed and utterly destroyed. That was all.

These things Mr. Fotheringay did not, of course, fully appreciate. But he perceived that his miracle had miscarried, and with that a great disgust of miracles came upon him. He was in darkness now, for the clouds had swept together and blotted out his momentary glimpse of the moon, and the air was full of fitful struggling tortured wraiths of hail. A great roaring of wind and waters filled earth and sky, and, peering under his hand through the dust and sleet to windward, he saw by the play of the lightnings a vast wall of water pouring towards him.

"Maydig!" screamed Mr. Fotheringay's feeble voice amid the elemental uproar. "Here!—Maydig!

"Stop!" cried Mr. Fotheringay to the advancing water. "Oh, for goodness' sake, stop!

"Just a moment," said Mr. Fotheringay to the lightnings and thunder. "Stop jest a moment while I collect my thoughts . . . And now what shall I do?" he said. "What *shall* I do? Lord! I wish Maydig was about.

"I know," said Mr. Fotheringay. "And for goodness' sake let's have it right *this* time."

He remained on all fours, leaning against the wind, very intent to have everything right.

"Ah!" he said. "Let nothing what I'm going to order hap-

pen until I say 'Off!' . . . Lord! I wish I'd thought of that before!"

He lifted his little voice against the whirlwind, shouting
louder and louder in the vain desire to hear himself speak.
"Now then!—here goes! Mind about that what I said just now.   5
In the first place, when all I've got to say is done, let me lose
my miraculous power, let my will become just like anybody
else's will, and all these dangerous miracles be stopped. I don't
like them. I'd rather I didn't work 'em. Ever so much. That's
the first thing. And the second is—let me be back just before   10
the miracles begin; let everything be just as it was before that
blessed lamp turned up. It's a big job, but it's the last. Have
you got it? No more miracles, everything as it was—me back
in the Long Dragon just before I drank my half-pint. That's it!
Yes."   15

He dug his fingers into the mould, closed his eyes, and said
"Off!"

Everything became perfectly still. He perceived that he was
standing erect.

"So *you* say," said a voice.   20

He opened his eyes. He was in the bar of the Long Dragon,
arguing about miracles with Toddy Beamish. He had a vague
sense of some great thing forgotten that instantaneously passed.
You see, except for the loss of his miraculous power, everything
was back as it had been; his mind and memory therefore were   25
now just as they had been at the time when this story began.
So that he knew absolutely nothing of all that is told here,
knows nothing of all that is told here to this day. And among
other things, of course, he still did not believe in miracles.

"I tell you that miracles, properly speaking, can't possibly   30
happen," he said, "whatever you like to hold. And I'm prepared
to prove it up to the hilt."

"That's what *you* think," said Toddy Beamish, and "Prove it
if you can."

"Looky here, Mr. Beamish," said Mr. Fotheringay. "Let us   35
clearly understand what a miracle is. It's something contrariwise to the course of nature done by power of Will. . . ."

Vocabulary

1. In paragraph one the author tells us that Fotheringay was "addicted to assertive argument." Does the statement in the following paragraph that Fotheringay is "determined to make an unusual rhetorical effort" support the author's original observation? What does Fotheringay mean when he defines a miracle as "something contrariwise to the course of nature done by power of Will . . ." (p. 148, ll. 2-3)?

2. The word "prosaic" (p. 148, l. 26) was also used in "The Monkey's Paw." Does it have the same meaning in both stories?

3. Mr. Cox's remark (p. 149, l. 3) is said to be "shorn of needless excrescences. . . ." What does that tell us about him?

4. What picture is brought to mind by the descriptive term "tornado of perplexity" used in describing Mr. Fotheringay's mind (p. 149, l. 12)?

5. What is meant by the admission that Mr. Fotheringay "inadvertently willed" his miracles (p. 149, ll. 25-26)?

Questions and Suggestions for Reading

POINT OF VIEW

1. This story is told in the third person omniscent point of view, that is to say, told as though the author knew everything about Mr. Fotheringay, what he thought, what he did, etc. However, the author says, "as I must admit" (p. 149, l. 33). The use of the word "I" tells us that the story is in the first person; yet we know it is in the third person. Why would the author change person? Are there any other instances in which the author shifts person?

PLOT

1. This is a story which is obviously built upon an impossibility. Does it interest the reader as a consequence of the impossibility or because of the impossibility?

2. The author states twice, once early in the story and once later on, that a miracle is "something contrariwise to the course of nature done by power of Will. . . ." Is this story an illustration of this statement?

John Steinbeck

FLIGHT

About fifteen miles below Monterey, on the wild coast, the Torres family had their farm, a few sloping acres above a cliff that dropped to the brown reefs and to the hissing white waters of the ocean. Behind the farm the stone mountains stood up against the sky. The farm buildings 5 huddled like little clinging aphids on the mountain skirts, crouched low to the ground as though the wind might blow them into the sea. The little shack, the rattling, rotting barn were grey-bitten with sea salt, beaten by the damp wind until they had taken on the color of the granite hills. Two horses, 10 a red cow and a red calf, half a dozen pigs and a flock of lean, multicolored chickens stocked the place. A little corn was raised on the sterile slope, and it grew short and thick under the wind, and all the cobs formed on the landward sides of the stalks.   15

Mama Torres, a lean, dry woman with ancient eyes, had ruled the farm for ten years, ever since her husband tripped over a stone in the field one day and fell full length on a rattlesnake. When one is bitten on the chest there is not much that can be done.   20

Mama Torres had three children, two undersized black ones of twelve and fourteen, Emilio and Rosy, whom Mamma kept fishing on the rocks below the farm when the sea was kind and when the truant officer was in some distant part of Monterey County. And there was Pepé, the tall smiling son of 25 nineteen, a gentle, affectionate boy, but very lazy. Pepé had a tall head, pointed at the top, and from its peak, coarse black

166

hair grew down like a thatch all around. Over his smiling little
eyes Mama cut a straight bang so he could see. Pepé had
sharp Indian cheekbones and an eagle nose, but his mouth was
as sweet and shapely as a girl's mouth, and his chin was fragile
and chiseled. He was loose and gangling, all legs and feet and   5
wrists, and he was very lazy. Mama thought him fine and brave,
but she never told him so. She said, "Some lazy cow must have
got into thy father's family, else how could I have a son like
thee." And she said, "When I carried thee, a sneaking lazy
coyote came out of the brush and looked at me one day. That   10
must have made thee so."

Pepé smiled sheepishly and stabbed at the ground with
his knife to keep the blade sharp and free from rust. It was his
inheritance, that knife, his father's knife. The long heavy blade
folded back into the black handle. There was a button on the   15
handle. When Pepé pressed the button, the blade leaped out
ready for use. The knife was with Pepé always, for it had been
his father's knife.

One sunny morning when the sea below the cliff was glinting and blue and the white surf creamed on the reef, when   20
even the stone mountain looked kindly, Mama Torres called
out the door of the shack, "Pepé, I have a labor for thee."

There was no answer. Mama listened. From behind the barn
she heard a burst of laughter. She lifted her full long skirt and
walked in the direction of the noise.   25

Pepé was sitting on the ground with his back against a box.
His white teeth glistened. On either side of him stood the two
black ones, tense and expectant. Fifteen feet away a redwood
post was set in the ground. Pepé's right hand lay limply in
his lap, and in the palm the big black knife rested. The blade   30
was closed back into the handle. Pepé looked smiling at the sky.

Suddenly Emilio cried, "Ya!"

Pepé's wrist flicked like the head of a snake. The blade
seemed to fly open in mid-air, and with a thump the point dug
into the redwood post, and the black handle quivered. The   35
three burst into excited laughter. Rosy ran to the post and
pulled out the knife and brought it back to Pepé. He closed

the blade and settled the knife carefully in his listless palm again. He grinned self-consciously at the sky.

"Ya!"

The heavy knife lanced out and sunk into the post again. Mama moved forward like a ship and scattered the play.

"All day you do foolish things with the knife, like a toy-baby," she stormed. "Get up on thy huge feet that eat up shoes. Get up!" She took him by one loose shoulder and hoisted at him. Pepé grinned sheepishly and came half-heartedly to his feet. "Look!" Mama cried. "Big lazy, you must catch the horse and put on him thy father's saddle. You must ride to Monterey. The medicine bottle is empty. There is no salt. Go thou now, Peanut! Catch the horse."

A revolution took place in the relaxed figure of Pepé. "To Monterey, me? Alone? *Si*, Mama."

She scowled at him. "Do not think, big sheep, that you will buy candy. No, I will give you only enough for the medicine and salt."

Pepé smiled. "Mama, you will put the hatband on the hat?"

She relented then. "Yes, Pepé. You may wear the hatband."

His voice grew insinuating. "And the green handkerchief, Mama?"

"Yes, if you go quickly and return with no trouble, the silk green handkerchief will go. If you make sure to take off the handkerchief when you eat so no spot may fall on it. . . ."

"*Si*, Mama. I will be careful. I am a man."

"Thou? A man? Thou art a peanut."

He went into the rickety barn and brought out a rope, and he walked agilely enough up the hill to catch the horse.

When he was ready and mounted before the door, mounted on his father's saddle that was so old that the oaken frame showed through torn leather in many places, then Mama brought out the round black hat with the tooled leather band, and she reached up and knotted the green silk handkerchief about his neck. Pepé's blue denim coat was much darker than his jeans, for it had been washed much less often.

Mama handed up the big medicine bottle and the silver coins. "That for the medicine," she said, "and that for the salt. That for a candle to burn for the papa. That for *dulces* for the little ones. Our friend Mrs. Rodriguez will give you dinner and maybe a bed for the night. When you go to the church say only ten Paternosters and only twenty-five Ave Marias. Oh! I know, big coyote. You would sit there flapping your mouth over Aves all day while you looked at the candles and the holy pictures. That is not good devotion to stare at the pretty things."

The black hat, covering the high pointed head and black thatched hair of Pepé, gave him dignity and age. He sat the rangy horse well. Mama thought how handsome he was, dark and lean and tall. "I would not send thee now alone, thou little one, except for the medicine," she said softly. "It is not good to have no medicine, for who knows when the toothache will come or the sadness of the stomach. These things are."

"Adios, Mama," Pepé cried. "I will come back soon. You may send me often alone. I am a man."

"Thou art a foolish chicken."

He straightened his shoulders, flipped the reins against the horse's shoulder and rode away. He turned once and saw that they still watched him, Emilio and Rosy and Mama. Pepé grinned with pride and gladness and lifted the tough buckskin horse to a trot.

When he had dropped out of sight over a little dip in the road, Mama turned to the black ones, but she spoke to herself. "He is nearly a man now," she said. "It will be a nice thing to have a man in the house again." Her eyes sharpened on the children. "Go to the rocks now. The tide is going out. There will be abalones to be found." She put the iron hooks into their hands and saw them down the steep trail to the reefs. She brought the smooth stone *metate* to the doorway and sat grinding her corn to flour and looking occasionally at the road over which Pepé had gone. The noonday came and then the afternoon, when the little ones beat the abalones on a rock to make them tender and Mama patted the tortillas to make them thin. They ate their dinner as the red sun was plunging down toward the ocean. They sat on the doorsteps and watched the big white moon come over the mountain tops.

Mama said, "He is now at the house of our friend Mrs. Rodriguez. She will give him nice things to eat and maybe a present." 5

Emilio said, "Some day I too will ride to Monterey for medicine. Did Pepé come to be a man today?"

Mama said wisely, "A boy gets to be a man when a man is needed. Remember this thing. I have known boys forty years old because there was no need for a man." 10

Soon afterwards they retired, Mama in her big oak bed on one side of the room, Emilio and Rosy in their boxes full of straw and sheepskins on the other side of the room.

The moon went over the sky and the surf roared on the rocks. The roosters crowed the first call. The surf subsided to a 15 whispering surge against the reef. The moon dropped toward the sea. The roosters crowed again.

The moon was near down to the water when Pepé rode on a winded horse to his home flat. His dog bounced out and circled the horse yelping with pleasure. Pepé slid off the 20 saddle to the ground. The weathered little shack was silver in the moonlight and the square shadow of it was black to the north and east. Against the east the piling mountains were misty with light; their tops melted into the sky.

Pepé walked wearily up the three steps and into the house. 25 It was dark inside. There was a rustle in the corner.

Mama cried out from her bed. "Who comes? Pepé, is it thou?"

"*Si*, Mama."

"Did you get the medicine?" 30

"Si, Mama."

"Well, go to sleep, then. I thought you would be sleeping at the house of Mrs. Rodriguez." Pepé stood silently in the dark room. "Why do you stand there, Pepé? Did you drink wine?"

"*Si*, Mama." 35

"Well, go to bed then and sleep out the wine."

His voice was tired and patient, but very firm. "Light the candle, Mama. I must go away into the mountains."

"What is this, Pepé? You are crazy." Mama struck a sulphur match and held the little blue burr until the flame spread up the stick. She set light to the candle on the floor beside her bed. "Now, Pepé, what is this you say?" She looked anxiously into his face.   5

He was changed. The fragile quality seemed to have gone from his chin. His mouth was less full than it had been, the lines of the lips were straighter, but in his eyes the greatest change had taken place. There was no laughter in them any more, nor any bashfulness. They were sharp and bright and 10 purposeful.

He told her in a tired monotone, told everything just as it had happened. A few people came into the kitchen of Mrs. Rodriguez. There was wine to drink. Pepé drank wine. The little quarrel—the man started toward Pepé and then the 15 knife—it went almost by itself. It flew, it darted before Pepé knew it. As he talked, Mama's face grew stern, and it seemed to grow more lean. Pepé finished. "I am a man now, Mama. The man said names to me I could not allow."

Mama nodded. "Yes, thou art a man, my poor little Pepé. 20 Thou art a man. I have seen it coming on thee. I have watched you throwing the knife into the post, and I have been afraid." For a moment her face had softened, but now it grew stern again. "Come! We must get you ready. Go. Awaken Emilio and Rosy. Go quickly."   25

Pepé stepped over to the corner where his brother and sister slept among the sheepskins. He leaned down and shook them gently. "Come, Rosy! Come, Emilio! The mama says you must arise."

The little black ones sat up and rubbed their eyes in the 30 candlelight. Mama was out of bed now, her long black skirt over her nightgown. "Emilio," she cried. "Go up and catch the other horse for Pepé. Quickly, now! Quickly!" Emilio put his legs in his overalls and stumbled sleepily out the door.

"You heard no one behind you on the road?" Mama de- 35 manded.

"No, Mama. I listened carefully. No one was on the road."

Mama darted like a bird about the room. From a nail on

the wall she took a canvas water bag and threw it on the floor. She stripped a blanket from her bed and rolled it into a tight tube and tied the ends with string. From a box beside the stove she lifted a flour sack half full of black stringy jerky "Your father's black coat, Pepé. Here, put it on."   5

Pepé stood in the middle of the floor watching her activity. She reached behind the door and brought out the rifle, a long 38-56, worn shiny the whole length of the barrel. Pepé took it from her and held it in the crook of his elbow. Mama brought a little leather bag and counted the cartridges into his hand.   10 "Only ten left," she warned. "You must not waste them."

Emilio put his head in the door. " '*Qui 'st 'l caballo*, Mama."

"Put on the saddle from the other horse. Tie on the blanket. Here, tie the jerky to the saddle horn."

Still Pepé stood silently watching his mother's frantic activity.   15 His chin looked hard, and his sweet mouth was drawn and thin. His little eyes followed Mama about the room almost suspiciously.

Rosy asked softly, "Where goes Pepé?"

Mama's eyes were fierce. "Pepé goes on a journey. Pepé is   20 a man now. He has a man's thing to do."

Pepé straightened his shoulders. His mouth changed until he looked very much like Mama.

At last the preparation was finished. The loaded horse stood outside the door. The water bag dripped a line of mois-   25 ture down the bay shoulder.

The moonlight was being thinned by the dawn and the big white moon was near down to the sea. The family stood by the shack. Mama confronted Pepé. "Look, my son! Do not stop until it is dark again. Do not sleep even though you are tired.   30 Take care of the horse in order that he may not stop of weariness. Remember to be careful with the bullets—there are only ten. Do not fill thy stomach with jerky or it will make thee sick. Eat a little jerky and fill thy stomach with grass. When thou comest to the high mountains, if thou seest any of the dark   35 watching men, go not near to them nor try to speak to them. And forget not thy prayers." She put her lean hands on Pepé's shoulders, stood on her toes and kissed him formally on both cheeks, and Pepé kissed her on both cheeks. Then he went to Emilio and Rosy and kissed both of their cheeks.

Pepé turned back to Mama. He seemed to look for a little softness, a little weakness in her. His eyes were searching, but Mama's face remained fierce. "Go now," she said. "Do not wait to be caught like a chicken."

Pepé pulled himself into the saddle. "I am a man," he said.

It was the first dawn when he rode up the hill toward the little canyon which let a trail into the mountains. Moonlight and daylight fought with each other, and the two warring qualities made it difficult to see. Before Pepé had gone a hundred yards, the outlines of his figure were misty; and long before he entered the canyon, he had become a gray, indefinite shadow.

Mama stood stiffly in front of her doorstep, and on either side of her stood Emilio and Rosy. They cast furtive glances at Mama now and then.

When the gray shape of Pepé melted into the hillside and disappeared, Mama relaxed. She began the high, whining keen of the death wail. "Our beautiful—our brave," she cried. "Our protector, our son is gone." Emilio and Rosy moaned beside her. "Our beautiful—our brave, he is gone." It was the formal wail. It rose to a high piercing whine and subsided to a moan. Mama raised it three times and then she turned and went into the house and shut the door.

Emilio and Rosy stood wondering in the dawn. They heard Mama whimpering in the house. They went out to sit on the cliff above the ocean. They touched shoulders. "When did Pepé come to be a man?" Emilio asked.

"Last night," said Rosy. "Last night in Monterey." The ocean clouds turned red with the sun that was behind the mountains.

"We will have no breakfast," said Emilio. "Mama will not want to cook." Rosy did not answer him. "Where is Pepé gone?" he asked.

Rosy looked around at him. She drew her knowledge from the quiet air. "He has gone on a journey. He will never come back."

"Is he dead? Do you think he is dead?"

Rosy looked back at the ocean again. A little steamer drawing a line of smoke sat on the edge of the horizon. "He is not dead," Rosy explained. "Not yet."

Pepé rested the big rifle across the saddle in front of him. He let the horse walk up the hill and he didn't look back. The stony slope took on a coat of short brush so that Pepé found the entrance to a trail and entered it.

When he came to the canyon opening, he swung once in his saddle and looked back, but the houses were swallowed in the misty light. Pepé jerked forward again. The high shoulder of the canyon closed in on him. His horse stretched out its neck and sighed and settled to the trail.

It was a well-worn path, dark soft leaf-mould earth strewn with broken pieces of sandstone. The trail rounded the shoulder of the canyon and dropped steeply into the bed of the stream. In the shallows the water ran smoothly, glinting in the first morning sun. Small round stones on the bottom were as brown as rust with sun moss. In the sand along the edges of the stream the tall, rich wild mint grew, while in the water itself the cress, old and tough, had gone to heavy seed.

The path went into the stream and emerged on the other side. The horse sloshed into the water and stopped. Pepé dropped his bridle and let the beast drink of the running water.

Soon the canyon sides became steep and the first giant sentinel redwoods guarded the trail, great round red trunks bearing foliage as green and lacy as ferns. Once Pepé was among the trees, the sun was lost. A perfumed and purple light lay in the pale green of the underbrush. Gooseberry bushes and blackberries and tall ferns lined the stream, and overhead the branches of the redwoods met and cut off the sky.

Pepé drank from the water bag, and he reached into the flour sack and brought out a black string of jerky. His white teeth gnawed at the string until the tough meat parted. He chewed slowly and drank occasionally from the water bag. His little eyes were slumberous and tired, but the muscles of his face were hard set. The earth of the trail was black now. It gave up a hollow sound under the walking hoofbeats.

The stream fell more sharply. Little waterfalls splashed on the stones. Five-fingered ferns hung over the water and dripped spray from their fingertips. Pepé rode half over in 5 his saddle, dangling one leg loosely. He picked a bay leaf from a tree beside the way and put it into his mouth for a moment to flavor the dry jerky. He held the gun loosely across the pommel.

Suddenly he squared in his saddle, swung the horse from 10 the trail and kicked it hurriedly up behind a big redwood tree. He pulled up the reins tight against the bit to keep the horse from whinnying. His face was intent and his nostrils quivered a little.

A hollow pounding came down the trail, and a horseman 15 rode by, a fat man with red cheeks and a white stubble beard. His horse put down its head and blubbered at the trail when it came to the place where Pepé had turned off. "Hold up!" said the man and he pulled up his horse's head.

When the last sound of the hoofs died away, Pepé came 20 back into the trail again. He did not relax in the saddle any more. He lifted the big rifle and swung the lever to throw a shell into the chamber, and then he let down the hammer to half cock.

The trail grew very steep. Now the redwood trees were 25 smaller and their tops were dead, bitten dead where the wind reached them. The horse plodded on; the sun went slowly overhead and started down toward the afternoon.

Where the stream came out of a side canyon, the trail left it. Pepé dismounted and watered his horse and filled up his 30 water bag. As soon as the trail had parted from the stream, the trees were gone and only the thick brittle sage and manzanita and chaparral edged the trail. And the soft black earth was gone, too, leaving only the light tan broken rock for the trail bed. Lizards scampered away into the brush as the horse 35 rattled over the little stones.

Pepé turned in his saddle and looked back. He was in the

open now: he could be seen from a distance. As he ascended
the trail the country grew more rough and terrible and dry.
The way wound about the bases of great square rocks. Little
gray rabbits skittered in the brush. A bird made a monotonous
high creaking. Eastward the bare rock mountaintops were pale 5
and powder-dry under the dropping sun. The horse plodded
up and up the trail toward a little V in the ridge which was the
pass.

Pepé looked suspiciously back every minute or so, and his
eyes sought the tops of the ridges ahead. Once, on a white 10
barren spur, he saw a black figure for a moment, but he looked
quickly away, for it was one of the dark watchers. No one
knew who the watchers were, nor where they lived, but it was
better to ignore them and never to show interest in them. They
did not bother one who stayed on the trail and minded his own 15
business.

The air was parched and full of light dust blown by the
breeze from the eroding mountains. Pepé drank sparingly from
his bag and corked it tightly and hung it on the horn again.
The trail moved up the dry shale hillside, avoiding rocks, drop- 20
ping under clefts, climbing in and out of old water scars. When
he arrived at the little pass he stopped and looked back for a
long time. No dark watchers were to be seen now. The trail behind was empty. Only the high tops of the redwoods indicated
where the stream flowed. 25

Pepé rode on through the pass. His little eyes were nearly
closed with weariness, but his face was stern, relentless and
manly. The high mountain wind coasted sighing through the
pass and whistled on the edges of the black blocks of broken
granite. In the air, a red-tailed hawk sailed over close to the 30
ridge and screamed angrily. Pepé went slowly through the
broken jagged pass and looked down on the other side.

The trail dropped quickly, staggering among broken rock. At
the bottom of the slope there was a dark crease, thick with
brush, and on the other side of the crease a little flat, in which 35
a grove of oak trees grew. A scar of green grass cut across the
flat. And behind the flat another mountain rose, desolate with

dead rocks and starving little black bushes. Pepé drank from
the bag again for the air was so dry that it encrusted his nostrils
and burned his lips. He put the horse down the trail. The
hooves slipped and struggled on the steep way, starting little
stones that rolled off into the brush. The sun was gone behind 5
the westward mountain now, but still it glowed brilliantly on
the oaks and on the grassy flat. The rocks and hillsides still
sent up waves of the heat they had gathered from the day's
sun.

Pepé looked up to the top of the next dry withered ridge. 10
He saw a dark form against the sky, a man's figure standing
on top of a rock, and he glanced away quickly not to appear
curious. When a moment later he looked up again, the figure
was gone.

Downward the trail was quickly covered. Sometimes the 15
horse floundered for footing, sometimes set his feet and slid a
little way. They came at last to the bottom where the dark
chaparral was higher than Pepé's head. He held up his rifle
on one side and his arm on the other to shield his face from
the sharp brittle fingers of the brush. 20

Up and out of the crease he rode, and up a little cliff. The
grassy flat was before him, and the round comfortable oaks.
For a moment he studied the trail down which he had come,
but there was no movement and no sound from it. Finally he
rode out over the flat, to the green streak, and at the upper 25
end of the damp he found a little spring welling out of the
earth and dropping into a dug basin before it seeped out over
the flat.

Pepé filled his bag first, and then he let the thirsty horse
drink out of the pool. He led the horse to the clump of oaks, 30
and in the middle of the grove, fairly protected from sight on
all sides, he took off the saddle and the bridle and laid them
on the ground. The horse stretched his jaws sideways and
yawned. Pepé knotted the lead rope about the horse's neck and
tied him to a sapling among the oaks, where he could graze in 35
a fairly large circle.

When the horse was gnawing hungrily at the dry grass,

Pepé went to the saddle and took a black string of jerky from the sack and strolled to an oak tree on the edge of the grove, from under which he could watch the trail. He sat down in the crisp dry oak leaves and automatically felt for his big black knife to cut the jerky, but he had no knife. He leaned back on his elbow and gnawed at the tough strong meat. His face was blank, but it was a man's face.

The bright evening light washed the eastern ridge, but the valley was darkening. Doves flew down from the hills to the spring, and the quail came running out of the brush and joined them, calling clearly to one another.

Out of the corner of his eye Pepé saw a shadow grow out of the bushy crease. He turned his head slowly. A big spotted wildcat was creeping toward the spring, belly to the ground, moving like thought.

Pepé cocked his rifle and edged the muzzle slowly around. Then he looked apprehensively up the trail and dropped the hammer again. From the ground beside him he picked an oak twig and threw it toward the spring. The quail flew up with a roar and the doves whistled away. The big cat stood up; for a long moment he looked at Pepé with cold yellow eyes, and then fearlessly walked back into the gulch.

The dusk gathered quickly in the deep valley. Pepé muttered his prayers, put his head down on his arm and went instantly to sleep.

The moon came up and filled the valley with cold blue light, and the wind swept rustling down from the peaks. The owls worked up and down the slopes looking for rabbits. Down in the brush of the gulch a coyote gabbled. The oak trees whispered softly in the night breeze.

Pepé started up, listening. His horse had whinnied. The moon was just slipping behind the western ridge, leaving the valley in darkness behind it. Pepé sat tensely gripping his rifle. From far up the trail he heard an answering whinny and the crash of shod hooves on the broken rock. He jumped to his feet, ran to his horse and led it under the trees. He threw on

the saddle and cinched it tight for the steep trail, caught the
unwilling head and forced the bit into the mouth. He felt the
saddle to make sure the water bag and the sack of jerky were
there. Then he mounted and turned up the hill.

It was velvet dark. The horse found the entrance to the trail 5
where it left the flat, and started up, stumbling and slipping on
the rocks. Pepé's hand rose up to his head. His hat was gone.
He had left it under the oak tree.

The horse had struggled far up the trail when the first change
of dawn came into the air, a steel grayness as light mixed thor- 10
oughly with dark. Gradually the sharp snaggled edge of the
ridge stood out above them, rotten granite tortured and eaten
by the winds of time. Pepé had dropped his reins on the horn,
leaving direction to the horse. The brush grabbed at his legs
in the dark until one knee of his jeans was ripped.   15

Gradually the light flowed down over the ridge. The
starved brush and rocks stood out in the half light, strange
and lonely in high perspective. Then there came warmth into
the light. Pepé drew up and looked back, but he could see
nothing in the darker valley below. The sky turned blue over 20
the coming sun. In the waste of the mountainside, the poor
dry brush grew only three feet high. Here and there, big out- /
croppings of unrotted granite stood up like mouldering houses.
Pepé relaxed a little. He drank from his water bag and bit off
a piece of jerky. A single eagle flew over, high in the light.   25

Without warning Pepé's horse screamed and fell on its side.
He was almost down before the rifle crash echoed up from the
valley. From a hole behind the struggling shoulder, a stream
of bright crimson blood pumped and stopped and pumped
and stopped. The hooves threshed on the ground. Pepé lay half 30
stunned beside the horse. He looked slowly down the hill. A
piece of sage clipped off beside his head and another crash
echoed up from side to side of the canyon. Pepé flung himself
frantically behind a bush.

He crawled up the hill on his knees and one hand. His right 35
hand held the rifle up off the ground and pushed it ahead of
him. He moved with the instinctive care of an animal. Rapidly

he wormed his way toward one of the big outcroppings of
granite on the hill above him. Where the brush was high he
doubled up and ran, but where the cover was slight he wriggled
forward on his stomach, pushing the rifle ahead of him. In the
last little distance there was no cover at all. Pepé poised and   5
then he darted across the space and flashed around the corner
of the rock.

He leaned panting against the stone. When his breath came
easier he moved along behind the big rock until he came to a
narrow split that offered a thin section of vision down the hill. 10
Pepé lay on his stomach and pushed the rifle barrel through
the slit and waited.

The sun reddened the western ridges now. Already the buz-
zards were settling down toward the place where the horse lay.
A small brown bird scratched in the dead sage leaves directly   15
in front of the rifle muzzle. The coasting eagle flew back toward the rising sun.

Pepé saw a little movement in the brush far below. His
grip tightened on the gun. A little brown doe stepped daintily
out on the trail and crossed it and disappeared into the brush 20
again. For a long time Pepé waited. Far below he could see the
little flat and the oak trees and the slash of green. Suddenly his
eyes flashed back at the trail again. A quarter of a mile down
there had been a quick movement in the chaparral. The rifle
swung over. The front sight nestled in the V of the rear sight. 25
Pepé studied for a moment and then raised the rear sight a
notch. The little movement in the brush came again. The sight
settled on it. Pepé squeezed the trigger. The explosion crashed
down the mountain and up the other side, and came rattling
back. The whole side of the slope grew still. No more move-   30
ment. And then a white streak cut into the granite of the slit
and a bullet whined away and a crash sounded up from below.
Pepé felt a sharp pain in his right hand. A sliver of granite was
sticking out from between his first and second knuckles and the
point protruded from his palm. Carefully he pulled out the   35
sliver of stone. The wound bled evenly and gently. No vein or
artery was cut.

Pepé looked into a little dusty cave in the rock and gathered a handful of spider web, and he pressed the mass into the cut, plastering the soft web into the blood. The flow stopped almost at once.

The rifle was on the ground. Pepé picked it up, levered a new shell into the chamber. And then he slid into the brush on his stomach. Far to the right he crawled, and then up the hill, moving slowly and carefully, crawling to cover and resting and then crawling again.

In the mountains the sun is high in its arc before it penetrates the gorges. The hot face looked over the hill and brought instant heat with it. The white light beat on the rocks and reflected from them and rose up quivering from the earth again, and the rocks and bushes seemed to quiver behind the air.

Pepé crawled in the general direction of the ridge peak, zigzagging for cover. The deep cut between his knuckles began to throb. He crawled close to a rattlesnake before he saw it, and when it raised its dry head and made a soft beginning whirr, he backed up and took another way. The quick gray lizards flashed in front of him, raising a tiny line of dust. He found another mass of spider web and pressed it against his throbbing hand.

Pepé was pushing the rifle with his left hand now. Little drops of sweat ran to the ends of his coarse black hair and rolled down his cheeks. His lips and tongue were growing thick and heavy. His lips writhed to draw saliva into his mouth. His little dark eyes were uneasy and suspicious. Once when a gray lizard paused in front of him on the parched ground and turned its head sideways he crushed it flat with a stone.

When the sun slid past noon he had not gone a mile. He crawled exhaustedly a last hundred yards to a patch of high sharp manzanita, crawled desperately, and when the patch was reached he wriggled in among the tough gnarly trunks and dropped his head on his left arm. There was little shade in the meager brush, but there was cover and safety. Pepé went to sleep as he lay and the sun beat on his back. A few little birds hopped close to him and peered and hopped away.

Pepé squirmed in his sleep and he raised and dropped his wounded hand again and again.

The sun went down behind the peaks and the cool evening came, and then the dark. A coyote yelled from the hillside. Pepé started awake and looked about with misty eyes. His hand was swollen and heavy; a little thread of pain ran up the inside of his arm and settled in a pocket in his armpit. He peered about and then stood up, for the mountains were black and the moon had not yet risen. Pepé stood up in the dark. The coat of his father pressed on his arm. His tongue was swollen until it nearly filled his mouth. He wriggled out of the coat and dropped it in the brush, and then he struggled up the hill, falling over rocks and tearing his way through the brush. The rifle knocked against stones as he went. Little dry avalanches of gravel and shattered stone went whispering down the hill behind him.

After a while the old moon came up and showed the jagged ridge top ahead of him. By moonlight Pepé traveled more easily. He bent forward so that his throbbing arm hung away from his body. The journey uphill was made in dashes and rests, a frantic rush up a few yards and then a rest. The wind coasted down the slope rattling the dry stems of the bushes.

The moon was at meridian when Pepé came at last to the sharp backbone of the ridge top. On the last hundred yards of the rise no soil had clung under the wearing winds. The way was on solid rock. He clambered to the top and looked down on the other side. There was a draw like the last below him, misty with moonlight, brushed with dry struggling sage and chaparral. On the other side the hill rose up sharply and at the top the jagged rotten teeth of the mountain showed against the sky. At the bottom of the cut the brush was thick and dark.

Pepé stumbled down the hill. His throat was almost closed with thirst. At first he tried to run, but immediately he fell and rolled. After that he went more carefully. The moon was just disappearing behind the mountains when he came to the bottom. He crawled into the heavy brush feeling with his fingers for water. There was no water in the bed of the stream, only

damp earth. Pepé laid his gun down and scooped up a handful
of mud and put it in his mouth, and then he spluttered and
scraped the earth from his tongue with his finger, for the mud
drew at his mouth like a poultice. He dug a hole in the stream
bed with his fingers, dug a little basin to catch water; but be- 5
fore it was very deep his head fell forward on the damp ground
and he slept.

The dawn came and the heat of the day fell on the earth,
and still Pepé slept. Late in the afternoon his head jerked
up. He looked slowly around. His eyes were slits of wariness. 10
Twenty feet away in the heavy brush a big tawny mountain
lion stood looking at him. Its long thick tail waved gracefully,
its ears were erect with interest, not laid back dangerously.
The lion squatted down on its stomach and watched him.

Pepé looked at the hole he had dug in the earth. A half inch 15
of muddy water had collected in the bottom. He tore the sleeve
from his hurt arm, with his teeth ripped out a little square,
soaked it in the water and put it in his mouth. Over and over
he filled the cloth and sucked it.

Still the lion sat and watched him. The evening came 20
down but there was no movement on the hills. No birds visited
the dry bottom of the cut. Pepé looked occasionally at the lion.
The eyes of the yellow beast drooped as though he were about
to sleep. He yawned and his long thin red tongue curled out.
Suddenly his head jerked around and his nostrils quivered. His 25
big tail lashed. He stood up and slunk like a tawny shadow
into the thick brush.

A moment later Pepé heard the sound, the faint far crash
of horses' hooves on gravel. And he heard something else, a
high whining yelp of a dog. 30

Pepé took his rifle in his left hand and he glided into the
brush almost as quietly as the lion had. In the darkening evening he crouched up the hill toward the next ridge. Only when
the dark came did he stand up. His energy was short. Once it
was dark he fell over the rocks and slipped to his knees on the 35
steep slope, but he moved on and on up the hill, climbing and
scrabbling over the broken hillside.

When he was far up toward the top, he lay down and slept for a little while. The withered moon, shining on his face, awakened him. He stood up and moved up the hill. Fifty yards away he stopped and turned back, for he had forgotten his rifle. He walked heavily down and poked about in the brush, 5 but he could not find his gun. At last he lay down to rest. The pocket of pain in his armpit had grown more sharp. His arm seemed to swell out and fall with every heartbeat. There was no position lying down where the heavy arm did not press against his armpit. 10

With the effort of a hurt beast, Pepé got up and moved again toward the top of the ridge. He held his swollen arm away from his body with his left hand. Up the steep hill he dragged himself, a few steps and a rest, and a few more steps. At last he was nearing the top. The moon showed the uneven 15 sharp back of it against the sky.

Pepé's brain spun in a big spiral up and away from him. He slumped to the ground and lay still. The rock ridge top was only a hundred feet above him.

The moon moved over the sky. Pepé half turned on his 20 back. His tongue tried to make words, but only a thick hissing came from between his lips.

When the dawn came, Pepé pulled himself up. His eyes were sane again. He drew his great puffed arm in front of him and looked at the angry wound. The black line ran up from his 25 wrist to his armpit. Automatically he reached in his pocket for the big black knife, but it was not there. His eyes searched the ground. He picked up a sharp blade of stone and scraped at the wound, sawed at the proud flesh and then squeezed the green juice out in big drops. Instantly he threw back his head 30 and whined like a dog. His whole right side shuddered at the pain, but the pain cleared his head.

In the gray light he struggled up the last slope of the ridge and crawled over and lay down behind a line of rocks. Below him lay a deep canyon exactly like the last, waterless and deso- 35 late. There was no flat, no oak trees, not even heavy brush in the bottom of it. And on the other side a sharp ridge stood up, thinly brushed with starving sage, littered with broken granite. Strewn over the hill there were giant outcroppings, and on the top the granite teeth stood out against the sky.

The new day was light now. The flame of the sun came over the ridge and fell on Pepé where he lay on the ground. His coarse black hair was littered with twigs and bits of spider web. His eyes had retreated back in to his head. Between his lips the tip of his black tongue showed.

He sat up and dragged his great arm into his lap and nursed it, rocking his body and moaning in his throat. He threw back his head and looked up into the pale sky. A big black bird circled nearly out of sight, and far to the left another was sailing near.

He lifted his head to listen, for a familiar sound had come to him from the valley he had climbed out of; it was the crying yelp of hounds, excited and feverish, on a trail.

Pepé bowed his head quickly. He tried to speak rapid words but only a thick hiss came from his lips. He drew a shaky cross on his breast with his left hand. It was a long struggle to get to his feet. He crawled slowly and mechanically to the top of a big rock on the ridge peak. Once there, he arose slowly, swaying to his feet, and stood erect. Far below he could see the dark brush where he had slept. He braced his feet and stood there, black against the morning sky.

There came a ripping sound at his feet. A piece of stone flew up and a bullet droned off into the next gorge. The hollow crash echoed up from below. Pepé looked down for a moment and then pulled himself straight again.

His body jarred back. His left hand fluttered helplessly toward his breast. The second crash sounded from below. Pepé swung forward and toppled from the rock. His body struck and rolled over and over, starting a little avalanche. And when at last he stopped against a bush, the avalanche slid slowly down and covered up his head.

Vocabulary

1. Describe in other terms what happened to Pepé's voice when it grew "insinuating" (p. 168, l. 22).

2. What action is the author describing or trying to indicate when he says that Pepé "walked agilely enough" to get the horse (p. 168, l. 30)?

3. Emilio and Rosy, watching Pepé leave, "cast furtive glances at Mama now and then." What were they doing (p. 173, ll. 16-17)?

4. The death wail Mama sang "subsided to a moan." What happened to the wail (p. 173, l. 23)?

Questions and Suggestions for Reading

DESCRIPTION

1. John Steinbeck is known as a master of description, and, as a consequence, his stories should be read slowly. He usually writes about California and the half-caste laboring class who live there. Notice how carefully Steinbeck sketches his scenes. He doesn't simply say, "The trail went up a hill," but rather, "The trail moved up the dry shale hillside, avoiding rocks, dropping under clefts, climbing in and out of old water scars" (p. 176, ll. 20-21). Select three other instances of this kind of descriptive writing.

2. Notice, too, that a number of days and nights pass during the story. How does Steinbeck make his readers believe that this has actually happened? Be specific.

MOTIVATION AND INTERPRETATION

1. Again we have a story in which motivation plays a great part, and, as a consequence, there are a number of problems of

interpretation. First, one might ask if Pepé went forth to Monterey with the idea of drinking wine and becoming a "man" or if these occurrences were simply a coincidence. Second, a reader might ask himself if Pepé, half man and half animal in his actions, would not have been more of a "man" if he had faced his pursuers instead of running away. And, third, one might ask himself if Pepé stood, facing inevitable death, outlined against the sky, in order to really become a "man" at the last; if he was simply taking the easiest way out and taking it because he was almost mad with pain; or if a combination of these two factors caused him to take the final action.

2. Pepé's mother prepares him for his journey and then sings a death wail and closes herself within the house. Does she do so because she believes she will never see Pepé again and that he will be dead to her in form if not in fact, or does she do so because she knows that he will undoubtedly be killed either by the creatures of the mountains into which he is going or by his pursuers?

3. Unless an author depicts the characters of whom he writes very clearly, it is often difficult to understand what he is trying to put across. He must also make his characters' backgrounds—their beliefs, habits, reactions to situations—very clear. In this story, Steinbeck assumes that his reader knows that Pepé, no matter what he does, is a doomed man from the moment he murders. He also assumes that his reader will realize that to be a "man" is the ultimate goal of any boy in Pepé's cultural group. Do we actually learn what Steinbeck assumes we know by reading the story?

Stephen Vincent Benét

BY THE WATERS
OF BABYLON

The north and the west and the south are good hunting ground, but it is forbidden to go east. It is forbidden to go to any of the Dead Places except to search for metal and then he who touches the metal must be a priest or the son of a priest. Afterwards, both the man and the metal must be puri- 5
fied. These are the rules and the laws; they are well made. It is forbidden to cross the great river and look upon the place that was the Place of the Gods—this is most strictly forbidden. We do not even say its name though we know its name. It is there that spirits live, and demons—it is there that there are the 10
ashes of the Great Burning. These things are forbidden—they have been forbidden since the beginning of time.

My father is a priest; I am the son of a priest. I have been in the Dead Places near us, with my father—at first, I was afraid. When my father went into the house to search for the 15
metal, I stood by the door and my heart felt small and weak. It was a dead man's house, a spirit house. It did not have the smell of man, though there were old bones in a corner. But it is not fitting that a priest's son should show fear. I looked at the bones in the shadow and kept my voice still. 20

Then my father came out with the metal—a good, strong piece. He looked at me with both eyes but I had not run away. He gave me the metal to hold—I took it and did not die. So he knew that I was truly his son and would be a priest in my time. That was when I was very young—nevertheless, my brothers 25

188

would not have done it, though they are good hunters. After that, they gave me the good piece of meat and the warm corner by the fire. My father watched over me—he was glad that I should be a priest. But when I boasted or wept without a reason, he punished me more strictly than my brothers. That was right.

After a time, I myself was allowed to go into the dead houses and search for metal. So I learned the ways of those houses—and if I saw bones, I was no longer afraid. The bones are light and old—sometimes they will fall into dust if you touch them. But that is a great sin.

I was taught the chants and the spells—I was taught how to stop the running of blood from a wound and many secrets. A priest must know many secrets—that was what my father said. If the hunters think we do all things by chants and spells, they may believe so—it does not hurt them. I was taught how to read in the old books and how to make the old writings—that was hard and took a long time. My knowledge made me happy—it was like a fire in my heart. Most of all, I liked to hear of the Old Days and the stories of the gods. I asked myself many questions that I could not answer, but it was good to ask them. At night, I would lie awake and listen to the wind—it seemed to me that it was the voice of the gods as they flew through the air.

We are not ignorant like the Forest People—our women spin wool on the wheel, our priests wear a white robe. We do not eat grubs from the tree, we have not forgotten the old writings, although they are hard to understand. Nevertheless, my knowledge and my lack of knowledge burned in me—I wished to know more. When I was a man at last, I came to my father and said, "It is time for me to go on my journey. Give me your leave."

He looked at me for a long time, stroking his beard, then he said at last, "Yes. It is time." That night, in the house of the priesthood, I asked for and received purification. My body hurt but my spirit was a cool stone. It was my father himself who questioned me about my dreams.

He bade me look into the smoke of the fire and see—I saw and told what I saw. It was what I have always seen—a river, and, beyond it, a great Dead Place and in it the gods walking. I have always thought about that. His eyes were stern when I told him—he was no longer my father but a priest. He said, 5 "This is a strong dream."

"It is mine," I said, while the smoke waved and my head felt light. They were singing the Star song in the outer chamber and it was like the buzzing of bees in my head.

He asked me how the gods were dressed and I told him how 10 they were dressed. We know how they were dressed from the book, but I saw them as if they were before me. When I had finished, he threw the sticks three times and studied them as they fell.

"This is a very strong dream," he said. "It may eat you up." 15

"I am not afraid," I said and looked at him with both eyes. My voice sounded thin in my ears but that was because of the smoke.

He touched me on the breast and the forehead. He gave me the bow and the three arrows. 20

"Take them," he said. "It is forbidden to travel east. It is forbidden to cross the river. It is forbidden to go to the Place of the Gods. All these things are forbidden."

"All these things are forbidden," I said, but it was my voice that spoke and not my spirit. He looked at me again. 25

"My son," he said. "Once I had young dreams. If your dreams do not eat you up, you may be a great priest. If they eat you, you are still my son. Now go on your journey."

I went fasting, as is the law. My body hurt but not my heart. When the dawn came, I was out of sight of the village. I prayed 30 and purified myself, waiting for a sign. The sign was an eagle. It flew east.

Sometimes signs are sent by bad spirits. I waited again on the flat rock, fasting, taking no food. I was very still—I could feel the sky above me and the earth beneath. I waited till the 35 sun was beginning to sink. Then three deer passed in the valley, going east—they did not wind me or see me. There was a white fawn with them—a very great sign.

I followed them, at a distance, waiting for what would happen. My heart was troubled about going east, yet I knew that I must go. My head hummed with my fasting—I did not even see the panther spring upon the white fawn. But, before I knew it, the bow was in my hand. I shouted and the panther lifted 5 his head from the fawn. It is not easy to kill a panther with one arrow but the arrow went through his eye and into his brain. He died as he tried to spring—he rolled over, tearing at the ground. Then I knew I was meant to go east—I knew that was my journey. When the night came, I made my fire and roasted 10 meat.

It is eight suns' journey to the east and a man passes by many Dead Places. The Forest People are afraid of them but I am not. Once I made my fire on the edge of a Dead Place at night and, next morning, in the dead house, I found a good 15 knife, little rusted. That was small to what came afterward but it made my heart feel big. Always when I looked for game it was in front of my arrow, and twice I passed hunting parties of the Forest People without their knowing. So I knew my magic was strong and my journey clean, in spite of the law. 20

Toward the setting of the eighth sun, I came to the banks of the great river. It was half-a-day's journey after I had left the god-road—we do not use the god-roads now for they are falling apart into great blocks of stone, and the forest is safer going. A long way off, I had seen the water through trees but 25 the trees were thick. At last, I came out upon an open place at the top of a cliff. There was the great river below, like a giant in the sun. It is very long, very wide. It could eat all the streams we know and still be thirsty. Its name is Ou-dis-sun, the Sacred, the Long. No man of my tribe had seen it, not even my father, 30 the priest. It was magic and I prayed.

Then I raised my eyes and looked south. It was there, the Place of the Gods.

How can I tell what it was like—you do not know. It was there, in the red light, and they were too big to be houses. It 35 was there with the red light upon it, mighty and ruined. I knew that in another moment the gods would see me. I covered my eyes with my hands and crept back into the forest.

Surely, that was enough to do, and live. Surely it was enough
to spend the night upon the cliff. The Forest People themselves
do not come near. Yet, all through the night, I knew that I
should have to cross the river and walk in the places of the
gods, although the gods ate me up. My magic did not help me   5
at all and yet there was a fire in my bowels, a fire in my mind.
When the sun rose, I thought, "My journey has been clean.
Now I will go home from my journey." But, even as I thought
so, I knew I could not. If I went to the Place of the Gods, I
would surely die, but, if I did not go, I could never be at peace   10
with my spirit again. It is better to lose one's life than one's
spirit, if one is a priest and the son of a priest.

Nevertheless, as I made the raft, the tears ran out of my
eyes. The Forest People could have killed me without fight, if
they had come upon me then, but they did not come. When   15
the raft was made, I said the sayings for the dead and painted
myself for death. My heart was cold as a frog and my knees
like water, but the burning in my mind would not let me have
peace. As I pushed the raft from the shore, I began my death
song—I had the right. It was a fine song.   20

"I am John, son of John," I sang. "My people are the Hill Peo-
      ple. They are the men.
I go into the Dead Places but I am not slain.
I take the metal from the Dead Places but I am not blasted.   25
I travel upon the god-roads and am not afraid. E-yah! I have
      killed the panther, I have killed the fawn!
E-yah! I have come to the great river. No man has come there
      before.
It is forbidden to go east, but I have gone, forbidden to go on   30
      the great river, but I am there.
Open your hearts, you spirits, and hear my song.
      Now I go to the Place of the Gods, I shall not return.
My body is painted for death and my limbs weak, but my heart
      is big as I go to the Place of the Gods!"   35

All the same, when I came to the Place of the Gods, I was
afraid, afraid. The current of the great river is very strong—it

gripped my raft with its hands. That was magic, for the river itself is wide and calm. I could feel evil spirits about me, in the bright morning; I could feel their breath on my neck as I was swept down the stream. Never have I been so much alone—I tried to think of my knowledge, but it was a squirrel's heap of winter nuts. There was no strength in my knowledge any more and I felt small and naked as a new-hatched bird—alone upon the great river, the servant of the gods.

Yet, after a while, my eyes were opened and I saw. I saw both banks of the river—I saw that once there had been god-roads across it, though now they were broken and fallen like broken vines. Very great they were, and wonderful and broken —broken in the time of the Great Burning when the fire fell out of the sky. And always the current took me nearer to the Place of the Gods, and the huge ruins rose before my eyes.

I do not know the customs of rivers—we are the People of the Hills. I tried to guide my raft with the pole but it spun around. I thought the river meant to take me past the Place of the Gods and out into the Bitter Water of the legends. I grew angry then—my heart felt strong. I said aloud, "I am a priest and the son of a priest!" The gods heard me—they showed me how to paddle with the pole on one side of the raft. The current changed itself—I drew near to the Place of the Gods.

When I was very near, my raft struck and turned over. I can swim in our lakes—I swam to the shore. There was a great spike of rusted metal sticking out into the river—I hauled myself up upon it and sat there, panting. I had saved my bow and two arrows and the knife I found in the Dead Place but that was all. My raft went whirling downstream toward the Bitter Water. I looked after it, and thought if it had trod me under, at least I would be safely dead. Nevertheless, when I had dried my bowstring and re-strung it, I walked forward to the Place of the Gods.

It felt like ground underfoot; it did not burn me. It is not true what some of the tales say, that the ground there burns forever, for I have been there. Here and there were the marks and stains of the Great Burning, on the ruins, that is true. But they were old marks and old stains. It is not true either, what

some of our priests say, that it is an island covered with fogs
and enchantments. It is not. It is a great Dead Place—greater
than any Dead Place we know. Everywhere in it there are god-
roads, though most are cracked and broken. Everywhere there
are the ruins of the high towers of the gods.   5

How shall I tell what I saw? I went carefully, my strung
bow in my hand, my skin ready for danger. There should have
been the wailings of spirits and the shrieks of demons, but there
were not. It was very silent and sunny where I had landed—the
wind and the rain and the birds that drop seeds had done their 10
work—the grass grew in the cracks of the broken stone. It is a
fair island—no wonder the gods built there. If I had come there,
a god, I also would have built.

How shall I tell what I saw? The towers are not all broken
—here and there one still stands, like a great tree in a forest, 15
and the birds nest high. But the towers themselves look blind,
for the gods are gone. I saw a fish-hawk, catching fish in the
river. I saw a little dance of white butterflies over a great heap
of broken stones and columns. I went there and looked about
me—there was a carved stone with cut-letters, broken in half. I 20
can read letters but I could not understand these. They said
UBTREAS. There was also the shattered image of a man or a
god. It had been made of white stone and he wore his hair tied
back like a woman's. His name was ASHING, as I read on the
cracked half of a stone. I thought it wise to pray to ASHING, 25
though I do not know that god.

How shall I tell what I saw? There was no smell of man left,
on stone or metal. Nor were there many trees in that wilderness
of stone. There are many pigeons, nesting and dropping in the
towers—the gods must have loved them, or, perhaps, they used 30
them for sacrifices. There are wild cats that roam the god-roads,
green-eyed, unafraid of man. At night they wail like demons
but they are not demons. The wild dogs are more dangerous,
for they hunt in a pack, but them I did not meet till later.
Everywhere there are the carved stones, carved with magical 35
numbers or words.

I went North—I did not try to hide myself. When a god or
a demon saw me, then I would die, but meanwhile I was no

longer afraid. My hunger for knowledge burned in me—there
was so much that I could not understand. After awhile, I knew
that my belly was hungry. I could have hunted for my meat,
but I did not hunt. It is known that the gods did not hunt as
we do—they got their food from enchanted boxes and jars.   5
Sometimes these are still found in the Dead Places—once, when
I was a child and foolish, I opened such a jar and tasted it and
found the food sweet. But my father found out and punished
me for it strictly, for, often, that food is death. Now, though, I
had long gone past what was forbidden, and I entered the like-   10
liest towers, looking for the food of the gods.

I found it at last in the ruins of a great temple in the mid-city.
A mighty temple it must have been, for the roof was painted
like the sky at night with its stars—that much I could see,
though the colors were faint and dim. It went down into great   15
caves and tunnels—perhaps they kept their slaves there. But
when I started to climb down, I heard the squeaking of rats, so
I did not go—rats are unclean, and there must have been many
tribes of them, from the squeaking. But near there, I found
food, in the heart of a ruin, behind a door that still opened. I   20
ate only the fruits from the jars—they had a very sweet taste.
There was drink, too, in bottles of glass—the drink of the gods
was strong and made my head swim. After I had eaten and
drunk, I slept on the top of a stone, my bow at my side.

When I woke, the sun was low. Looking down from where   25
I lay, I saw a dog sitting on his haunches. His tongue was hanging out of his mouth; he looked as if he were laughing. He was
a big dog, with a gray-brown coat, as big as a wolf. I sprang up
and shouted at him but he did not move—he just sat there as if
he were laughing. I did not like that. When I reached for a   30
stone to throw, he moved swiftly out of the way of the stone.
He was not afraid of me; he looked at me as if I were meat. No
doubt I could have killed him with an arrow, but I did not
know if there were others. Moreover, night was falling.

I looked about me—not far away there was a great, broken   35
god-road, leading North. The towers were high enough, but not
so high, and while many of the dead-houses were wrecked,
there were some that stood. I went toward this god-road, keep-

ing to the heights of the ruins, while the dog followed. When I
had reached the god-road, I saw that there were others behind
him. If I had slept later, they would have come upon me asleep
and torn out my throat. As it was, they were sure enough of
me; they did not hurry. When I went into the dead-house, they   5
kept watch at the entrance—doubtless they thought they
would have a fine hunt. But a dog cannot open a door and I
knew, from the books, that the gods did not like to live on the
ground but on high.

I had just found a door I could open when the dogs decided   10
to rush. Ha! They were surprised when I shut the door in their
faces—it was a good door, of strong metal. I could hear their
foolish baying beyond it but I did not stop to answer them. I
was in darkness—I found stairs and climbed. There were many
stairs, turning around till my head was dizzy. At the top was   15
another door—I found the knob and opened it. I was in a long
small chamber—on one side of it was a bronze door that could
not be opened, for it had no handle. Perhaps there was a magic
word to open it but I did not have the word. I turned to the
door in the opposite side of the wall. The lock of it was broken   20
and I opened it and went in.

Within, there was a place of great riches. The god who lived
there must have been a powerful god. The first room was a
small anteroom—I waited there for some time, telling the spirits
of the place that I came in peace and not as a robber. When it   25
seemed to me that they had had time to hear me, I went on.
Ah, what riches! Few, even, of the windows had been broken—
it was all as it had been. The great windows that looked over
the city had not been broken at all though they were dusty
and streaked with many years. There were coverings on the   30
floors, the colors not greatly faded, and the chairs were soft and
deep. There were pictures upon the walls, very strange, very
wonderful—I remember one of a bunch of flowers in a jar—if
you came close to it, you could see nothing but bits of color,
but if you stood away from it, the flowers might have been   35
picked yesterday. It made my heart feel strange to look at this
picture—and to look at the figure of a bird, in some hard clay,
on a table and see it so like our birds. Everywhere there were

books and writings, many in tongues that I could not read. The
god who lived there must have been a wise god and full of
knowledge. I felt I had right there, as I sought knowledge also.

Nevertheless, it was strange. There was a washing-place but
no water—perhaps the gods washed in air. There was a cooking-   5
place but no wood, and though there was a machine to cook
food, there was no place to put fire in it. Nor were there candles
or lamps—there were things that looked like lamps but they
had neither oil nor wick. All these things were magic, but I
touched them and lived—the magic had gone out of them. Let   10
me tell one thing to show. In the washing-place, a thing said
"Hot" but it was not hot to the touch—another thing said "Cold"
but it was not cold. This must have been a strong magic but
the magic was gone. I do not understand—they had ways—I
wish that I knew.   15

It was close and dry and dusty in their house of the gods. I
have said the magic was gone but that is not true—it had gone
from the magic things but it had not gone from the place. I felt
the spirits about me, weighing upon me. Nor had I ever slept
in a Dead Place before—and yet, tonight, I must sleep there.   20
When I thought of it, my tongue felt dry in my throat, in spite
of my wish for knowledge. Almost I would have gone down
again and faced the dogs, but I did not.

I had not gone through all the rooms when the darkness fell.
When it fell, I went back to the big room looking over the city   25
and made fire. There was a place to make fire and a box with
wood in it, though I do not think they cooked there. I wrapped
myself in a floor-covering and slept in front of the fire—I was
very tired.

Now I tell what is very strong magic. I woke in the midst   30
of the night. When I woke, the fire had gone out and I was cold.
It seemed to me that all around me there were whisperings
and voices. I closed my eyes to shut them out. Some will say
that I slept again, but I do not think that I slept. I could feel
the spirits drawing my spirit out of my body as a fish is drawn   35
on a line.

Why should I lie about it? I am a priest and the son of a
priest. If there are spirits, as they say, in the small Dead Places

near us, what spirits must there not be in that great Place of
the Gods? And would not they wish to speak? After such long
years? I know that I felt myself drawn as a fish is drawn on a
line. I had stepped out of my body—I could see my body asleep
in front of the cold fire, but it was not I. I was drawn to look out   5
upon the city of the gods.

It should have been dark, for it was night, but it was not
dark. Everywhere there were lights—lines of light—circles and
blurs of light—ten thousand torches would not have been the
same. The sky itself was alight—you could barely see the stars   10
for the glow in the sky. I thought to myself "This is strong
magic" and trembled. There was a roaring in my ears like the
rushing of rivers. Then my eyes grew used to the light and my
ears to the sound. I knew that I was seeing the city as it had
been when the gods were alive.   15

That was a sight indeed—yes, that was a sight: I could not
have seen it in the body—my body would have died. Everywhere went the gods, on foot and in chariots—there were gods
beyond number and counting and their chariots blocked the
streets. They had turned night to day for their pleasure—they   20
did not sleep with the sun. The noise of their coming and going was the noise of many waters. It was magic what they could
do—it was magic what they did.

I looked out of another window—the great vines of their
bridges were mended and the god-roads went East and West.   25
Restless, restless, were the gods and always in motion! They
burrowed tunnels under rivers—they flew in the air. With unbelievable tools they did giant works—no part of the earth was
safe from them, for, if they wished for a thing, they summoned
it from the other side of the world. And always, as they labored 30
and rested, as they feasted and made love, there was a drum
in their ears—the pulse of the giant city, beating and beating
like a man's heart.

Were they happy? What is happiness to the gods? They were
great, they were mighty, they were wonderful and terrible. As   35
I looked upon them and their magic, I felt like a child—but a
little more, it seemed to me, and they would pull down the
moon from the sky. I saw them with wisdom beyond wisdom

and knowledge beyond knowledge. And yet not all they did was well done—even I could see that—and yet their wisdom could not but grow until all was peace.

Then I saw their fate come upon them and that was terrible past speech. It came upon them as they walked the streets of their city. I have been in the fights with the Forest People—I have seen men die. But this was not like that. When gods war with gods, they use weapons we do not know. It was fire falling out of the sky and a mist that poisoned. It was the time of the Great Burning and the Destruction. They ran about like ants in the streets of their city—poor gods, poor gods! Then the towers began to fall. A few escaped—yes, a few. The legends tell it. But, even after the city had become a Dead Place, for many years the poison was still in the ground. I saw it happen, I saw the last of them die. It was darkness over the broken city and I wept.

All this, I saw. I saw it as I have told it, though not in the body. When I woke in the morning, I was hungry, but I did not think first of my hunger for my heart was perplexed and confused. I knew the reason for the Dead Places but I did not see why it had happened. It seemed to me it should not have happened, with all the magic they had. I went through the house looking for an answer. There was so much in the house I could not understand—and yet I am a priest and the son of a priest. It was like being on one side of the great river, at night, with no light to show the way.

Then I saw the dead god. He was sitting in his chair, by the window, in a room I had not entered before and, for the first moment, I thought that he was alive. Then I saw the skin on the back of his hand—it was like dry leather. The room was shut, hot and dry—no doubt that had kept him as he was. At first I was afraid to approach him—then the fear left me. He was sitting looking out over the city—he was dressed in the clothes of the gods. His age was neither young nor old—I could not tell his age. But there was wisdom in his face and great sadness. You could see that he would have not run away. He had sat at his window, watching his city die—then he himself had died. But it is better to lose one's life than one's spirit—and

you could see from the face that his spirit had not been lost. I
knew that, if I touched him, he would fall into dust—and yet,
there was something unconquered in the face.

That is all of my story, for then I knew he was a man—I knew
then that they had been men, neither gods nor demons. It is a
great knowledge, hard to tell and believe. They were men—
they went a dark road, but they were men. I had no fear after
that—I had no fear going home, though twice I fought off the
dogs and once I was hunted for two days by the Forest People.
When I saw my father again, I prayed and was purified. He
touched my lips and my breast, he said, "You went away a boy.
You come back a man and a priest." I said, "Father, they were
men! I have been in the Place of the Gods and seen it! Now
slay me, if it is the law—but still I know they were men."

He looked at me out of both eyes. He said, "The law is not
always the same shape—you have done what you have done. I
could not have done it in my time, but you come after me. Tell!"

I told and he listened. After that, I wished to tell all the people but he showed me otherwise. He said, "Truth is a hard
deer to hunt. If you eat too much truth at once, you may die of
the truth. It was not idly that our fathers forbade the Dead
Places." He was right—it is better the truth should come little
by little. I have learned that, being a priest. Perhaps, in the old
days, they ate knowledge too fast.

Nevertheless, we make a beginning. It is not for the metal
alone we go to the Dead Places now—there are the books and
the writings. They are hard to learn. And the magic tools are
broken—but we can look at them and wonder. At least, we make
a beginning. And, when I am chief priest we shall go beyond
the great river. We shall go to the Place of the Gods—the place
Newyork—not one man but a company. We shall look for the
images of the gods and find the god ASHING and the others—
the god LICOLN and BILTMORE and MOSES. But they were
men who built the city, not gods or demons. They were men.
I remember the dead man's face. They were men who were
here before us. We must build again.

Vocabulary

1. What are the differences in "chants" and "spells"?
2. Why are the expressions "Dead Places," "Great Burning," "Old Days" capitalized in the story?
3. Can you identify these words: UBTREAS, ASHING, LICOLN, BILTMORE, and MOSES?
4. Notice that there is little dialogue in this story. Instead the boy simply reveals his simple and rather primitive thoughts.

Questions and Suggestions for Reading

SETTING

1. This story is more like a detective story than any other in this collection. We wonder about the setting—when the story took place and where. At first it seems to have been written about an age long ago, but later we are told that the gods in the "Dead Places" got their food from boxes and jars. After seeing a dead man through John's eyes, we can definitely conclude that these gods were not "mythological." Exactly what has happened? Where is the "Dead Place"? In what age or century did the boy John go there?

THEME

1. One of the author's main concerns in this story is the moral, the lesson the story teaches which he believes touches all men. When John goes forth to the "Dead Place" he sees and experiences a great deal, and he tells his father about everything that has happened. However, his father refuses to let John tell all he knows to the other people of the tribe. Why? Is it better that truth "should come little by little"?

2. Twice in the story John thinks "it is better to lose one's life than one's spirit." The first time he thinks this he adds, "if one is a priest and the son of a priest." The second time he thinks this is when he sees the dead "god."

3. Does the author seem to believe that the Hill People under John's leadership will be wiser, in the future, than the people who had lived in Newyork earlier? Support your answer.

4. What caused the downfall of these "gods"?

Wilbur Daniel Steele

HOW BEAUTIFUL
WITH SHOES

By the time the milking was finished, the sow, which had farrowed the past week, was making such a row that the girl spilled a pint of the warm milk down the trough-lead to quiet the animal before taking the pail to the well-house. Then in the quiet she heard a sound of hoofs on the bridge, where the road crossed the creek a hundred yards below the house, and she set the pail down on the ground beside her bare, barn-soiled feet. She picked it up again. She set it down. It was as if she calculated its weight.

That was what she was doing, as a matter of fact, setting off against its pull toward the well-house the pull of that wagon team in the road, with little more of personal wish or will in the matter than has a wooden weathervane between two currents in the wind. And as with the vane, so with the wooden girl—the added behest of a whip-lash cracking in the distance was enough; leaving the pail at the barn door, she set off in a deliberate, docile beeline through the cow-yard, over the fence, and down in a diagonal across the farm's one tilled field toward the willow brake that walled the road at the dip. And once under way, though her mother came to the kitchen door and called in her high flat voice, 'Amarantha, where you goin', Amarantha?' the girl went on apparently unmoved, as though she had been as deaf as the woman in the doorway; indeed, if there was emotion in her it was the purely sensuous one of feeling the clods of the furrows breaking softly between her toes. It was springtime in the mountains.

'Amarantha, why don't you answer me, Amarantha?'

For moments after the girl had disappeared beyond the willows the widow continued to call, unaware through long habit of how absurd it sounded, the name which the strange man her husband had put upon their daughter in one of his moods. Mrs. Doggett had been deaf so long she did not realize that nobody else ever thought of it for the broad-fleshed, slow-minded girl, but called her Mary or, even more simply, Mare.

Ruby Herter had stopped his team this side of the bridge, the mules' heads turned into the lane to his father's farm beyond the road. A big-barreled, heavy-limbed fellow with a square, sallow, not unhandsome face, he took out youth in ponderous gestures of masterfulness; it was like him to have cracked his whip above his animals' ears the moment before he pulled them to a halt. When he saw the girl getting over the fence under the willows he tongued the wad of tobacco out of his mouth into his palm, threw it away beyond the road, and drew a sleeve of his jumper across his lips.

'Don't run yourself out o' breath, Mare; I got all night.'

'I was comin'!' It sounded sullen only because it was matter of fact.

'Well, keep a-comin' and give us a smack.' Hunched on the wagon seat, he remained motionless for some time after she had arrived at the hub, and when he stirred it was but to cut a fresh bit of tobacco, as if already he had forgotten why he threw the old one away. Having satisfied his humor, he unbent, climbed down, kissed her passive mouth, and hugged her up to him, roughly and loosely, his hands careless of contours. It was not out of the way; they were used to handling animals both of them; and it was spring. A slow warmth pervaded the girl, formless, nameless, almost impersonal.

Her betrothed pulled her head back by the braid of her yellow hair. He studied her face, his brows gathered and his chin out.

'Listen, Mare, you wouldn't leave nobody else hug and kiss you, dang you!'

She shook her head, without vehemence or anxiety.

'Who's that?' She hearkened up the road. 'Pull your team out,' she added, as a Ford came in sight around the bend above the house, driven at speed. 'Geddap!' she said to the mules herself.

But the car came to a halt near them, and one of the five 5 men crowded in it called, 'Come on, Ruby, climb in. They's a loony loose out o' Dayville Asylum, and they got him trailed over somewheres on Split Ridge, and Judge North phoned up to Slosson's store for ever'body come help circle him—come on, hop the runnin'-board!' 10

Ruby hesitated, an eye on his team.

'Scared, Ruby?' The driver raced his engine. 'They say this boy's a killer.'

'Mare, take the team in and tell pa.' The car was already moving when Ruby jumped it. A moment after it had sounded 15 on the bridge it was out of sight.

'Amarantha, Amarantha, why don't you come, Amarantha?'

Returning from her errand, fifteen minutes later, Mare heard the plaint lifted in the twilight. The sun had dipped behind the back ridge, and though the sky was still bright with day, 20 the dusk began to smoke up out of the plowed field like a ground-fog. The girl had returned through it, got the milk, and started toward the well-house before the widow saw her.

'Daughter, seems to me you might?' she expostulated without change of key. 'Here's some young man friend o' yourn 25 stopped to say howdy, and I been rackin' my lungs out after you . . . Put that milk in the cool and come!'

Some young man friend? But there was no good to be got from puzzling. Mare poured the milk in the pan in the dark of the low house over the well, and as she came out, stooping, she 30 saw a figure waiting for her, black in silhouette against the yellowing sky.

'Who are you?' she asked, a native timidity making her sound sulky.

' "Amarantha!" ' the fellow mused. 'That's poetry.' And she 35 knew then that she did not know him.

She walked past, her arms straight down and her eyes front.

Strangers always affected her with a kind of muscular terror simply by being strangers. So she gained the kitchen steps, aware by his tread that he followed. There, taking courage at sight of her mother in the doorway, she turned on him, her eyes down at the level of his knees.

'Who are you and what d'y' want?'

He still mused. 'Amarantha! Amarantha in Carolina! That makes me happy!'

Mare hazarded one upward look. She saw that he had red hair, brown eyes, and hollows under his cheek-bones, and though the green sweater he wore on top of a gray overall was plainly not meant for him, sizes too large as far as girth went, yet he was built so long of limb that his wrists came inches out of the sleeves and made his big hands look even bigger.

Mrs. Doggett complained. 'Why don't you introduce us, daughter?'

The girl opened her mouth and closed it again. Her mother, unaware that no sound had come out of it, smiled and nodded, evidently taking to the tall, homely fellow and tickled by the way he could not seem to get his eyes off her daughter. But the daughter saw none of it, all her attention centered upon the stranger's hands.

Restless, hard-fleshed, and chap-bitten, they were like a countryman's hands; but the fingers were longer than the ordinary, and slightly spatulate at their ends, and these ends were slowly and continuously at play among themselves.

The girl could not explain how it came to her to be frightened and at the same time to be calm, for she was inept with words. It was simply that in an animal way she knew animals, knew them in health and ailing, and when they were ailing she knew by instinct, as her father had known, how to move so as not to fret them.

Her mother had gone in to light up; from beside the lamp-shelf she called back, 'If he's aimin' to stay to supper you should've told me, Amarantha, though I guess there's plenty of the side-meat to go 'round, if you'll bring me in a few more turnips and potatoes, though it is late.'

At the words the man's cheeks moved in and out. 'I'm very hungry,' he said.

Mare nodded deliberately. Deliberately, as if her mother could hear her, she said over her shoulder, 'I'll go get the potatoes and turnips, ma.' While she spoke she was moving, slowly, softly, at first, toward the right of the yard, where the fence gave over into the field. Unluckily her mother spied her through the window.

'Amarantha, where *are* you goin'?'

'I'm goin' to get the potatoes and turnips.' She neither raised her voice nor glanced back, but lengthened her stride. 'He won't hurt her,' she said to herself. 'He won't hurt her; it's me, not her,' she kept repeating, while she got over the fence and down into the shadow that lay more than ever like a fog on the field.

The desire to believe that it actually did hide her, the temptation to break from her rapid but orderly walk grew till she could no longer fight it. She saw the road willows only a dash ahead of her. She ran, her feet floundering among the furrows.

She neither heard nor saw him, but when she realized he was with her she knew he had been with her all the while. She stopped, and he stopped, and so they stood, with the dark open of the field all around. Glancing sidewise presently, she saw he was no longer looking at her with those strangely importunate brown eyes of his, but had raised them to the crest of the wooded ridge behind her.

By and by, 'What does it make you think of?' he asked. And when she made no move to see, 'Turn around and look!' he said, and though it was low and almost tender in its tone, she knew enough to turn.

A ray of the sunset hidden in the west struck through the tops of the topmost trees, far and small up there, a thin, bright hem.

'What does it make you think of, Amarantha? . . . Answer!'

'Fire,' she made herself say.

'Or blood.'

'Or blood, yeh. That's right, or blood.' She had heard a Ford

going up the road beyond the willows, and her attention was
not on what she said.

The man soliloquized. 'Fire and blood, both; spare one or
the other, and where is beauty, the way the world is? It's an
awful thing to have to carry, but Christ had it. Christ came 5
with a sword. I love beauty, Amarantha . . . I say, I love
beauty!'

'Yeh, that's right, I hear.' What she heard was the car stopping at the house.

'Not prettiness. Prettiness'll have to go with ugliness, because 10
it's only ugliness trigged up. But beauty!' Now again he was
looking at her. 'Do you know how beautiful you are, Amarantha, "Amarantha sweet and fair"?' Of a sudden, reaching behind her, he began to unravel the meshes of her hair-braid, the
long, flat-tipped fingers at once impatient and infinitely gentle. 15
' "Braid no more that shining hair!" '

Flat-faced Mare Doggett tried to see around those glowing
eyes so near to hers, but wise in her instinct, did not try too
hard. 'Yeh,' she temporized. 'I mean, no, I mean.'

'Amarantha, I've come a long way for you. Will you come 20
away with me now?'

'Yeh—that is—in a minute I will, mister—yeh . . .'

'Because you want to, Amarantha? Because you love me as I
love you? Answer!'

'Yeh—sure—uh . . . *Ruby!*' 25

The man tried to run, but there were six against him, coming up out of the dark that lay in the plowed ground. Mare
stood where she was while they knocked him down and got a
rope around him; after that she walked back toward the house
with Ruby and Older Haskins, her father's cousin. 30

Ruby wiped his brow and felt of his muscles. 'Gees, you're
lucky we come, Mare. We're no more'n past the town, when
they came hollerin' he'd broke over this way.'

When they came to the fence the girl sat on the rail for a
moment and rebraided her hair before she went into the house, 35
where they were making her mother smell ammonia.

Lots of cars were coming. Judge North was coming, some-

body said. When Mare heard this she went into her bedroom off
the kitchen and got her shoes and put them on. They were
brand new two-dollar shoes with cloth tops, and she had only
begun to break them in last Sunday; she wished afterwards
she had put her stockings on too, for they would have eased   5
the seams. Or else that she had put on the old button pair,
even though the soles were worn through.

Judge North arrived. He thought first of taking the loony
straight through to Dayville that night, but then decided to
keep him in the lock-up at the courthouse till morning and   10
make the drive by day. Older Haskins stayed in, gentling Mrs.
Doggett, while Ruby went out to help get the man into the
Judge's sedan. Now that she had them on, Mare didn't like to
take the shoes off till Older went; it might make him feel small,
she thought.   15

Older Haskins had a lot of facts about the loony.

'His name's Humble Jewett,' he told them. 'They belong
back in Breed County, all them Jewetts, and I don't reckon
there's none on 'em that's not a mite unbalanced. He went to
college though, worked his way, and he taught somethin' 'rother 20
in some academy-school a spell, till he went off his head all of
a sudden and took after folks with an axe. I remember it in the
paper at the time. They give out one while how the Principal
wasn't goin' to live, and there was others—there was a girl he
tried to strangle. That was four—five year back.'   25

Ruby came in guffawing. 'Know the only thing they can get
him to say, Mare? Only God thing he'll say is, "Amarantha, she's
goin' with me." . . . Mare!'

'Yeh, I know.'

The cover of the kettle the girl was handling slid off the   30
stove with a clatter. A sudden sick wave passed over her. She
went out to the back, out into the air. It was not till now she
knew how frightened she had been.

Ruby went home, but Older Haskins stayed to supper with
them, and helped Mare do the dishes afterward; it was nearly   35
nine when he left. The mother was already in bed, and Mare
was about to sit down to get those shoes off her wretched feet

at last, when she heard the cow carrying on up at the barn, lowing and kicking, and next minute the sow was in it with a horning note. It might be a fox passing by to get at the hen-house, or a weasel. Mare forgot her feet, took a broom-handle they used in boiling clothes, opened the back door, and stepped out. Blinking the lamplight from her eyes, she peered up toward the out-buildings, and saw the gable end of the barn standing like a red arrow in the dark, and the top of a butternut tree beyond it drawn in skeleton traceries, and just then a cock crowed.

She went to the right corner of the house and saw where the light came from, ruddy above the woods down the valley. Returning into the house, she bent close to her mother's ear and shouted, 'Somethin's a-fire down to the town, looks like,' then went out again and up to the barn. 'Soh! Soh!' she called in to the animals. She climbed up and stood on the top rail of the cow-pen fence, only to find she could not locate the flame even there.

Ten rods behind the buildings a mass of rock mounted higher than their ridgepoles, a chopped-off buttress of the back ridge, covered with oak scrub and wild grapes and blackberries, whose thorny ropes the girl beat away from her skirt with the broom-handle as she scrambled up in the wine-colored dark. Once at the top, and the brush held aside, she could see the tongue-tip of the conflagration half a mile away at the town. And she knew by the bearing of the two church steeples that it was the building where the lock-up was that was burning.

There is a horror in knowing animals trapped in a fire, no matter what the animals.

'Oh, my God!' Mare said.

A car went down the road. Then there was a horse galloping. That would be Older Haskins probably. People were out at Ruby's father's farm; she could hear their voices raised. There must have been another car up from the other way, for lights wheeled and shouts were exchanged in the neighborhood of the bridge. Next thing she knew, Ruby was at the house below, looking for her probably.

He was telling her mother. Mrs. Doggett was not used to him, so he had to shout even louder than Mare had to.

'What y' reckon he done, the hellion! he broke the door and killed Lew Fyke and set the courthouse afire! . . . Where's Mare?'   5

Her mother would not know. Mare called. 'Here, up the rock here.'

She had better go down, Ruby would likely break his bones if he tried to climb the rock in the dark, not knowing the way. But the sight of the fire fascinated her simple spirit, the fearful   10
element, more fearful than ever now, with the news. 'Yes, I'm comin',' she called sulkily, hearing feet in the brush. 'You wait; I'm comin'.'

When she turned and saw it was Humble Jewett, right be-hind her among the branches, she opened her mouth to screech.   15
She was not quick enough. Before a sound came out he got one hand over her face and the other arm around her body.

Mare had always thought she was strong, and the loony looked gangling, yet she was so easy for him that he need not hurt her. He made no haste and little noise as he carried her   20
deeper into the undergrowth. Where the hill began to mount it was harder though. Presently he set her on her feet. He let the hand that had been over her mouth slip down to her throat, where the broad-tipped fingers wound tender as yearn-ing, weightless·as caress.   25

'I was afraid you'd scream before you knew who 'twas. Amarantha. But I didn't want to hurt your lips, dear heart, your lovely, quiet lips.'

It was so dark under the trees she could hardly see him, but she felt his breath on her mouth, near to. But then, instead of   30
kissing her, he said, 'No! No!' took from her throat for an instant the hand that had held her mouth, kissed its palm, and put it back softly against her skin.

'Now, my love, let's go before they come.'

She stood stock still. Her mother's voice was to be heard in   35
the distance, strident and meaningless. More cars were on the road. Nearer, around the rock, there were sounds of tramping

and thrashing. Ruby fussed and cursed. He shouted, 'Mare, dang you, where are you, Mare?' his voice harsh with uneasy anger. Now, if she aimed to do anything, was the time to do it. But there was neither breath nor power in her windpipe. It was as if those yearning fingers had paralyzed the muscles.

'Come!' The arm he put around her shivered against her shoulder blades. It was anger. 'I hate killing. It's a dirty, ugly thing. It makes me sick.' He gagged, judging by the sound. But then he ground his teeth. 'Come away, my love!'

She found herself moving. Once when she broke a branch underfoot with an instinctive awkwardness he chided her. 'Quiet, my heart, else they'll hear!' She made herself heavy. He thought she grew tired and bore more of her weight till he was breathing hard.

Men came up the hill. There must have been a dozen spread out, by the angle of their voices as they kept touch. Always Humble Jewett kept caressing Mare's throat with one hand; all she could do was hang back.

'You're tired and you're frightened,' he said at last. 'Get down here.'

There were twigs in the dark, the overhang of a thicket of some sort. He thrust her in under this, and lay beside her on the bed of groundpine. The hand that was not in love with her throat reached across her; she felt the weight of its forearm on her shoulder and its fingers among the strands of her hair, eagerly, but tenderly, busy. Not once did he stop speaking, no louder than breathing, his lips to her ear.

' "*Amarantha sweet and fair—Ah, braid no more that shining hair . . .*" '

Mare had never heard of Lovelace, the poet; she thought the loony was just going on, hardly listened, got little sense. But the cadence of it added to the lethargy of all her flesh.

"*Like a clew of golden thread—Most excellently ravelléd . . .*" '

Voices loudened; feet came trampling; a pair went past not two rods away.

' ". . . *Do not then wind up the light—In ribbands, and o'ercloud in night . . .*" '

The search went on up the woods, men shouting to one another and beating the brush.

' ". . . *But shake your head and scatter day!*" I've never loved,
Amarantha. They've tried me with prettiness, but prettiness is
too cheap, yes, it's too cheap.'   5

Mare was cold, and the coldness made her lazy. All she knew
was that he talked on.

'But dogwood blowing in the spring isn't cheap. The earth
of a field isn't cheap. Lots of times I've lain down and kissed
the earth of a field, Amarantha. That's beauty, and a kiss for   10
beauty.' His breath moved up her cheek. He trembled violently. 'No, no, not yet!' He got to his knees and pulled her by
an arm. 'We can go now.'

They went back down the slope, but at an angle, so that
when they came to the level they passed two hundred yards to   15
the north of the house, and crossed the road there. More and
more her walking was like sleep-walking, the feet numb in
their shoes. Even where he had to let go of her, crossing the
creek on stones, she stepped where he stepped with an obtuse
docility. The voices of the searchers on the back ridge were   20
small in distance when they began to climb the face of Coward
Hill, on the opposite side of the valley.

There is an old farm on top of Coward Hill, big hay-fields as
flat as tables. It had been half-past nine when Mare stood on
the rock above the barn; it was toward midnight when Humble   25
Jewett put aside the last branches of the woods and let her out
on the height, and half a moon had risen. And a wind blew
there, tossing the withered tops of last year's grasses, and mists
ran with the wind, and ragged shadows with the mists, and
mares'-tails of clear moonlight among the shadows, so that now   30
the boles of birches on the forest's edge beyond the fences
were but opal blurs and now cut alabaster. It struck so cold
against the girl's cold flesh, this wind, that another wind of
shivers blew through her, and she put her hands over her face
and eyes. But the madman stood with his eyes open wide and   35
his mouth open, drinking the moonlight and the wet wind.

His voice, when he spoke at last, was thick in his throat.

'Get down on your knees.' He got down on his and pulled her after. 'And pray!'

Once in England a poet sang four lines. Four hundred years have forgotten his name, but they have remembered his lines. The daft man knelt upright, his face raised to the wild scud, his long wrists hanging to the dead grass. He began simply:

> ' "O western wind, when wilt thou blow
> "That the small rain down can rain?" '

The Adam's-apple was big in his bent throat. As simply he finished.

> ' "Christ, that my love were in my arms
> "And I in my bed again!" '

Mare got up and ran. She ran without aim or feeling in the power of the wind. She told herself again that the mists would hide her from him, as she had done at dusk. And again, seeing that he ran at her shoulder, she knew he had been there all the while, making a race of it, flailing the wind with his long arms for joy of play in the cloud of spring, throwing his knees high, leaping the moon-blue waves of the brown grass, shaking his bright hair; and her own hair was a weight behind her, lying level on the wind. Once a shape went bounding ahead of them for instants; she did not realize it was a fox till it was gone.

She never thought of stopping; she never thought anything, except once, 'Oh, my God, I wish I had my shoes off!' And what would have been the good in stopping or in turning another way, when it was only play? The man's ecstasy magnified his strength. When a snake-fence came at them he took the top rail in flight, like a college hurdler and, seeing the girl hesitate and half turn as if to flee, he would have releaped it without touching a hand. But then she got a loom of buildings, climbed over quickly, before he should jump, and ran along the lane that ran with the fence.

Mare had never been up there, but she knew that the farm and the house belonged to a man named Wyker, a kind of cousin of Ruby Herter's, a violent, bearded old fellow who lived by himself. She could not believe her luck. When she had run half the distance and Jewett had not grabbed her, doubt grabbed her instead. 'Oh, my God, go careful!' she told herself. 'Go slow!' she implored herself, and stopped running, to walk.

Here was a misgiving the deeper in that it touched her special knowledge. She had never known an animal so far gone that its instincts failed it; a starving rat will scent the trap sooner than a fed one. Yet, after one glance at the house they approached, Jewett paid it no further attention, but walked with his eyes to the right, where the cloud had blown away, and wooded ridges, like black waves rimmed with silver, ran down away toward the Valley of Virginia.

'I've never lived!' In his single cry there were two things, beatitude and pain.

Between the bigness of the falling world and his eyes the flag of her hair blew. He reached out and let it whip between his fingers. Mare was afraid it would break the spell then, and he would stop looking away and look at the house again. So she did something almost incredible; she spoke.

'It's a pretty—I mean—a beautiful view down that-a-way.'

'God Almighty beautiful, to take your breath away. I knew I'd never loved, Belovéd—' He caught a foot under the long end of one of the boards that covered the well and went down heavily on his hands and knees. It seemed to make no difference. 'But I never knew I'd never lived,' he finished in the same tone of strong rapture, quadruped in the grass, while Mare ran for the door and grabbed the latch.

When the latch would not give, she lost what little sense she had. She pounded with her fists. She cried with all her might: 'Oh—hey—in there—hey—in there!' Then Jewett came and took her gently between his hands and drew her away, and then, though she was free, she stood in something like an awful embarrassment while he tried shouting.

'Hey! Friend! whoever you are, wake up and let my love and me come in!'

'No!' wailed the girl.

He grew peremptory. 'Hey, wake up.' He tried the latch.

He passed to full fury in a wink's time; he cursed, he kicked, he beat the door till Mare thought he would break his hands. Withdrawing, he ran at it with his shoulder; it burst at the latch, went slamming in, and left a black emptiness. His anger dissolved in a big laugh. Turning in time to catch her by a wrist, he cried joyously, 'Come, my Sweet One!'

'No! No! Please—aw—listen. There ain't nobody there. He ain't to home. It wouldn't be right to go in anybody's house if they wasn't to home, you know that.'

His laugh was blither than ever. He caught her high in his arms.

'I'd do the same by his love and him if 'twas my house, I would.' At the threshold he paused and thought, 'That is, if she was the true love of his heart forever.'

The room was the parlor. Moonlight slanted in at the door, and another shaft came through a window and fell across a sofa, its covering dilapidated, showing its wadding in places. The air was sour, but both of them were farm-bred.

'Don't, Amarantha!' His words were pleading in her ear. 'Don't be so frightened.'

He set her down on the sofa. As his hands let go of her they were shaking.

'But look, I'm frightened too.' He knelt on the floor before her, reached out his hands, withdrew them. 'See, I'm afraid to touch you.' He mused, his eyes round. 'Of all the ugly things there are, fear is the ugliest. And yet, see, it can be the very beautifulest. That's a strange queer thing.'

The wind blew in and out of the room, bringing the thin, little bitter sweetness of new April at night. The moonlight that came across Mare's shoulders fell full upon his face but hers it left dark, ringed by the aureole of her disordered hair.

'Why do you wear a halo, Love?' He thought about it. 'Because you're an angel, is that why?' The swift, untempered logic of the mad led him to dismay. His hands came flying to hers, to make sure they were of earth; and he touched her breast, her shoulders, and her hair. Peace returned to his eyes as his fingers twined among the strands.

' "Thy hair is as a flock of goats that appear from Gilead . . ." '
He spoke like a man dreaming. ' "Thy temples are like a piece
of pomegranate within thy locks." '

Mare never knew that he could not see her for the moon-
light.   5

'Do you remember, Love?'

She dared not shake her head under his hand. 'Yeh, I
reckon,' she temporized.

'You remember how I sat at your feet, long ago, like this, and
made up a song? And all the poets in all the world have never   10
made one to touch it, have they, Love?'

'Ugh-ugh—never.'

' "How beautiful are thy feet with shoes . . . " Remember?'

'Oh, my God, what's he sayin' now?' she wailed to herself.

' *"How beautiful are thy feet with shoes, O prince's daughter!*   15
   the joints of thy thighs are like jewels, the work of the
   hands of a cunning workman.
   "Thy navel is like a round goblet, which wanteth not liquor;
      thy belly is like a heap of wheat set about with lilies.
   "Thy two breasts are like two young roes that are twins." '   20

Mare had not been to church since she was a little girl,
when her mother's black dress wore out. 'No, no!' she wailed
under her breath. 'You're awful to say such awful things.' She
might have shouted it; nothing could have shaken the man now,
rapt in the immortal, passionate periods of Solomon's Song.   25

' *". . . now also thy breast shall be as clusters of the vine, and the*
   smell of thy nose like apples." '

Hotness touched Mare's face for the first time. 'Aw, no,
don't talk so!'

' *"And the roof of thy mouth like the best wine for my belovéd*   30
   . . . causing the lips of them that are asleep to speak." '

He had ended. His expression changed. Ecstasy gave place
to anger, love to hate. And Mare felt the change in the weight
of the fingers in her hair.

'What do you mean, I mustn't say it like that?' But it was   35
not to her his fury spoke, for he answered himself straightway.

'Like poetry, Mr. Jewett; I won't have blasphemy around my school.'

'Poetry! My God! if that isn't poetry—if that isn't music—' . . . 'It's Bible, Jewett. What you're paid to teach here is *litera-* *ture.'* 5

'Doctor Ryeworth, you're the blasphemer and you're an ig- norant man.' . . . 'And your Principal. And I won't have you go- ing around reading sacred allegory like earthly love.'

'Ryeworth, you're an old man, a dull man, a dirty man, and you'd be better dead.' 10

Jewett's hands had slid down from Mare's head. 'Then I went to put my fingers around his throat, so. But my stomach turned, and I didn't do it. I went to my room. I laughed all the way to my room. I sat in my room at my table and I laughed. I laughed all afternoon and long after dark came. And, then, 15 about ten, somebody came and stood beside me in my room.'

' "Wherefore dost thou laugh, son?"

'Then I knew who He was, He was Christ.

' "I was laughing about that dirty, ignorant, crazy old fool, Lord." 20

' "Wherefore dost thou laugh?"

'I didn't laugh any more. He didn't say any more. I kneeled down, bowed my head.

' "Thy will be done! Where is he, Lord?"

' "Over at the girls' dormitory, waiting for Blossom Sinck- 25 ley."

'Brassy Blossom, dirty Blossom . . .'

It had come so suddenly it was nearly too late. Mare tore at his hands with hers, tried with all her strength to pull her neck away. 30

'Filthy Blossom! and him an old filthy man, Blossom! and you'll find him in Hell when you reach there, Blossom . . .'

It was more the nearness of his face than the hurt of his hands that gave her power of fright to choke out three words.

'*I—ain't—Blossom!'* 35

Light ran in crooked veins. Through the veins she saw his face bewildered. His hands loosened. One fell down and hung;

the other he lifted and put over his eyes, took it away again
and looked at her.

'Amarantha!' His remorse was fearful to see. 'What have I
done!' His hands returned to hover over the hurts, ravening
with pity, grief and tenderness. Tears fell down his cheeks. 5
And with that, dammed desire broke its dam.

'Amarantha, my love, my dove, my beautiful love—'

*'And I ain't Amarantha neither, I'm Mary! Mary, that's my
name!'*

She had no notion what she had done. He was like a crystal 10
crucible that a chemist watches, changing hue in a wink with
one adeptly added drop; but hers was not the chemist's eye.
All she knew was that she felt light and free of him; all she
could see of his face as he stood away above the moonlight
were the whites of his eyes.   15

'Mary!' he muttered. A slight paroxysm shook his frame. So
in the transparent crucible desire changed its hue. He retreated
farther, stood in the dark by some tall piece of furniture. And
still she could see the whites of his eyes.

'Mary! Mary Adorable!' A wonder was in him. 'Mother of 20
God!'

Mare held her breath. She eyed the door, but it was too far.
And already he came back to go on his knees before her, his
shoulders so bowed and his face so lifted that it must have
cracked his neck, she thought; all she could see on the face was 25
pain.

'Mary Mother, I'm sick to my death. I'm so tired.'

She had seen a dog like that, one she had loosed from a trap
after it had been there three days, its caught leg half gnawed
free. Something about the eyes.   30

'Mary Mother, take me in your arms . . .'

Once again her muscles tightened. But he made no move.

'. . . and give me sleep.'

No, they were worse than the dog's eyes.

'Sleep, sleep! why won't they let me sleep? Haven't I done 35
it all yet, Mother? Haven't I washed them yet of all their sins?
I've drunk the cup that was given me; is there another? They've

mocked me and reviled me, broken my brow with thorns and my hands with nails, and I've forgiven them, for they knew not what they did. Can't I go to sleep now, Mother?'

Mare could not have said why, but now she was more frightened than she had ever been. Her hands lay heavy on her knees, side by side, and she could not take them away when he bowed his head and rested his face upon them.

After a moment he said one thing more. 'Take me down gently when you take me from the Tree.'

Gradually the weight of his body came against her shins, and he slept.

The moon streak that entered by the eastern window crept north across the floor, thinner and thinner; the one that fell through the southern doorway traveled east and grew fat. For a while Mare's feet pained her terribly and her legs too. She dared not move them, though, and by and by they did not hurt so much.

A dozen times, moving her head slowly on her neck, she canvassed the shadows of the room for a weapon. Each time her eyes came back to a heavy earthenware pitcher on a stand some feet to the left of the sofa. It would have had flowers in it when Wyker's wife was alive; probably it had not been moved from its dust-ring since she died. It would be a long grab, perhaps too long; still it might be done if she had her hands.

To get her hands from under the sleeper's head was the task she set herself. She pulled first one, then the other, infinitesimally. She waited. Again she tugged a very, very little. The order of his breathing was not disturbed. But at the third trial he stirred.

'Gently! gently!' His own muttering waked him more. With some drowsy instinct of possession he threw one hand across her wrists, pinning them together between thumb and fingers. She kept dead quiet, shut her eyes, lengthened her breathing, as if she too slept.

There came a time when what was pretense grew a peril; strange as it was, she had to fight to keep her eyes open. She never knew whether or not she really napped. But something

changed in the air, and she was wide awake again. The moonlight was fading on the doorsill, and the light that runs before
dawn waxed in the window behind her head.

And then she heard a voice in the distance, lifted in maun-
dering song. It was old man Wyker coming home after a night,   5
and it was plain he had had some whiskey.

Now a new terror laid hold of Mare.

'Shut up, you fool you!' she wanted to shout. 'Come quiet,
quiet!' She might have chanced it now to throw the sleeper
away from her and scramble and run, had his powers of   10
strength and quickness not taken her simple imagination utterly
in thrall.

Happily the singing stopped. What had occurred was that
the farmer had espied the open door and, even befuddled as
he was, wanted to know more about it quietly. He was so quiet   15
that Mare began to fear he had gone away. He had the squir-
rel-hunter's foot, and the first she knew of him was when she
looked and saw his head in the doorway, his hard, soiled,
whiskery face half up-side-down with craning.

He had been to the town. Between drinks he had wandered   20
in and out of the night's excitement; had even gone a short distance with one search party himself. Now he took in the situation in the room. He used his forefinger. First he held it to his
lips. Next he pointed it with a jabbing motion at the sleeper.
Then he tapped his own forehead and described wheels.   25
Lastly, with his whole hand, he made pushing gestures, for
Mare to wait. Then he vanished as silently as he had appeared.

The minutes dragged. The light in the east strengthened and
turned rosy. Once she thought she heard a board creaking in
another part of the house, and looked down sharply to see if   30
the loony stirred. All she could see of his face was a temple
with freckles on it and the sharp ridge of a cheekbone, but even
from so little she knew how deeply and peacefully he slept.
The door darkened. Wyker was there again. In one hand he
carried something heavy; with the other he beckoned.   35

'Come jumpin'!' he said out loud.

Mare went jumping, but her cramped legs threw her down
halfway to the sill; the rest of the distance she rolled and

crawled. Just as she tumbled through the door it seemed as if the world had come to an end above her; two barrels of a shotgun discharged into a room make a noise. Afterwards all she could hear in there was something twisting and bumping on the floorboards. She got up and ran. 5

Mare's mother had gone to pieces; neighbor women put her to bed when Mare came home. They wanted to put Mare to bed, but she would not let them. She sat on the edge of her bed in her lean-to bedroom off the kitchen, just as she was, her hair down all over her shoulders and her shoes on, and stared away 10 from them, at a place in the wallpaper.

'Yeh, I'll go myself. Lea' me be!'

The women exchanged quick glances, thinned their lips, and left her be. 'God knows,' was all they would answer to the questionings of those that had not gone in, 'but she's gettin' 15 herself to bed.'

When the doctor came though he found her sitting just as she had been, still dressed, her hair down on her shoulders and her shoes on.

'What d' y' want?' she muttered and stared at the place in 20 the wallpaper.

How could Doc Paradise say, when he did not know himself?

'I didn't know if you might be—might be feeling very smart, Mary.' 25

'I'm all right. Lea' me be.'

It was a heavy responsibility. Doc shouldered it. 'No, it's all right,' he said to the men in the road. Ruby Herter stood a little apart, chewing sullenly and looking another way. Doc raised his voice to make certain it carried. 'Nope, nothing.' 30

Ruby's ears got red, and he clamped his jaws. He knew he ought to go in and see Mare, but he was not going to do it while everybody hung around waiting to see if he would. A mule tied near him reached out and mouthed his sleeve in idle innocence; he wheeled and banged a fist against the side of 35 the animal's head.

'Well, what d' y' aim to do 'bout it?' he challenged its owner.

He looked at the sun then. It was ten in the morning. 'Hell, I got work!' he flared, and set off down the road for home. Doc looked at Judge North, and the Judge started after Ruby. But Ruby shook his head angrily. 'Lea' me be!' He went on, and the Judge came back.   5

It got to be eleven and then noon. People began to say, 'Like enough she'd be as thankful if the whole neighborhood wasn't camped here.' But none went away.

As a matter of fact they were no bother to the girl. She never saw them. The only move she made was to bend her   10
ankles over and rest her feet on edge; her shoes hurt terribly and her feet knew it, though she did not. She sat all the while staring at that one figure in the wallpaper, and she never saw the figure.

Strange as the night had been, this day was stranger. Fright   15
and physical pain are perishable things once they are gone. But while pain merely dulls and telescopes in memory and remains diluted pain, terror looked back upon has nothing of terror left. A gambling chance taken, at no matter what odds, and won was a sure thing since the world's beginning; perils   20
come through safely were never perilous. But what fright does do in retrospect is this—it heightens each sensuous recollection, like a hard, clear lacquer laid on wood, bringing out the color and grain of it vividly.

Last night Mare had lain stupid with fear on groundpine be-   25
neath a bush, loud foot-falls and light whispers confused in her ear. Only now, in her room, did she smell the groundpine.

Only now did the conscious part of her brain begin to make words of the whispering.

'*Amarantha*,' she remembered, '*Amarantha sweet and fair.*'   30
That was as far as she could go for the moment, except that the rhyme with 'fair' was 'hair.' But then a puzzle, held in abeyance, brought other words. She wondered what 'ravel Ed' could mean. '*Most excellently ravelléd.*' It was left to her mother to bring the end.   35

They gave up trying to keep her mother out at last. The poor woman's prostration took the form of fussiness.

'Good gracious, daughter, you look a sight. Them new shoes, half ruined; ain't your feet *dead?* And look at your hair, all tangled like a wild one!'

She got a comb.

"Be quiet, daughter; what's ailin' you? Don't shake your head!"

' *"But shake your head and scatter day."* '

'What you say, Amarantha?' Mrs. Doggett held an ear down. 'Go away! Lea' me be!'

Her mother was hurt and left. And Mare ran, as she stared at the wallpaper.

'*Christ, that my love were in my arms . . .*'

Mare ran. She ran through a wind white with moonlight and wet with 'the small rain.' And the wind she ran through, it ran through her, and made her shiver as she ran. And the man beside her leaped high over the waves of the dead grasses and gathered the wind in his arms, and her hair was heavy and his was tossing, and a little fox ran before them across the top of the world. And the world spread down around in waves of black and silver, more immense than she had ever known the world could be, and more beautiful.

'*God Almighty beautiful, to take your breath away!*'

Mare wondered, and she was not used to wondering. 'Is it only crazy folks ever run like that and talk that way?'

She no longer ran; she walked; for her breath was gone. And there was some other reason, some other reason. Oh, yes, it was because her feet were hurting her. So, at last, and roundabout, her shoes had made contact with her brain.

Bending over the side of her bed, she loosened one of them mechanically. She pulled it half off. But then she looked down at it sharply, and pulled it on again.

'*How beautiful . . .*'

Color overspread her face in a low wave.

'*How beautiful are thy feet with shoes . . .*'

'Is it only crazy folks ever say such things?'

'*O prince's daughter!*'

'Or call you that?'

By and by there was a knock at the door. It opened, and
Ruby Herter came in.

'Hello, Mare old girl!' His face was red. He scowled and
kicked at the floor. 'I'd 'a' been over sooner, except we got a
mule down sick.' He looked at his dumb betrothed. 'Come on, 5
cheer up, forget it! He won't scare you no more, not that boy,
not what's left o' him. What you lookin' at, sourface? Ain't you
glad to see me?'

Mare quit looking at the wallpaper and looked at the floor.
'Yeh,' she said.   10

'That's more like it, babe.' He came and sat beside her;
reached down behind her and gave her a spank. 'Come on, give
us a kiss, babe!' He wiped his mouth on his jumper sleeve, a
good farmer's sleeve, spotted with milking. He put his hands
on her; he was used to handling animals. 'Hey, you, warm up 15
a little; reckon I'm goin' to do all the lovin'?'

'Ruby, lea' me be!'

'What!'

She was up, twisting. He was up, purple.

'What's ailin' of you, Mare? What you bawlin' about?'   20
'Nothin'—only go 'way!'

She pushed him to the door and through it with all her
strength, and closed it in his face, and stood with her weight
against it, crying, 'Go 'way! Go 'way! Lea' me be!'

Vocabulary

1. Describe the emotion of Mare's (p. 202, l. 24) which the
author says is "purely sensuous." Remember that she sets off in
a "docile beeline through the cow-yard" and is herself "docile"
(p. 202, l. 17). Also the author says (p. 212, l. 20) that she walks
in the path of Jewett with "docility," another form of the word.

2. Ruby Herter "took out youth in ponderous gestures of
masterfulness" (p. 203, ll. 12-13). Describe this phrase some other
way.

3. What happens when "A slow warmth pervades the girl"
(p. 203, l. 30)?

4. If Mare had shaken her head with "vehemence" (p. 203, l.
37), what would she have been doing?

5. What is indicated when the author says that the lunatic "chided" Mare (p. 211, l. 11)?

6. Jewett's strength is "magnified" (to an amazing degree) by his "ecstasy" (p. 213, ll. 26-27). This is not a simple example of joy or bliss. The author is being quite exact, as he is later (p. 216, ll. 32-33) when he says Jewett's "Ecstasy gave place to anger, love to hate."

Questions and Suggestions for Reading

EVALUATION

"How Beautiful with Shoes" is a simple story of a farm girl, Mare, who is betrothed to a farm boy, Ruby. Mare meets a madman who says beautiful things to her, and for the first time in her life she hears words which were written simply because they describe the beauty of the surrounding world and suggest beautiful thoughts. Her initial reaction reflects her present life: she thinks that a man who recites poetry is mad. She reacts as an animal does—naturally, directly, intuitively.

Early in the story Steele tells us that the girl has sensuous emotions which are evoked by clods of earth "breaking softly between her toes," and by the rude embrace of Ruby. But Steele also tells us that the response Ruby arouses is "formless, nameless, almost impersonal." The girl does not recognize the emotion. However, the reader realizes later that this response is the same one which later was stimulated in her by sound combined with imagination.

The structure of the story, like the character of Mare, is uncomplicated. First we are introduced to Mare and Ruby and hear the voice of her mother. Next we meet the madman who pursues Mare, is captured, escapes, returns to woo the girl, and is finally recaptured and killed. Up to this point, the story is presented as one long scene, a scene which seems to flow like an uninterrupted memory of a day and a night which have passed. However, there is more to the story. There is a second scene in which we see the result of the experience on Mare. This scene has been set apart because it is the effect and not the events themselves which are so important.

Although this story has a simple structure, there is a great deal of action. The heroine of this story, like the hero of "To Build a Fire," is not capable of much intellectual action, so physical action dominates. Mare is in the milking shed when the story opens; she moves along the path, hears hoofbeats on the bridge, goes across the farm, meets Ruby, and embraces him. Then, while he is joining a search party, she walks to her home, goes to find Ruby—after meeting, recognizing, and escaping the madman—finds herself succumbing to the latter's salving gestures after he returns to her; and, finally, crawls away from the lunatic when she is rescued. These are all physical actions. Even the recognition scene—when Mare realizes who the madman is—calls up an instinctive response. Jewett himself is incapable of clear thinking, and no one can suppose that Ruby or Mare's mother and neighbors can understand what happens to her. Except for the small glimmering of understanding within Mare at the very last, mental action is almost completely absent. Once again, physical action predominates.

This story has little dialogue, but what it does have suggests much about the characters speaking the lines and about those characters spoken of. For example, when Jewett says, "Amarantha! Amarantha in Carolina! That makes me happy!" one knows immediately that the man is not mentally responsible, since he is, after all, answering the simple question: "Who are you and what d'y' want?" Mare is practically monosyllabic except when she says near the end of the story: "It's a pretty—I mean—a beautiful view down that-a-way." Her dialogue, consisting of words of one syllable, indicates that she herself is simple.

In this story suspense is measured in small amounts. One wonders whether Mare will be strangled as the girl Blossom was, whether Mare will call to the search party when they are nearby, whether Jewett will wake up before old man Wyker returns; but the element of suspense is never of primary importance—nor is motivation. The reasons for Jewett's and Mare's actions are always clear. He is an escapee, and he has committed several murders. Because he is mad, he is not responsible for his actions. Mare acts as she does simply to try to save her own life.

There are two further considerations—the conflict and the way in which the story is told. First let us turn to conflict. One may wonder why such a story is interesting and gripping. The structure is neither complicated nor contrived, the plot is straightforward, the ending is curious, and the dialogue is simple. What, then, makes the story so interesting? Surely, one says, it is the conflict, but what is this unstated conflict? Is it simply the conflict of a girl and a madman? Is it the conflict of a group of people against an escaped murderer? Or is it perhaps the conflict of an unawakened girl, living in a callous world, who is shown a world of tenderness, gentleness, and loveliness, even though she is shown this world by a lunatic? Why does she cry at the end of the story? Why does she ask, "Is it only crazy folks ever say such things? . . . Or call you that?" Here, then, is the conflict: a sympathetic, ignorant girl who lives in a rude world is thrown violently into contact with another pleasanter, kinder world by a madman, a man who himself could not cope with a narrow world of intolerance and ugliness. Mare sees that there are two worlds—one of hard, uncouth men and another of madmen who gently speak of loveliness. Can she choose between the two? Must there be a separation?

At the end of the story, Steele leaves us with a sense of frustration and indecision. We hear the girl's lament and understand her newly awakened state perhaps better than she does. We feel pity for her because her present situation is intolerable. It seems no one in her world knows what she knows. The reader can only hope that she will either leave her old world or forget what has been awakened in her.

Finally, one should notice the style—the language Steele uses. The story is comparatively long even though the dialogue is scant. It is the description that sets this story apart. In the vocabulary section of this exercise, attention was drawn to Steele's description of Ruby, poetic in itself. There are many such touches of beautifully moving and perceptive description. As Mare runs, attempting to elude Jewett, the author describes Jewett as "making a race of it, flailing the wind with his long arms for joy of play in the cloud of spring, throwing his knees high, leaping the moon-blue waves of brown grass, shaking his bright hair . . . ." Again, when Mare tells him she is not Blossom, Jewett's response is merely indicated as the author says, "Light ran in crooked veins." And, as Mare sits with Jewett's head cradled in her hands, the author describes the scene: "The moon streak that entered by the eastern window crept north across the floor, thinner and thinner; the one that fell through the southern doorway traveled east and grew fat." When he is not quoting poetry directly, Steele creates his own.

Shirley Jackson

THE LOTTERY

The morning of June 27th was clear and sunny, with the fresh warmth of a full-summer day; the flowers were blossoming profusely and the grass was richly green. The people of the village began to gather in the square, between the post office and the bank, around ten o'clock; in some towns there were so many people that the lottery took two days and had to be started on June 26th, but in this village, where there were only about three hundred people, the whole lottery took less than two hours, so it could begin at ten o'clock in the morning and still be through in time to allow the villagers to get home for noon dinner.

The children assembled first, of course. School was recently over for the summer, and the feeling of liberty sat uneasily on most of them; they tended to gather together quietly for a while before they broke into boisterous play, and their talk was still of the classroom and the teacher, of books and reprimands. Bobby Martin had already stuffed his pockets full of stones, and the other boys soon followed his example, selecting the smoothest and roundest stones; Bobby and Harry Jones and Dickie Delacroix—the villagers pronounced this name "Dellacroy"—eventually made a great pile of stones in one corner of the square and guarded it against the raids of the other boys. The girls stood aside, talking among themselves, looking over their shoulders at the boys, and the very small children rolled in the dust or clung to the hands of their older brothers or sisters.

Soon the men began to gather, surveying their own children, speaking of planting and rain, tractors and taxes. They stood together, away from the pile of stones in the corner, and their jokes were quiet and they smiled rather than laughed. The women, wearing faded house dresses and sweaters, came shortly after their menfolk. They greeted one another and exchanged bits of gossip as they went to join their husbands. Soon the women, standing by their husbands, began to call to their children, and the children came reluctantly, having to be called four or five times. Bobby Martin ducked under his mother's grasping hand and ran, laughing, back to the pile of stones. His father spoke up sharply, and Bobby came quickly and took his place between his father and his oldest brother.

The lottery was conducted—as were the square dances, the teen-age club, the Halloween program—by Mr. Summers, who had time and energy to devote to civic activities. He was a round-faced, jovial man and he ran the coal business, and people were sorry for him, because he had no children and his wife was a scold. When he arrived in the square, carrying the black wooden box, there was a murmur of conversation among the villagers, and he waved and called, "Little late today, folks." The postmaster, Mr. Graves, followed him, carrying a three-legged stool, and the stool was put in the center of the square and Mr. Summers set the black box down on it. The villagers kept their distance, leaving a space between themselves and the stool, and when Mr. Summers said, "Some of you fellows want to give me a hand?" there was a hesitation before two men, Mr. Martin and his oldest son, Baxter, came forward to hold the box steady on the stool while Mr. Summers stirred up the papers inside it.

The original paraphernalia for the lottery had been lost long ago, and the black box now resting on the stool had been put into use even before Old Man Warner, the oldest man in town, was born. Mr. Summers spoke frequently to the villagers about making a new box, but no one liked to upset even as much tradition as was represented by the black box. There was a story that the present box had been made with some pieces of the box that had preceded it, the one that had been con-

structed when the first people settled down to make a village
here. Every year, after the lottery, Mr. Summers began talking
again about a new box, but every year the subject was allowed
to fade off without anything's being done. The black box grew
shabbier each year; by now it was no longer completely black   5
but splintered badly along one side to show the original wood
color, and in some places faded or stained.

Mr. Martin and his oldest son, Baxter, held the black box
securely on the stool until Mr. Summers had stirred the papers
thoroughly with his hand. Because so much of the ritual had   10
been forgotten or discarded, Mr. Summers had been successful
in having slips of papers substituted for the chips of wood that
had been used for generations. Chips of wood, Mr. Summers
had argued, had been all very well when the village was tiny,
but now that the population was more than three hundred and   15
likely to keep on growing, it was necessary to use something
that would fit more easily into the black box. The night before
the lottery, Mr. Summers and Mr. Graves made up the slips of
paper and put them in the box, and it was then taken to the
safe of Mr. Summers' coal company and locked up until Mr.   20
Summers was ready to take it to the square next morning. The
rest of the year, the box was put away, sometimes one place,
sometimes another; it had spent one year in Mr. Graves's barn
and another year underfoot in the post office, and sometimes it
was set on a shelf in the Martin grocery and left there.   25

There was a great deal of fussing to be done before Mr. Summers declared the lottery open. There were the lists to make
up—of heads of families, heads of households in each family,
members of each household in each family. There was the
proper swearing-in of Mr. Summers by the postmaster, as the   30
official of the lottery; at one time, some people remembered,
there had been a recital of some sort, performed by the official
of the lottery, a perfunctory, tuneless chant that had been rattled off duly each year; some people believed that the official
of the lottery used to stand just so when he said or sang it,   35
others believed that he was supposed to walk among the people, but years and years ago this part of the ritual had been

allowed to lapse. There had been, also, a ritual salute, which the official of the lottery had had to use in addressing each person who came up to draw from the box, but this also had changed with time, until now it was felt necessary only for the official to speak to each person approaching. Mr. Summers was very good at all this; in his clean white shirt and blue jeans, with one hand resting carelessly on the black box, he seemed very proper and important as he talked interminably to Mr. Graves and the Martins.

Just as Mr. Summers finally left off talking and turned to the assembled villagers, Mrs. Hutchinson came hurriedly along the path to the square, her sweater thrown over her shoulders, and slid into place in the back of the crowd. "Clean forgot what day it was," she said to Mrs. Delacroix, who stood next to her, and they both laughed softly. "Thought my old man was out back stacking wood," Mrs. Hutchinson went on, "and then I looked out the window and the kids were gone, and then I remembered it was the twenty-seventh and came a-running." She dried her hands on her apron, and Mrs. Delacroix said, "You're in time, though. They're still talking away up there."

Mrs. Hutchinson craned her neck to see through the crowd and found her husband and children standing near the front. She tapped Mrs. Delacroix on the arm as a farewell and began to make her way through the crowd. The people separated good-humoredly to let her through; two or three people said, in voices just loud enough to be heard across the crowd, "Here comes your Missus, Hutchinson," and "Bill, she made it after all." Mrs. Hutchinson reached her husband, and Mr. Summers, who had been waiting, said cheerfully, "Thought we were going to have to get on without you, Tessie." Mrs. Hutchinson said, grinning, "Wouldn't have me leave m'dishes in the sink, now, would you, Joe?," and soft laughter ran through the crowd as the people stirred back into position after Mrs. Hutchinson's arrival.

"Well, now," Mr. Summers said soberly, "guess we better get started, get this over with, so's we can go back to work. Anybody ain't here?"

"Dunbar," several people said. "Dunbar, Dunbar."

Mr. Summers consulted his list. "Clyde Dunbar," he said. "That's right. He's broke his leg, hasn't he? Who's drawing for him?"

"Me, I guess," a woman said, and Mr. Summers turned to   5
look at her. "Wife draws for her husband," Mr. Summers said. "Don't you have a grown boy to do it for you, Janey?" Although Mr. Summers and everyone else in the village knew the answer perfectly well, it was the business of the official of the lottery to ask such questions formally. Mr. Summers waited with an   10
expression of polite interest while Mrs. Dunbar answered.

"Horace's not but sixteen yet," Mrs. Dunbar said regretfully. "Guess I gotta fill in for the old man this year."

"Right," Mr. Summers said. He made a note on the list he was holding. Then he asked, "Watson boy drawing this year?"   15

A tall boy in the crowd raised his hand. "Here," he said. "I'm drawing for m'mother and me." He blinked his eyes nervously and ducked his head as several voices in the crowd said things like "Good fellow, Jack," and "Glad to see your mother's got a man to do it."   20

"Well," Mr. Summers said, "guess that's everyone. Old Man Warner make it?"

"Here," a voice said, and Mr. Summers nodded.

A sudden hush fell on the crowd as Mr. Summers cleared his throat and looked at the list. "All ready?" he called. "Now,   25
I'll read the names—heads of families first—and the men come up and take a paper out of the box. Keep the paper folded in your hand without looking at it until everyone has had a turn. Everything clear?"

The people had done it so many times that they only half   30
listened to the directions; most of them were quiet, wetting their lips, not looking around. Then Mr. Summers raised one hand high and said, "Adams." A man disengaged himself from the crowd and came forward. "Hi, Steve," Mr. Summers said, and Mr. Adams said, "Hi, Joe." They grinned at one another   35
humorlessly and nervously. Then Mr. Adams reached into the black box and took out a folded paper. He held it firmly by

one corner as he turned and went hastily back to his place in the crowd, where he stood a little apart from his family, not looking down at his hand.

"Allen," Mr. Summers said. "Andrews. . . . Bentham."

"Seems like there's no time at all between lotteries any   5
more," Mrs. Delacroix said to Mrs. Graves in the back row. "Seems like we got through with the last one only last week."

"Time sure goes fast," Mrs. Graves said.

"Clark. . . . Delacroix."

"There goes my old man," Mrs. Delacroix said. She held her   10
breath while her husband went forward.

"Dunbar," Mr. Summers said, and Mrs. Dunbar went steadily to the box while one of the women said, "Go on, Janey," and another said, "There she goes."

"We're next," Mrs. Graves said. She watched while Mr.   15
Graves came around from the side of the box, greeted Mr. Summers gravely, and selected a slip of paper from the box. By now, all through the crowd there were men holding the small folded papers in their large hands, turning them over over nervously. Mrs. Dunbar and her two sons stood together,   20
Mrs. Dunbar holding the slip of paper.

"Harburt. . . . Hutchinson."

"Get up there, Bill," Mrs. Hutchinson said, and the people near her laughed.

"Jones."   25

"They do say," Mr. Adams said to Old Man Warner, who stood next to him, "that over in the north village they're talking of giving up the lottery."

Old Man Warner snorted. "Pack of crazy fools," he said. "Listening to the young folks, nothing's good enough for *them*.   30
Next thing you know, they'll be wanting to go back to living in caves, nobody work any more, live *that* way for a while. Used to be a saying about 'Lottery in June, corn be heavy soon.' First thing you know, we'd all be eating stewed chickweed and acorns. There's *always* been a lottery," he added petulantly.   35
"Bad enough to see young Joe Summers up there joking with everybody."

"Some places have already quit lotteries," Mrs. Adams said.

"Nothing but trouble in *that*," Old Man Warner said stoutly. "Pack of young fools."

"Martin." And Bobby Martin watched his father go forward. "Overdyke. . . . Percy." 5

"I wish they'd hurry," Mrs. Dunbar said to her older son. "I wish they'd hurry."

"They're almost through," her son said.

"You get ready to run tell Dad," Mrs. Dunbar said.

Mr. Summers called his own name and then stepped forward 10 precisely and selected a slip from the box. Then he called, "Warner."

"Seventy-seventh year I been in the lottery," Old Man Warner said as he went through the crowd. "Seventy-seventh time." 15

"Watson." The tall boy came awkwardly through the crowd. Someone said, "Don't be nervous, Jack," and Mr. Summers said, "Take your time, son."

"Zanini."

After that, there was a long pause, a breathless pause, until 20 Mr. Summers, holding his slip of paper in the air, said, "All right, fellows." For a minute, no one moved, and then all the slips of paper were opened. Suddenly, all women began to speak at once, saying, "Who is it?," "Who's got it?," "Is it the Dunbars?," "Is it the Watsons?" Then the voices began to say, 25 "It's Hutchinson. It's Bill." "Bill Hutchinson got it."

"Go tell your father," Mrs. Dunbar said to her older son.

People began to look around to see the Hutchinsons. Bill Hutchinson was standing quiet, staring down at the paper in his hand. Suddenly, Tessie Hutchinson shouted to Mr. Summers, 30 "You didn't give him time enough to take any paper he wanted. I saw you. It wasn't fair."

"Be a good sport, Tessie," Mrs. Delacroix called, and Mrs. Graves said, "All of us took the same chance."

"Shut up, Tessie," Bill Hutchinson said. 35

"Well, everyone," Mr. Summers said, "that was done pretty fast, and now we've got to be hurrying a little more to get done in time." He consulted his next list. "Bill," he said, "you draw for the Hutchinson family. You got any other households in the Hutchinsons?"

"There's Don and Eva," Mrs. Hutchinson yelled. "Make *them* take their chance!"

"Daughters draw with their husbands' families, Tessie," Mr. Summers said gently. "You know that as well as anyone else."

"It wasn't *fair*," Tessie said.

"I guess not, Joe," Bill Hutchinson said regretfully. "My daughter draws with her husband's family, that's only fair. And I've got no other family except the kids."

"Then as far as drawing for families is concerned, it's you," Mr. Summers said in explanation, "and as far as drawing for households is concerned, that's you, too. Right?"

"Right," Bill Hutchinson said.

"How many kids, Bill?" Mr. Summers asked formally.

"Three," Bill Hutchinson said. "There's Bill, Jr., and Nancy, and little Dave. And Tessie and me."

"All right, then," Mr. Summers said. "Harry, you got their tickets back?"

Mr. Graves nodded and held up the slips of paper. "Put them in the box, then," Mr. Summers directed. "Take Bill's and put it in."

"I think we ought to start over," Mrs. Hutchinson said, as quietly as she could. "I tell you it wasn't *fair*. You didn't give him time enough to choose. *Every*body saw that."

Mr. Graves had selected the five slips and put them in the box, and he dropped all the papers but those onto the ground, where the breeze caught them and lifted them off.

"Listen, everybody," Mrs. Hutchinson was saying to the people around her.

"Ready, Bill?" Mr. Summers asked, and Bill Hutchinson, with one quick glance around at his wife and children, nodded.

"Remember," Mr. Summers said, "take the slips and keep them folded until each person has taken one. Harry, you help little Dave." Mr. Graves took the hand of the little boy, who came willingly with him up to the box. "Take a paper out of

the box, Davy," Mr. Summers said. Davy put his hand into the box and laughed. "Take just *one* paper," Mr. Summers said. "Harry, you hold it for him." Mr. Graves took the child's hand and removed the folded paper from the tight fist and held it while little Dave stood next to him and looked up at him won- 5
deringly.

"Nancy next," Mr. Summers said. Nancy was twelve, and her school friends breathed heavily as she went forward, switching her skirt, and took a slip daintly from the box. "Bill, Jr.," Mr. Summers said, and Billy, his face red and his feet over-large, 10
nearly knocked the box over as he got a paper out. "Tessie," Mr. Summers said. She hesitated for a minute, looking around defiantly, and then set her lips and went up to the box. She snatched a paper out and held it behind her.

"Bill," Mr. Summers said, and Bill Hutchinson reached into 15
the box and felt around, bringing his hand out at last with the slip of paper in it.

The crowd was quiet. A girl whispered, "I hope it's not Nancy," and the sound of the whisper reached the edges of the crowd. 20

"It's not the way it used to be," Old Man Warner said clearly. "People ain't the way they used to be."

"All right," Mr. Summers said. "Open the papers. Harry, you open little Dave's."

Mr. Graves opened the slip of paper and there was a general 25
sigh through the crowd as he held it up and everyone could see that it was blank. Nancy and Bill, Jr., opened theirs at the same time, and both beamed and laughed, turning around to the crowd and holding their slips of paper above their heads.

"Tessie," Mr. Summers said. There was a pause, and then 30
Mr. Summers looked at Bill Hutchinson, and Bill unfolded his paper and showed it. It was blank.

"It's Tessie," Mr. Summers said, and his voice was hushed. "Show us her paper, Bill."

Bill Hutchinson went over to his wife and forced the slip of 35
paper out of her hand. It had a black spot on it, the black spot Mr. Summers had made the night before with the heavy pen-

cil in the coal-company office. Bill Hutchinson held it up, and there was a stir in the crowd.

"All right, folks," Mr. Summers said, "Let's finish quickly."

Although the villagers had forgotten the ritual and lost the original black box, they still remembered to use stones. The pile of stones the boys had made earlier was ready; there were stones on the ground with the blowing scraps of paper that had come out of the box. Mrs. Delacroix selected a stone so large she had to pick it up with both hands and turned to Mrs. Dunbar. "Come on," she said. "Hurry up."

Mrs. Dunbar had small stones in both hands, and she said, gasping for breath, "I can't run at all. You'll have to go ahead and I'll catch up with you."

The children had stones already, and someone gave little Davy Hutchinson a few pebbles.

Tessie Hutchinson was in the center of a cleared space by now, and she held her hands out desperately as the villagers moved in on her. "It isn't fair," she said. A stone hit her on the side of the head.

Old Man Warner was saying, "Come on, come on, everyone." Steve Adams was in the front of the crowd of villagers, with Mrs. Graves beside him.

"It isn't fair, it isn't right," Mrs. Hutchinson screamed, and then they were upon her.

William Faulkner

A ROSE FOR EMILY

When Miss Emily Grierson died, our whole town went to her funeral: the men through a sort of respectful affection for a fallen monument, the women mostly out of curiosity to see the inside of her house, which no one save an old man-servant—a combined gardener and cook—had seen in at least ten years.

It was a big, squarish frame house that had once been white, decorated with cupolas and spires and scrolled balconies in the heavily lightsome style of the Seventies, set on what had once been our most select street. But garages and cotton gins had encroached and obliterated even the august names of that neighborhood; only Miss Emily's house was left, lifting its stubborn and coquettish decay above the cotton wagons and the gasoline pumps—an eyesore among eyesores. And now Miss Emily had gone to join the representatives of those august names where they lay in the cedar-bemused cemetery among the ranked and anonymous graves of Union and Confederate soldiers who fell at the battle of Jefferson.

Alive, Miss Emily had been a tradition, a duty, and a care; a sort of hereditary obligation upon the town, dating from that day in 1894 when Colonel Sartoris, the mayor—he who fathered the edict that no Negro woman should appear on the streets without an apron—remitted her taxes, the dispensation dating from the death of her father on into perpetuity. Not that Miss Emily would have accepted charity. Colonel Sartoris invented an involved tale to the effect that Miss Emily's father had loaned money to the town, which the town, as a matter of business, preferred this way of repaying. Only a man of Colonel

650
750

750-050-008

sum 150

1story

40,40,20

hunts 2n?

Sartoris' generation and thought could have invented it, and only a woman could have believed it.

When the next generation, with its more modern ideas, became mayors and aldermen, this arrangement created some little dissatisfaction. On the first of the year they mailed her a tax notice. February came, and there was no reply. They wrote her a formal letter, asking her to call at the sheriff's office at her convenience. A week later the mayor wrote her himself, offering to call or to send his car for her, and received in reply a note on paper of an archaic shape, in a thin, flowing calligraphy in faded ink, to the effect that she no longer went out at all. The tax notice was also enclosed, without comment.

They called a special meeting of the Board of Aldermen. A deputation waited upon her, knocked at the door through which no visitor had passed since she ceased giving china-painting lessons eight or ten years earlier. They were admitted by the old Negro into a dim hall from which a stairway mounted into still more shadow. It smelled of dust and disuse—a close, dank smell. The Negro led them into the parlor. It was furnished in heavy, leather-covered furniture. When the Negro opened the blinds of one window, they could see that the leather was cracked; and when they sat down, a faint dust rose sluggishly about their thighs, spinning with slow motes in the single sun-ray. On a tarnished gilt easel before the fireplace stood a crayon portrait of Miss Emily's father.

They rose when she entered—a small, fat woman in black, with a thin gold chain descending to her waist and vanishing into her belt, leaning on an ebony cane with a tarnished gold head. Her skeleton was small and spare; perhaps that was why what would have been merely plumpness in another was obesity in her. She looked bloated, like a body long submerged in motionless water, and of that pallid hue. Her eyes, lost in the fatty ridges of her face, looked like two small pieces of coal pressed into a lump of dough as they moved from one face to another while the visitors stated their errand.

She did not ask them to sit. She just stood in the door and listened quietly until the spokesman came to a stumbling halt.

Then they could hear the invisible watch ticking at the end of the gold chain.

Her voice was dry and cold. "I have no taxes in Jefferson. Colonel Sartoris explained it to me. Perhaps one of you can gain access to the city records and satisfy yourselves."   5

"But we have. We are the city authorities, Miss Emily. Didn't you get a notice from the sheriff, signed by him?"

"I received a paper, yes," Miss Emily said. "Perhaps he considers himself the sheriff . . . I have no taxes in Jefferson."

"But there is nothing on the books to show that, you see. 10 We must go by the—"

"See Colonel Sartoris. I have no taxes in Jefferson."

"But, Miss Emily—"

"See Colonel Sartoris." (Colonel Sartoris had been dead almost ten years.) "I have no taxes in Jefferson. Tobe!" The Ne- 15 gro appeared. "Show these gentlemen out."

II

So she vanquished them, horse and foot, just as she had vanquished their fathers thirty years before about the smell. That 20 was two years after her father's death and a short time after her sweetheart—the one we believed would marry her—had deserted her. After her father's death she went out very little; after her sweetheart went away, people hardly saw her at all. A few of the ladies had the temerity to call, but were not re- 25 ceived, and the only sign of life about the place was the Negro man—a young man then—going in and out with a market basket.

"Just as if a man—any man—could keep a kitchen properly," the ladies said; so they were not surprised when the smell de- 30 veloped. It was another link between the gross, teeming world and the high and mighty Griersons.

A neighbor, a woman, complained to the mayor, Judge Stevens, eighty years old.

"But what will you have me do about it, madam?" he said. 35

"Why, send her word to stop it," the woman said. "Isn't there a law?"

"I'm sure that won't be necessary," Judge Stevens said. "It's probably just a snake or a rat that nigger of hers killed in the yard. I'll speak to him about it."

The next day he received two more complaints, one from a man who came in diffident deprecation. "We really must do something about it, Judge. I'd be the last one in the world to bother Miss Emily, but we've got to do something." That night the Board of Aldermen met—three graybeards and one younger man, a member of the rising generation.

"It's simple enough," he said. "Send her word to have her place cleaned up. Give her a certain time to do it in, and if she don't . . ."

"Dammit, sir," Judge Stevens said, "will you accuse a lady to her face of smelling bad?"

So the next night, after midnight, four men crossed Miss Emily's lawn and slunk about the house like burglars, sniffing along the base of the brickwork and at the cellar openings while one of them performed a regular sowing motion with his hand out of a sack slung from his shoulder. They broke open the cellar door and sprinkled lime there, and in all the outbuildings. As they recrossed the lawn, a window that had been dark was lighted and Miss Emily sat in it, the light behind her, and her upright torso motionless as that of an idol. They crept quietly across the lawn and into the shadow of the locusts that lined the street. After a week or two the smell went away.

That was when people had begun to feel really sorry for her. People in our town, remembering how Old Lady Wyatt, her great-aunt, had gone completely crazy at last, believed that the Griersons held themselves a little too high for what they really were. None of the young men were quite good enough for Miss Emily and such. We had long thought of them as a tableau: Miss Emily a slender figure in white in the background, her father a spraddled silhouette in the foreground, his back to her and clutching a horse-whip, the two of them framed by the back-flung front door. So when she got to be thirty and was still single, we were not pleased exactly, but vindicated; even with insanity in the family she wouldn't have turned down all of her chances if they had really materialized.

When her father died, it got about that the house was all

that was left to her; and in a way, people were glad. At last they could pity Miss Emily. Being left alone, and a pauper, she had become humanized. Now she too would know the old thrill and the old despair of a penny more or less.

The day after his death all the ladies prepared to call at the house and offer condolence and aid, as is our custom. Miss Emily met them at the door, dressed as usual and with no trace of grief on her face. She told them that her father was not dead. She did that for three days, with the ministers calling on her, and the doctors, trying to persuade her to let them dispose of the body. Just as they were about to resort to law and force, she broke down, and they buried her father quickly.

We did not say she was crazy then. We believed she had to do that. We remembered all the young men her father had driven away, and we knew that with nothing left, she would have to cling to that which had robbed her, as people will.

III

She was sick for a long time. When we saw her again, her hair was cut short, making her look like a girl, with a vague resemblance to those angels in colored church windows—sort of tragic and serene.

The town had just let the contracts for paving the sidewalks, and in the summer after her father's death they began the work. The construction company came with niggers and mules and machinery, and a foreman named Homer Barron, a Yankee—a big, dark, ready man, with a big voice and eyes lighter than his face. The little boys would follow in groups to hear him cuss the niggers, and the niggers singing in time to the rise and fall of picks. Pretty soon he knew everybody in town. Whenever you heard a lot of laughing anywhere about the square, Homer Barron would be in the center of the group. Presently we began to see him and Miss Emily on Sunday afternoons driving in the yellow-wheeled buggy and the matched team of bays from the livery stable.

At first we were glad that Miss Emily would have an interest, because the ladies all said, "Of course a Grierson would not think seriously of a Northerner, a day laborer." But there were still others, older people, who said that even grief could not cause a real lady to forget *noblesse oblige*—without calling it *noblesse oblige*. They just said, "Poor Emily. Her kinsfolk should come to her." She had some kin in Alabama; but years ago her father had fallen out with them over the estate of Old Lady Wyatt, the crazy woman, and there was no communication between the two families. They had not even been represented at the funeral.

And as soon as the old people said, "Poor Emily," the whispering began. "Do you suppose it's really so?" they said to one another. "Of course it is. What else could . . . " This behind their hands; rustling of craned silk and satin behind jalousies closed upon the sun of Sunday afternoon as the thin, swift clop-clop-clop of the matched team passed: "Poor Emily."

She carried her head high enough—even when we believed that she was fallen. It was as if she demanded more than ever the recognition of her dignity as the last Grierson; as if it had wanted that touch of earthiness to reaffirm her imperviousness. Like when she bought the rat poison, the arsenic. That was over a year after they had begun to say "Poor Emily," and while the two female cousins were visiting her.

"I want some poison," she said to the druggist. She was over thirty then, still a slight woman, though thinner than usual, with cold, haughty black eyes in a face the flesh of which was strained across the temples and about the eye-sockets as you imagine a lighthouse-keeper's face ought to look. "I want some poison," she said.

"Yes, Miss Emily. What kind? For rats and such? I'd recom—"

"I want the best you have. I don't care what kind."

The druggist named several. "They'll kill anything up to an elephant. But what you want is—"

"Arsenic," Miss Emily said. "Is that a good one?"

"Is . . . arsenic? Yes, ma'am. But what you want—"

"I want arsenic."

The druggist looked down at her. She looked back at him,

erect, her face like a strained flag. "Why, of course," the druggist said. "If that's what you want. But the law requires you
to tell what you are going to use it for."

Miss Emily just stared at him, her head tilted back in order
to look him eye for eye, until he looked away and went and   5
got the arsenic and wrapped it up. The Negro delivery boy
brought her the package; the druggist didn't come back. When
she opened the package at home there was written on the box,
under the skull and bones: "For rats."

IV

So the next day we all said, "She will kill herself"; and we said   10
it would be the best thing. When she had first begun to be seen
with Homer Barron, we had said, "She will marry him." Then
we said, "She will persuade him yet," because Homer himself
had remarked—he liked men, and it was known that he drank
with the younger men in the Elks' Club—that he was not a   15
marrying man. Later we said, "Poor Emily," behind the jalousies
as they passed on Sunday afternoon in the glittering buggy,
Miss Emily with her head high and Homer Barron with his hat
cocked and a cigar in his teeth, reins and whip in a yellow
glove.   20

Then some of the ladies began to say that it was a disgrace
to the town and a bad example to the young people. The men
did not want to interfere, but at last the ladies forced the Bap-
· tist minister—Miss Emily's people were Episcopal—to call upon
her. He would never divulge what happened during that inter-   25
view, but he refused to go back again. The next Sunday they
again drove about the streets, and the following day the minister's wife wrote to Miss Emily's relations in Alabama.

So she had blood-kin under her roof again and we sat back
to watch developments. At first nothing happened. Then we   30
were sure that they were to be married. We learned that Miss
Emily had been to the jeweler's and ordered a man's toilet set
in silver, with the letter H. B. on each piece. Two days later we
learned that she had bought a complete outfit of men's clothing, including a nightshirt, and we said, "They are married."   35

We were really glad. We were glad because the two female cousins were even more Grierson than Miss Emily had ever been.

So we were not surprised when Homer Barron—the streets had been finished some time since—was gone. We were a little disappointed that there was not a public blowing-off, but we believed that he had gone on to prepare for Miss Emily's coming, or to give her a chance to get rid of the cousins. (By that time it was a cabal, and we were all Miss Emily's allies to help circumvent the cousins.) Sure enough, after another week they departed. And, as we had expected all along, within three days Homer Barron was back in town. A neighbor saw the Negro man admit him at the kitchen door at dusk one evening.

And that was the last we saw of Homer Barron. And of Miss Emily for some time. The Negro man went in and out with the market basket, but the front door remained closed. Now and then we would see her at a window for a moment, as the men did that night when they sprinkled the lime, but for almost six months she did not appear on the streets. Then we knew that this was to be expected too; as if that quality of her father which had thwarted her woman's life so many times had been too virulent and too furious to die.

When we next saw Miss Emily, she had grown fat and her hair was turning gray. During the next few years it grew grayer and grayer until it attained an even pepper-and-salt iron-gray, when it ceased turning. Up to the day of her death at seventy-four it was still that vigorous iron-gray, like the hair of an active man.

From that time on her front door remained closed, save for a period of six or seven years, when she was about forty, during which she gave lessons in china-painting. She fitted up a studio in one of the downstairs rooms, where the daughters and granddaughters of Colonel Sartoris' contemporaries were sent to her with the same regularity and in the same spirit that they were sent to church on Sundays with a twenty-five-cent piece for the collection plate. Meanwhile her taxes had been remitted.

Then the newer generation became the backbone and the

spirit of the town, and the painting pupils grew up and fell away and did not send their children to her with boxes of color and tedious brushes and pictures cut from the ladies' magazines. The front door closed upon the last one and remained closed for good. When the town got free postal delivery, Miss 5
Emily alone refused to let them fasten the metal numbers above her door and attach a mailbox to it. She would not listen to them.

Daily, monthly, yearly we watched the Negro grow grayer and more stooped, going in and out with the market basket. 10
Each December we sent her a tax notice, which would be returned by the post office a week later, unclaimed. Now and then we would see her in one of the downstairs windows—she had evidently shut up the top floor of the house—like the carven torso of an idol in a niche, looking or not looking at us, 15
we could never tell which. Thus she passed from generation to generation—dear, inescapable, impervious, tranquil, and perverse.

And so she died. Fell ill in the house filled with dust and shadows, with only a doddering Negro man to wait on her. We 20
did not even know she was sick; we had long since given up trying to get any information from the Negro. He talked to no one, probably not even to her, for his voice had grown harsh and rusty, as if from disuse.

She died in one of the downstairs rooms, in a heavy walnut 25
bed with a curtain, her gray head propped on a pillow yellow and moldy with age and lack of sunlight.

V

The Negro met the first of the ladies at the front door and let 30
them in, with their hushed, sibilant voices and their quick, curious glances, and then he disappeared. He walked right through the house and out the back and was not seen again.

The two female cousins came at once. They held the funeral on the second day, with the town coming to look at Miss Emily 35
beneath a mass of bought flowers, with the crayon face of her father musing profoundly above the bier and the ladies sibilant

and macabre; and the very old men—some in their brushed Confederate uniforms—on the porch and the lawn, talking of Miss Emily as if she had been a contemporary of theirs, believing that they had danced with her and courted her perhaps, confusing time with its mathematical progression, as the old do, to whom all the past is not a diminishing road but, instead, a huge meadow which no winter ever quite touches, divided from them now by the narrow bottle-neck of the most recent decade of years.

Already we knew that there was one room in that region above stairs which no one had seen in forty years, and which would have to be forced. They waited until Miss Emily was decently in the ground before they opened it.

The violence of breaking down the door seemed to fill this room with pervading dust. A thin, acrid pall as of the tomb seemed to lie everywhere upon this room decked and furnished as for a bridal: upon the valance curtains of faded rose color, upon the rose-shaded lights, upon the dressing table, upon the delicate array of crystal and the man's toilet things backed with tarnished silver, silver so tarnished that the monogram was obscured. Among them lay a collar and tie, as if they had just been removed, which, lifted, left upon the surface a pale crescent in the dust. Upon a chair hung the suit, carefully folded; beneath it the two mute shoes and the discarded socks.

The man himself lay in the bed.

For a long while we just stood there, looking down at the profound and fleshless grin. The body had apparently once lain in the attitude of an embrace, but now the long sleep that outlasts love, that conquers even the grimace of love, had cuckolded him. What was left of him, rotted beneath what was left of the nightshirt, had become inextricable from the bed in which he lay; and upon him and upon the pillow beside him lay that even coating of the patient and biding dust.

Then we noticed that in the second pillow was the indentation of a head. One of us lifted something from it, and leaning forward, that faint and invisible dust dry and acrid in the nostrils, we saw a long strand of iron-gray hair.

TERMS TO KNOW

ACTION—what happens in a story; what the characters do, including what they say and think. Some stories depend primarily upon external or physical action, others upon internal or mental action. Reaction, external or internal, is response to action, and is therefore also a kind of action. Action of whatever kind has two primary functions: to further the plot and to clarify the characters.

CHARACTERIZATION—the result of the method or methods used by the short story writer to create characters, realistic or not depending upon his purpose, but believable within the story. Because the form is brief, the short story normally reveals rather than develops character. It does so mainly through action, speech, environment, physical appearance, reactions of other characters, thought, and the author's statements.

(a) Action—what a person does in a given situation speaks eloquently of what he is. The behavior of a character reveals his nature. (See *Action* above.)

(b) Speech—what a person says (a kind of action) helps reveal his inner self. Unless the writer indicates that what the character is saying is not what that character thinks, the reader is obliged to assume that what he says, including both content and manner, is an accurate reflection of the character. If it is not, the result may be irony. (See *Dialogue* and *Irony* below.)

(c) Environment—surroundings also help to characterize. If a character is in a slum and seems to fit there, he is one kind of person; if he is in a slum and does not seem to fit there, he is another kind. A person's choice of friends, food, recreation, and clothing, among other things, says something about him. (See *Setting* below.)

(d) Physical Appearance—a person's physical make-up, and his care and use of it, is important in showing what kind of character he is. A woman with habitually unkempt hair and fingernails, no matter what her other characteristics, is different from the woman who is always meticulously groomed. Slouching may reveal either defiance or weariness, while an upright bearing may show pride or confidence.

(e) Reactions of Other Characters—what his contemporaries think of a character, as revealed by their speech or actions, is important in establishing the nature of that character. Who speaks and who reacts will, of course, be a factor in the degree to which we heed what is said or done: the charges of an irresponsible person would not influence us to any great degree in our judgment of the character.

(f) Thought—to the extent that the author reveals them, a character's thoughts reflect what he is, just as his physical actions and speech do. Every character is the total of his thoughts, his speech, and his action.

(g) Author's Statement—the author may choose to tell us about the character he is creating rather than to let actions or other factors do the work. This method of characterization is largely expository rather than narrative, is used sparingly by modern writers, and is most effective when scattered throughout a story rather than presented in a block.

The writer creates his characters by using these means and by presenting significant detail. He seeks not to make complete people—they are too complex to be set down on paper—but to create the illusion of completeness. Unless the author does create an illusion of reality, we are not interested in the characters as people but only as figures. For some stories, figures are enough; for most, characters who seem alive are necessary.

Characters who do not achieve the status of individuals but remain typical of classes or reminiscent of previously created characters are called *stock characters:* the prissy old maid, the shrewd Yankee, the dumb blond. While they have a certain usefulness, as characters, they are not created fresh for each particular story, but are reproduced in the image of a literary ancestor.

CLIMAX—the high point of a story. Usually a story presents a series of actions which culminate in some crisis which determines how the story will end; that crisis is the climax. Sometimes the climax is not entirely physical, but a moment of illumination or realization that makes the significance of the action plain. The climax normally occurs near the end of a story. (See *Plot* below.)

COINCIDENCE—the chance happening of two unrelated actions at the same time. While such accidents do happen in life, we hesitate to accept in a story any incident which is not prepared for in some way. We expect some believable cause for every effect. If a non-smoker just happens to find a match in his pocket at the moment he needs to build a fire to save the life of a freezing friend, we have a case of unbelievable coincidence. But if the friends enter a cafe and one is heard to say to the other: "When you pay the check, get me some matches and keep them; I'm always running out," we may think little of the incident at the moment but we may later believe the coincidental possession of matches by the non-smoker who saves the life of his freezing friend.

CONFLICT—the physical or psychological clash of opposing forces or interests. Two men engaged in a fist fight over a woman are in physical conflict with each other. A man trying to make up his mind about which of two women to marry is in psychological conflict within himself. (See *Plot* below.)

DIALOGUE—what the characters in a story say to one another. Dialogue, like action, is used mainly to further the plot and to delineate character. It should also be interesting in its own right. Dialogue in which only one character speaks is called monologue.

FORESHADOWING—preparing early in the story for what happens later. Events in a plot must be motivated either by action, dialogue, or character if they are to be credible, and not merely coincidence. If one character warns another of the dangers of a particular place and later the warned character has need to go to that particular place, the reader may expect danger because danger has been foreshadowed.

IRONY—the contrast between intent and performance, verbal or otherwise. For example, if two young men see an ugly girl and one says, "Now there's a real beauty," both will know that the speaker means just the opposite. This is *verbal* irony. Another example: A man works hard for twenty years in order to provide for a comfortable old age and then dies at the end of the twentieth year of a condition brought about by working too hard. This is *cosmic* irony. A final example: A character in a play goes to great lengths to obtain a certain jewel, thinking it is very valuable. The audience knows all the time that it is not. This is *dramatic* irony.

MOTIVATION—the causes which bring about effects in human relationships. Usually such causes are implicit in the personality of the characters, although outside forces may also motivate action. (See *Plot* below.)

PERSONA—the voice of the story. The author of a story chooses a character who speaks the author's thoughts. This created narrator is the persona. (See *Point of View* below.)

PLOT—the tightly designed and carefully controlled series of related and motivated events developing a conflict which is finally resolved in one way or another within the story or within the mind of the reader.

A sequence of events by itself is not a plot. E. M. Forster in differentiating plot and sequence has said that this is a sequence: "The queen died; then the king died." This, on the other hand, is a plot: "The queen died; then the king died of grief." The difference is that the plot reveals relationships between events and gives those events significance, while a sequence does not.

Most plots are concerned with a conflict of some kind, internal or external (see *Conflict* above), and with its resolution, complete or partial. The resolution or settling of the conflict may take place either within the story itself, as when the hero triumphs over the villain as an opposing force, or within the mind of the reader, as when he realizes that the hero's apparent failure in business is really the beginning of a better life for him.

The crux of the matter, the high point of the narrative as the story proceeds to its resolution, is called the climax. It will vary depending upon the nature of the conflict involved. Frequently the climax will be heightened by the use of suspense. (See *Suspense* below.)

If a story is to be believable as a reflection of life and not as a fantasy, the incidents of the plot must result from the motivated actions of the characters and not from coincidence or chance. People in life act and react in response to causes, and the characters in a story must do the same. Without characters who are motivated either consciously or unconsciously, a sequence of events does not make a coherent and meaningful plot.

POINT OF VIEW—the character through which the author relates his story to the reader. There are essentially four points of view, with variations.

(a) Omniscient Point of View—the persona knows everything about all of the characters, including their thoughts and even what is going to happen to them in the future, and relates it directly to the reader. He may or may not interpret the thoughts and experiences of the characters, but he will *report* them.

(b) Limited Omniscient Point of View—the persona reports the thoughts of only one selected character and has that one character tell us if the things said and done are good or not. The persona may provide narration and descriptions of all the characters, but he penetrates into only one mind. This narrator may be in the story himself or he may be simply a person who has heard the story and is in turn telling it to us.

(c) Effaced Narrator Point of View—the persona narrates and describes, but he does not penetrate the consciousness of any of the characters, and he does not usually interpret action. He is objective, he tells what was done and what was said, but he does not tell us whether what was done or said is good or bad. This point of view comes closest to the method of drama.

(d) First Person Point of View—the persona is one of the characters in the story, and reports what he sees, thinks, and does. He cannot penetrate the minds of the other characters but can report their actions and interpret them from his own

understanding of them. The first person narrator may be the
main character in a story, or he may be a secondary one
whose main function is observing and reporting.

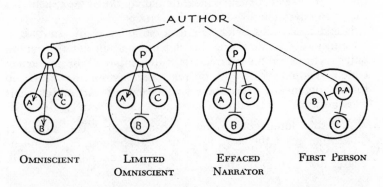

| OMNISCIENT | LIMITED OMNISCIENT | EFFACED NARRATOR | FIRST PERSON |

SETTING—the physical background for the action of a story.
This includes both geography in a broad way and more limited
surroundings in a narrow way, the time in history, and the
social and occupational environment. Sometimes the general
feeling of a locale, called *atmosphere,* is an important part of
the setting, as in some Poe stories. In "The Fall of the House of
Usher" the gloom can almost be felt. The setting of a story may
be important in suggesting character traits or in providing
motivation for action.

STRUCTURE—the way a story is put together to achieve its purpose and effect. Some stories are simple chronological progres-
sions, with few complications. Others are more complex, prob-
ing into the past by flashbacks and relating the past to the
present. Some rely primarily upon narration, while others com-
bine narration and dialogue. Some use a good deal of description, some little. Structure is the architecture of the story.

SUSPENSE—the deliberate prolongation of states of anxiety,
indecision, or irresolution. A good plot often suspends the resolution of the conflict to heighten excitement, or prolongs the
periods of waiting before relating what has been inevitable or
anticipated from early in the story. Suspense is a basic in-
gredient of almost all fiction.

SYMBOLISM—a literary process by which a writer expresses two levels of meaning at the same time. A rose, for instance, exists at one level of meaning as a flower, but it has also come to stand for beauty. Some public or conventional symbols have become relatively fixed, like the cross, which suggests the whole rich complex of Christianity. Some symbols are created for and by a specific literary work, and can be fully understood only in the context of that work. An example might be a poem which symbolizes rebirth by the germination of a seed in spring. By means of symbols writers extend and enrich their meanings.

THEME—the intellectual point or concept that the author is conveying; what the story is about. It is the core of the meaning of the story growing out of the *significance* of the action. Although westerns and detective stories have as their basic appeal action or suspense of some kind they usually also have a basic theme: good conquers evil. The theme is not what happens in a story but the idea or concept that the actions convey. Some stories stress theme more than others; some, indeed, have no theme at all. However, some of the attraction of fiction derives from its power to state a theme indirectly. Through concrete representation of people in action, fiction can present an abstract concept with an accompanying strong emotional appeal that expository prose on the same general subject cannot match.